CONCEIVING THE SELF: PRESENCE AND ABSENCE IN PSYCHOANALYTIC THEORY

CONCEIVING THE SELF:
PRESENCE AND ABSENCE IN
PSYCHOANALYTIC THEORY

by

Barbara J. Socor, Ph.D.

INTERNATIONAL UNIVERSITIES PRESS, INC.
Madison   Connecticut

Copyright © 1997, International Universities Press, Inc.

INTERNATIONAL UNIVERSITIES PRESS and IUP (& design) ® are registered trademarks of International Universities Press, Inc.

Library of Congress Cataloging-in-Publication Data

Socor, Barbara J.
    Conceiving the self : presence and absence in psychoanalytic theory / by Barbara J. Socor.
        p.   cm.
    Includes bibliographical references and indexes.
    ISBN 0-8236-1030-6 (hardcover)
    1. Self.   2. Psychoanalysis.   3. Self psychology.   I. Title.
BF697.S672   1996
155.2—dc20   96-29441
                                                                        CIP

Manufactured in the United States of America

This Book is Dedicated in Love and Gratitude to My Parents
Pearl and Philip Feld

TABLE OF CONTENTS

PART IV:
THE THOUGHT OF THE UNKNOWN   261

ACKNOWLEDGMENTS

I am grateful to International Universities Press, and particularly to Dr. Margaret Emery, for the generous encouragement and enthusiasm given for this volume. My gratitude as well to Adrienne Franco, and particularly to Robert Monteleone, both of the Ryan Library at Iona College for their very important assistance in tracking down essential material. I wish to acknowledge The New York University School of Social Work Doctoral Program, and to express gratitude for the atmosphere of intellectual openness encouraged by Dr. George Frank. I am especially grateful to Dr. Jeffrey Seinfeld, whose remarkable intelligence and keen insights frequently left me breathless and always left me thinking. I am indebted to his guidance. To my colleagues Dr. Kevin Phillips, Steve Roithmayr, Dr. Cindy Tannenbaum, and especially Dr. Eileen Taylor-Appleby, thank you for your support, your interest, and for sharing so much of the journey. For Sandy Wolf, whose invaluable friendship and sustaining presence means so much, there truly is no adequate way to speak my gratitude. And to my parents, Pearl and Philip Feld, for whose lifelong confidence and love, gratitude is a pale word indeed.

ACKNOWLEDGMENTS

This sense of *sameness* is the very keel and backbone
of our thinking. . . . We do not care whether there be any
real sameness in *things* or not, or whether the mind
be true or false in its assumptions of it. Our principle
only lays it down that the mind makes continual
use of the *notion* of sameness, and if deprived of it,
would have a different structure from what it has
                    [William James, 1890, pp. 459–460].

When we speak of presentability, we do not mean
presence alone, but presence and absence taken as a
couple. When we speak of identifiability, we do not
mean sameness alone, but same and other taken as a
couple. . .
                    [Robert Sokolowski, 1978, p. 162].

The final belief is to believe in a fiction, which
you know to be a fiction, there being nothing else.
The exquisite truth is to know that it is a fiction
and that you believe in it willingly
                    [Wallace Stevens, 1957, p. 157].

PREFACE

One of the fundamental themes implicit in this book is that the self concept, indeed, the very idea of the self, is a manifestation of what T. S. Eliot has called a "raid on the inarticulate." In other words, the experience of being a self is fundamentally outside the domain of language, and theories represent verbal incursions into the realm of the unspoken. Such incursions seek to specify the indeterminate, and to formulate the ineffable, by effecting an expressive capture, within the contextual confines of the word, of that entity which, in being defined, eludes its meaning, and which cannot be found without also and immediately being lost. For words are imperfect and inherently static tools which can only approximate the dynamic experience of being. Words represent, and seek in their effect, to literally *re*present and make present again, that which is fundamentally absent—or else it would not require representing. In this way, to speak of the self is always to say what is not; to engage in incantatory conjuring of what is absent.

Yet it remains that words *do* invoke presences. They can "call to mind" images not there before the utterance, and stir associated affects not felt (in the same way) before they were spoken. Thus do words confer meaning and serve as guides in mapping, indeed in representing, the world and ourselves to our selves. Thus, the other side of our assertion that words represent what is irremediably beyond capture, is that they also are the primary vehicle through which the self is realized. We become as we come to represent ourselves (in words and images) to the mind. We associate self with the spoken and "imagined" representation of sameness over time. We are what we recognize ourselves to be; what we *say* we are. The self so spoken, so represented, is experienced as affectively real, if nonetheless a verbal reification. Words breach the void and fill the silence. They make what is absent by its silence present by its sounded utterance.

In this volume we shall investigate selected theories of the self which, with the exception of Greenwald's (1980) paper, derive from within the psychoanalytic tradition, and which are more or less frankly associated with one or the other side of the couplet of absence and presence. We undertake to illustrate that these theories have largely, though surely not exclusively and fixedly, adhered to one or the other of these notions in constructing a concept of self. Thus, for example, we shall see that many of the formulations of self associated with the influential school of American ego psychology address a self whose efficacy rests in establishing a sense of sameness imparted by representing the self as (the same as) the (strange and unspeakable and thus unknowable) other. On the other hand, we shall follow the assertion, principally elucidated here within the context of the work of Jacques Lacan, that the self which we represent ourselves to be is a fundamental and inevitable distortion wrought by the equally inevitable demands of language.

So, broadly speaking, this review of the literature is an effort to understand the variety of ways in which theorists have sought to ''raid the inarticulate'' and speak the self. And in this way it seeks as well to offer an alternative reading of those efforts, endeavoring to put into words and context—to make present—what has yet to be spoken. For we concur that ''one has only learnt to get the better of words for the thing one no longer has to say, or the way in which one is no longer disposed to say it'' (Eliot, 1943, p. 16).

INTRODUCTION:
THE CERTAIN SELF AND THE ROLE OF THE OTHER

> Like the physical, the psychical is not necessarily in reality what it appears to us to be
>
> [Freud, 1915, p. 171].

When Descartes declared that the only certainty was the doubting subject itself, reasoning that he who is capable of doubting all else must himself be the only surety, he was already elaborating upon the much earlier distinction made by Aristotle, between the physical and nonphysical aspects of being. Indeed, it is not so much the dualism, but its having been coupled with and compatible with an increasing grasp and mastery of the physical world by the subject (we think here of Copernicus, of Galileo, and the coming discoveries of Newton) which distinguishes the Cartesian axiom of certainty as it conceived the certain subject.

The preoccupation with self, and its distinction from all *res extensa*, is an ancient Western tradition. Indeed it was through the Logos that, "in the beginning," God assigned to man the rights and burdens of dominion over the rest of creation, and in dominion a particular relationship to all otherness was engaged.

But it was the Cartesian assertion which established the primacy of the self and made of this absolutely certain subject the central object of philosophic inquiry. For since Descartes, the doubting and discrete subject has certainly been beyond doubt, and doubtless a source of much speculation both within and without philosophy. Certainly, a central preoccupation with the self, in its origins, relationships, responsibilities, angst, and very efficacy, within the many disciplines, professions, and indeed, artistic and literary pursuits, has come to characterize considerable portions of the culturally and intellectually modern world. Disciplines such as psychology, sociology, and psychiatry, for example, may be the latter-day chroniclers, explainers, healers, and in countless other ways, true legatees of the Cartesian project. For Descartes established the subject, and we have been pursuing it ever since.

1

It is the basic intent of this volume, in a somewhat circumscribed fashion, to join in the pursuit of the selfsame subject. By aiming to examine a selected number of classic and contemporary theories of the self within the psychoanalytic tradition, as well as surveying some recent developments within the humanistic branch of psychology, which is adapting postmodern thinking to the matter, I will elucidate not only the particulars of different theories of the self, but more broadly, employ those theories to illustrate two distinctive, overarching themes.

Specifically, I will argue that theories of self themselves reflect a larger epistemological struggle with the nature of what can be known, and how such knowledge is apprehended by human beings. This "struggle" may be dichotomously and variously conceptualized as *presence/absence, immanence/transcendence,* or *desire/fulfillment.* I contend that within the psychoanalytic tradition itself, theories of self may be understood in terms of these distinctive ways of knowing. These ways differentially engage the idea of "otherness," and of the unknown, of the "strange" and "unseen," equally with the "known," the "seen," and the familiar, to define and characterize the self. Psychoanalysis, as a theoretical project seeking to explain the nature of psychological being, established and yet maintains a significant relationship to the idea of otherness.

But just what do we mean when we refer to "presence," and to "absence," to "otherness" and the "unknown," and what is the role of psychoanalysis in this seemingly unrelated matter?

Central Themes

As suggested, we shall take as our starting point the inward turn effected by the Cartesian elevation of the subject, and the subsequent flowering of thought about the nature of the relationship between the subjective self and the objective other.

This turn, by proclaiming the subject as the only source of palpable certainty, of knowing and of knowledge, leads to the assertion that all we may ever claim to know with certainty of the objective world must, of Cartesian necessity, derive from the subjective. So viewed, the objective world of others is no longer strange (i.e., absent from subjective knowledge) because it originated in, and in its essence remains a part of, the subjective self. Rather, the objective is familiar (i.e., present to subjective knowledge). Thus, the objective is the same as the subjective, and all certain knowledge shares an identity of character. The subjective is *present* in all that appears to be objective and not self. Thus, the impression of alterity is illusory, and *res extensa* a thoughtful construction. All otherness is a presence of mind.

This idea, that the world is not strange and irremediably beyond subjective grasp (i.e., that it is a *presence of mind*, just as the subject itself is) will serve as one central organizing principle of this work and is complemented by its dialectical opposite, that of a kind of *absence of mind*, or absent-mindedness.

Here, conversely, all that is not self is subject to actual alterity. The world is radically objective in its seamless and eternal indifference to the subjective; and all nonself, all otherness, is irremediably absent and cannot be made same.

These two epistemologies are employed as they differentially characterize the theoretical undertakings within the mainly psychoanalytic tradition explored in this volume and will, as we have suggested, be characterized as *presence/fulfillment* and *absence/desire*. The former describes concepts which formulate the self as a psychological experience of the palpable and the achieved; the *realized*. The latter conceives a self most authentically experienced in the psychic embrace of the intangible; of that which is eternally anticipated. And while presence is the nominal descriptor of the psychological experience of "fullness," of solidity (i.e., of fulfillment), absence bespeaks the experience of wanting, of longing, for what is not (i.e., desire). Thus, one of the outcomes of this book will be to underscore the fundamental epistemological distinction between those theories of self which originate in a conceptual commitment to absence that the French tradition of theorizing suggests, and those of the Anglo-American literature which illuminate the idea of presence and fulfillment.

Postmodern Paradigms

Psychoanalysis, and hence theories of self which derive from it, is largely a subparadigm of modernism as a distinct and defining worldview, and this overarching model, which has shaped thought at least since the early twentieth century, and arguably, in some respects, much earlier, is currently being challenged by the assertions of a postmodern sensibility. It is this sensibility which directly challenges the long standing modern (and romantic) conviction that, regardless of its various particularities and modes of being, there is a singular, persistent and identifiable psychological entity known as the self. Indeed, the postmodern view essentially argues that the self is a social construction erected upon the uncertain sands of shifting sociocultural formulations about the world.

Surely it is possible to argue that the two fundamental ways of knowing the self addressed in this work (i.e., in terms of presence or absence) themselves may be understood to represent and to describe a particular worldview, though these arguments will not be undertaken in this volume, whose focus rests elsewhere. For theories of self, like the disciplines from which they emerge, often reflect the more encompassing cultural and intellectual contexts which father, nurture, and confirm them. Thus, many postmodern theorists contend that these cultural and intellectual contexts themselves are, for a variety of reasons, giving way and can no longer support the idea of a singular identity.

Indeed, the very idea of the certainty and centrality of the self is, many have argued (e.g., Foucault, and Derrida among numerous other philosophers and theorists loosely grouped as postmodern or deconstructionist), itself a product of other and anonymous forces, such as power or language or narrative.

Foucault (1965, 1977), for example, has been a historian of discontinuities; that is, rather than reaffirming the traditional proclivity to insert events into a system of rational explanation (i.e., into a ''totalizing'' framework), Foucault has underscored the frequently unarticulated ruptures between the present and the past. His intent, thus, is to assert that there are no constants, and surely no rational or reasonable continuities which connect the past to the present. Indeed, reason is a retrospective imposition on fundamentally discontinuous and disparate events—and this imposition accounts as well for the mistaken assumption of an immutable, singular self.

Not unlike Lacan in this regard, Foucault has also focused upon ''otherness.'' For Foucault, however, this otherness signifies the discontinuous events of history, which are dealt with through a silence which serves to ignore and to deny those events which do not conform with a ''reasonable,'' favorable, and continuous explanation of history.

Thus, in *Madness and Civilization* (1965), for example, Foucault describes how "madness" became "illness" and how madmen—free to wander the countryside as just another form of being during the Renaissance—soon became *sick* men, confined to hospitals and subject to treatment. The nature of being, and being a self, was redefined.

Derrida (1967a,b) also engages the idea of endless mutability, by focusing rather more explicitly on the formative influence of language in constituting the self. In all these early works Derrida argues that language, as a system of signifiers and those things which are signified, offers a profoundly misleading sense of certain and immutable meaning. On the contrary, Derrida (1967a,b) asserts that linguistic signifiers are not inherently tied to what they signify, but rather are constantly signifying other things. Indeed, signifiers can themselves become the signified, as words—all meaning—is fragmented across the "chain of signifiers." And this does not exclude the self, which itself is a product of (changeable) language. The self, in this view, is a linguistic signification; inherently as unstable as any other signifier-signified relationship.

Derrida's (1967a,b) linguistic deconstruction of the self owes much to his radical extension of the work of the linguist Ferdinand de Saussure (1915). Saussure argued that all linguistic signs are arbitrary and, further, that they themselves do not refer back to any transcendent signified. This was, at the time, a radical notion, challenging as it did the general assertions of transcendence made, notably, by Hegel (1807). For Saussure (1915) is saying that signs have no other meaning aside from that which is assigned them within a temporal context. That is to say, meaning is man-made; there is no "prime mover." Derrida (1967a,b) takes this Saussurian notion further when he claims no inherent meaning for the signifier even within the network of temporality. All things are always mutable, and elusive, perhaps especially the self. And because, Derrida (1967a,b) asserts, signs point to what is not present, the signification of the self indicates its essential absence.

The postmodern formulation of the self has, of course, been advanced in many quarters, not least among those theoreticians of the self variously referred to as sociocognitive or humanist psychologists. Among these we would briefly note the work of Kenneth Gergen (1985, 1990, 1991) who addresses the idea that the self "exist[s] in a state of continuous construction and reconstruction" (p. 7). In his work we encounter intrinsically mutable selves, in a world which itself recognizes no permanent, and certainly no transcendent reality. For transcendence has yielded to immanence and the self in a postmodern world exists, if at all, in a perpetual state of changeable "nowness." The idea of "oneness" submits to "manyness," and the singular voice of the identifiable self is seduced—indeed, is "saturated"—by a chorus of plurality.

Similar arguments regarding the essential instability of objects in general and of the self in particular are taken up by George Rosenwald (1988a,b) and Edward Sampson (1985, 1988, 1989), and may perhaps be well summarized in the latter's assertion that "individualism is a sociohistorical rather than a natural event" (1988, p. 18).

As we have suggested, however, we will not be engaging the postmodern argument for the demise of the bounded self concept in this work. Indeed, the question of the viability of the self and the associated inquiry into the stability of the romantic-modern paradigm which supports and informs that viability, is a substantial but very different one from that raised in this context. Here, rather, we are interested in investigating the conceptions of self organized mainly within psychoanalytic thought (with the single exception of Greenwald's work), and exploring the differential relationship of the known and subjective self to the unknown and objective other that the principles of *presence* and *absence* suggest.

This idea of otherness, and of the absent Other, while seemingly the intellectual property of more postmodern times, has played an important theoretical role in the work of Jacques Lacan, and was a very real presence in the early theoretical reckonings of the Freudian enterprise as well.

The capitalized Lacanian Other is an ambiguous term whose meaning is not easily captured, but it is perhaps most often employed to suggest the subject's unconscious. This unconscious, however, is not simply the repository of repressed or forbidden wishes. Lacan's Other is the ever present, if always absent, "third term" in all dyadic relationships and "not even an apparent monologue can take place without the mediation of 'Otherness' " (Wilden, 1968, p. 264). This Otherness is Lacan's expression of the absent made present, and he accomplishes this through language, via "the Word." For by speaking we conjure what is not there, we literally "call it to mind," and it is the Other, Lacan asserts, that speaks this absence which (unconsciously)

controls us. All "others" speak the distortions of a knowing consciousness, but the Other speaks the truth of the self which is always an
unknown and unconscious absence. The Other is the absent guest at
the table of consciousness.

Aspects of Lacan's contribution to the notion of absence in formu-
lating the self will be undertaken in some detail below. Here, we briefly
explore the presence of the Other even as psychoanalysis undertook
its earliest investigations, for this idea of otherness, of the formative
impact of the unknown, played a central role in the construction of the
Freudian enterprise, and an understanding of the role it has played
in subsequent analytic theories to be explored here asks for a brief
consideration of its rather "orthodox" origins.

Psychoanalysis and Its Relationship to the Other

This volume, as it follows the evolution of the concept of the self
within significant portions of the American, French, and British schools
of psychoanalytic thought, observes that while these traditions have
produced their own rather distinctive theoretical assertions, all retain
an intellectual commitment to the generative formulation of psychoanalysis, to wit, that "the division of the psychical into what is conscious and what is unconscious is the fundamental premise of psychoanalysis" (Freud, 1923, p. 13). In this all traditions agree, though
admittedly with varying degrees of emphasis. In thus dividing the psyche, the psychoanalytic tradition itself is a fair reflection of the larger
Cartesian project of which it is a certain product.

Thus we shall observe that all the psychoanalytic schools of
thought addressed herein developed theory from the more or less explicit starting point of the divided, or split, subject; partly conscious,
and partly unconscious. In some respects accessible to its own knowing, while in other respects profoundly alienated from essential features
of its being, the distinctly psychoanalytic subject was, from its very
inception, depicted in terms of what was not present but was actually
an absent influence. The absent other, conceived as the unconscious,
was present from the outset.

This concern with the felt, or sensed, influence of what was not
present was inherent in, indeed may be said to have been the very
impetus for, the emergence and subsequent evolution of psychoanalytic

thought. Thus did Breuer and Freud (1895) initially observe of Anna
O that:

> [t]wo entirely distinct states of consciousness were present which
> alternated very frequently . . . [and] at this stage of her illness if
> something had been moved in the room or someone had entered
> or left [during her other state of consciousness] she would com-
> plain of having "lost" some time and would remark upon the
> gap in her train of conscious thoughts . . . these *"absences"* had
> already been observed before she took to her bed [p. 24].

This problematic issue, of the influence of "other states" upon
the behavioral and existential qualities of being, will, as we shall see,
cast a conceptual shadow across the face of subsequently developed
analytic theories of the self even unto this day. How did psychoanalysis
understand the relationship of the object (i.e., the objective nonself) to
the subject (i.e., the subjective self); what was its theory with respect
to these relations?

Just as the issue of the relationship of self to the world was the
broader philosophic focus, psychoanalysis undertook its work with an
exploration of the relationship of the self to itself, or what would
become its own strange "other" world. Thus, while early analytic
pursuits were not directly framed in terms of the self, and while the
manifest concerns of theory were not characterized in the language of
the known and the unknown, or the present and the absent, such issues
were surely present nonetheless.

Perhaps no statement more decidedly reflects this presence, or the
psychoanalytic relationship to the Cartesian problematic, than when
Freud (1915) asserted, "that without any special reflection we attribute
to everyone else our own constitution and therefore our consciousness
as well, and [this] identification is a *sine qua non* of our understanding"
(p. 169).

The consciousness of others, Freud (1915) continues, can only be
inferred by what appears to be similar behavior, and we can presume
to know the other only by a Cartesian inference of sameness. We are
capable of knowing only that which *is* our self or is perceived (i.e.,
recognized) as the same and identical to our self. The other is made
present and familiar by attribution.

And so, much before Lacan but reflecting his concerns, psychoanalysis undertook to discover what could be known of the unknown.

And thus did psychoanalysis carry the Cartesian split of the subject from the object world to the very heart of the knowing subject itself, arguing that even at the center of such knowing, of such certainty, there also rests the unknown; and even the self contains the other. The nature of the self, and its relation to otherness, then, has been a latent substrate of the psychoanalytic tradition virtually from the start, and the resonance of earlier ponderings are experienced even today when we say, with Freud (1915), that "all the acts and manifestations which I notice in myself and do not know how to link up with the rest of my mental life must be judged as if they belonged to someone else: they are to be explained by a mental life ascribed to the other person" (p. 169).

Organization of This Volume

Divided into four parts, the book seeks to take a closer look not only at the theories themselves, though this will be done; nor only at the theories as they address the self concept, though this too will be undertaken. It aims, more broadly, to understand these theories as characteristic representations of a larger story. Thus, we shall explore a selected number of psychoanalytic theories addressing the origin and elaboration of the self as particular illustrative instances of the more encompassing narrative of *presence-absence.*

In Part I, "The Self of Realization," selected American ego psychology and object relations theories will be examined in light of this dichotomy in order to demonstrate that on the whole, they depict the self as a realization, or more accurately, as a signification, or sign, of the *actual.* We shall argue that these theories, in the aggregate, tell of an increasingly substantial, existent, and veridical self, made manifest especially in the establishment of the image, the (internal-eternal) vision attesting by *its* presence to the coincident presence of the self. This has been frequently expressed, for example, in the concept of object constancy. We shall see that other sensory manifestations, as that of smell, sound, and touch, also serve a presencing purpose. Variations in approach aside, we note that all theories within this framework assert the realization of the self when an internal sense of coherence and order are achieved; as personal control and increasing mastery of the environment are attained; and as firm boundaries are established.

The realized self is distinctly separate—indeed separation and individuation are central hallmarks of personhood—and unambiguously differentiated from all others.

Part II, "The Self of Anticipation," engages that aspect of the narrative which chronicles a self whose very nature rests in the experience of anticipation—of desire which remains unrequited. Here, the self is most closely approached as it recedes; most truly known as it suggests the unknowable. It is a self which is "realized" as it embraces what is most profoundly absent in its nature. Thus, Jacques Lacan, whose work we shall discuss here, will maintain that the self which is often psychologically recognized is a distorted product of "ego," that is, of received culture. A "true" self, on the other hand, is knowable, but only in the sense that the absent is desired. In the knowledgeable experience of desiring that which shall never be fulfilled, the self is "known." And that which is desired is a kind of union with a vast and profoundly impersonal "Otherness," which suggests that identity is discoverable only in the strange; and self can be completed only in the experience of the incomplete and absent.

In Part III, "Anomalous Selves," we undertake to examine theoretically significant formulations of the self concept which represent, in varying degree, anomalies within the traditions from which they originate. Thus, in the relatively unexplored work of Paul Federn, for example, we encounter an alternative formulation, indeed, an alternative ego psychology, which has, for the most part, remained within the shadow of the Hartmannian paradigm. Didier Anzieu, the contemporary French analyst, has also made some interesting assertions with regard to the self which bear little particular kinship to the Lacanian tradition.

We explore here as well the rather better known theorists of the British "middle group," including Winnicott, Balint, and Guntrip. In part due to the particular nature of theory development in Britain, these theorists have constructed a paradox in which, as Janus, the self (concept) looks in both directions, facing a self of presence which yet points toward a self of absence.

In Part IV, "The Thought of the Unknown," we take a close look at the important work of Christopher Bollas, whose own constructions contain, in my view, the possibility of an interesting narrative reconciliation.

Finally, we conclude this volume by proposing a conceptual modification of the idea of self. Containing both the thesis of presence and the antithesis of absence, the *supplemental object* and the *allusional self* will endeavor to contain the immanence and the transcendence which characterize the paradox of the self, serving thus to introduce a degree of symmetry among these seemingly incommensurate formulations. And in so doing, we contribute, in a paraphrase of Barrett (1986), to the gathering of some of "the significant strands of . . . [theoretical] history and [make] them [more] fully explicit" (p. 122).

Part I:
THE SELF OF REALIZATION

The self is a substitute for the lost other . . . our identity is always
a case of mistaken identity

[Brown, 1966, p. 144].

In what follows, we shall pursue an exploration of the formulation and evolution of the concept of the self as it increasingly, if not exclusively, moves toward an implicit assumption of realization. Theory, particularly, and I would argue, for reasons of cultural predilection, as it evolved within the American tradition of analytic ego psychology, and to a large extent, in American cognitive psychology as well, conceived of the self largely as a substantive rather than a metaphorical entity.

The self, as we suggested in the introduction, can be recognized to have unfolded in at least two epistemologically distinct directions, that of presence and that of absence. Here, we shall undertake an examination of the former, expressed as realization, in order to convey the sense of "here and nowness," of actuality, indeed of "realness" that is conveyed by a self which has been given a range of empirical referents observable in the real (i.e., the outside) world. Perhaps among the more significant of these referents is the visual image, for the capacity to visualize, to conjure up, and to see, has long been one of humankind's most convincing, if not always reliable, methods of testing and asserting the real. We shall see that the self as a composite of functions and visualizations becomes an affirmation of the psychologically knowable, and a distancing from charges of mysticism to which the Americans, perhaps more than the British and certainly in this respect, the French, are especially sensitive.

We shall concentrate here on the elaboration of the self concept within the ego psychological tradition of American analytic theorizing, which illuminates an epistemology of presence. In doing so, we do not suggest that there is a monolithic American tradition. On the contrary, we recognize that within Freudian theory, for example, many interpretative outposts have been established in the United States, just as they have been in France and in England.

13

Thus, for instance, we acknowledge, but will not be addressing in this work, that influential group of analytic acolytes, perhaps most often associated with Karen Horney (1937, 1939), Erich Fromm (1941, 1947, 1955), and H. S. Sullivan (1940, 1950, 1953), whose work may be understood as an effort to adapt Freudian principles to patterns of social and cultural behavior. Indeed, though different in many respects, their work came to be thought of as an *interpersonal* psychoanalysis for the commonly held conviction among its adherents that classical psychoanalysis had neglected the formative influence of the broader cultural and social context in seeking to account for the development of personality.

Thus, Sullivan, like Horney and Fromm, subscribed to the view that to fully appreciate the insights of psychoanalysis they needed to be placed within a broader, sociocultural framework. Fromm, for example, argued that the force of socialization is not only profound but often pernicious, compelling the individual as it does to engage in considerable self-deception in the interests of conforming to social demands. Much of Fromm's work also sought to make the Freudian unconscious compatible with a Marxist view of history which may, perhaps, account for the relatively marginal role it has played in the development of American ego psychology, particularly during the 1950s.

It was, however, Sullivan who devoted a substantial portion of his theoretical efforts to developing a specific formulation of the concept of self. He assigned the concept different, and often somewhat arcane, meanings over the course of his theoretical career, beginning with his early efforts to differentiate among the self and the personality, conceiving of the former as a repository of those images which reflect the person's own experience of his being, while understanding the latter as that which a person actually is. Somewhat later, and taking his cue from the work of G. H. Mead (1934), Sullivan (1940) conceptualized the self as a composite of "reflected appraisals." Finally, Sullivan (1953) modified his view of the self so that it became more than simply a collection of reflections. The self became a psychic organization whose primary function was to moderate anxiety, and to protect the rest of the personality from it.

A second illustration of the diversity of theoretical proclivities within the "tradition" of American psychoanalysis, is the work of

Franz Alexander (Alexander and Szasz, 1952), who applied modifications of psychoanalytic principles to the treatment of patients suffering from somatic illnesses, particularly gastric and duodenal ulcers. It was in large part as a result of his particular slant on psychoanalysis that aspects of it would become more or less assimilated to a form of psychosomatic medicine.

A third trend within American analytic circles, of course, was and is ego psychology. Long associated with the pioneering work of Heinz Hartmann, as well as Ernst Kris and David Rapaport, ego psychology, in what amounted to a reformulation of psychoanalytic metapsychology, proposed a model in which the ego assumed a predominant role vis-à-vis the other two components of the structured mind. In this respect, the ego's role was to promote adaptation to the environment and autonomy from the demands of the drives. It is within this tradition of analytic theory construction that much of the following discussion will pursue the elaboration of the idea of self.

We recognize as well that academic psychology in America has a long and complex history, and taken as a whole represents a number of methodological and conceptual byways, the subject matter of which is well beyond the scope and intent of this book. However, the considerably more circumscribed consideration of the role played by cognitive structures in the elaboration, indeed the construction, of self, variously referred to as "mind," "identity," and "ego," pursued by Greenwald (1980) is within the purview of this project, and we shall address his classic paper as it bears upon our topic.

Each of the chapters within this section will undertake a discussion of the work of a selected theorist, addressing the emergence and particular character of the self within the work. In addition to an elucidation of the particular theory, we aim to demonstrate that, for all the variation in content and emphasis, a concept of self emerges from each construction which bears the mark of *presence*. Thus, from the moment that Hartmann explicitly introduces the concept of self into analytic thinking, as a construct distinct from and no longer coterminous with the ego, as it more or less had been for Freud, we shall observe that through the various structural, interpersonal, and representational vicissitudes of Spiegel, Mahler, Jacobson, Kernberg, Kohut, and Stern, as well as in Greenwald's contribution, a self which asserts the concept of presence. That is to say, a self with a substantive signification of actual, not potential, being. It is an idea of self which, by way primarily, but not exclusively, of the visual image, and the spoken as opposed to the written word asserts the realization "I am."

However, before we embark upon this aspect of our exploration, it will, I believe, prove useful to briefly review the somewhat shifting bases upon which all that follows is so delicately and thought-provokingly balanced.

Freud's Ambiguous Legacy

Although the psychoanalytic project stands as a remarkable explanatory instance of the timeless effort to explain ourselves to ourselves, the self as a psychoanalytic formulation has been incompletely realized. Implied in the very nature of analytic inquiry from the beginning, a rigorous theoretical elaboration and formal conceptualization of the self was perhaps forestalled by a nineteenth century Weltanschauung of materialist determinism and detached objectivity inimical to the intensely personal and inevitably subjective nature of the idea of self. Still, its influence, variously expressed as the I, the subject, or the whole person, continued to make itself felt, if not always explicitly, throughout the course of theory development.

Thus, while psychoanalysis did not, at the outset, directly engage the idea of the self, its presence was surely felt and even frequently, if obscurely, addressed. Indeed, very generally speaking, psychoanalysis could be said to have been prompted into formal existence as Breuer and Freud (1893–1895) were confronted with the curious, and seemingly inexplicable, conundrum of a woman, Anna O, whose very being appeared divided and beyond her direction; whose body seemed to have visited upon her a chain of experiences she neither wished for, nor could direct. Thus did Anna O endure "disorders of vision and hearing of every sort, neuralgias, coughing, tremors [and] disturbances of speech" (Breuer and Freud, 1893–1895, p. 35). Accompanying these puzzling and seemingly unbidden manifestations were frequent experiences of psychic dissociation, or separation, in which Anna did not seem to know where she herself had been.

How was it that things were happening to her that she herself did not want to happen? Indeed, she did not appear to have control of her own *self*. The larger question is posed, if not immediately articulated: What is the nature of self that it may be thus divided, or hidden? And so the inquiry is engaged, the pursuit of the self undertaken, even if not yet expressed as such, within the parameters of the evolving viewpoint of Freudian psychoanalysis. Increasingly, however, a disciplined focus upon the nature and influence of the self in psychic development was obscured, but not obviated, by the priority accorded first to instinctual, and then ego-structural determinants in the course of building an analytic model of the mind. But what, we might ask at the outset of this work, was Freud's own idea of the self? Did he have a distinct view? Was it different from the ego, commensurate with it, or irrelevant to it?

How, then, did the introduction of the self concept come to pass? For it amounted, in terms of theoretical "purity" with respect to the structural theory, to the introduction of the fox to the chickens. What issues were at stake? A review of the Freudian *oeuvre*, tracing the elusive threads of the self through the theoretical fabric of the ego, will serve to highlight some of the challenges faced by Hartmann and subsequent theoreticians who worked to find and account for the self within the strictures of a structural theory.

Nowhere in the vast body of theoretical work that is the Freudian opus does the concept of the self assert a claim to direct elaboration, though everywhere it is either the silent partner or the unarticulated deus ex machina of the ego, or of the id. Nowhere does Freud find it necessary to clearly address the constituency of that which is in relationship to, indeed is the "experiencer" of and "container" for concepts with which it is intimately associated, such as autoeroticism, narcissism, melancholia, and the object world at large.

Aspects of Freud's work, perhaps particularly those which antedate the structural theory, suggest that the ego is largely understood as commensurate with the individual qua person, though this is not always the case. There are, as well, instances in which Freud does seem to be drawing a distinction, as when, for example, he discusses self-regard as "an expression of the size of the ego" (1914, p. 98) and then allows that self-regard consists of "everything a *person* possesses or achieves . . . " (1914, p. 98; emphasis added). If the level of self-regard reflects the "size" of the ego, but at the same time self-regard consists of those things a person achieves, is not *person* something other than, and seemingly supraordinate to, ego?

Again, in a similar vein, Freud (1914) will maintain, in "On Narcissism," that the ego does not exist from the outset, but that autoeroticism (i.e., a state of *self* eroticism) does. To what is the auto-erotic instinct attached if not the ego?

On the other hand, Freud (1914) suggests an easy interchangeability between these two concepts when, for example, he speaks of the narcissistic equivalence of illness and sleep; saying of the former that the ill person withdraws libido "back upon his own ego" (p. 82), while in sleep there is a "narcissistic withdrawal . . . of the libido on to the *subject's own self*. . . " (p. 83; emphasis added).

While the psychoanalytic emphasis surely shifted subsequent to the introduction of the structural theory of the mind, there yet remained no stated demarcation between the idea of a self and any of the newly elaborated elements of the mind. Was the individual subject the same as the ego, the id, and did it matter theoretically? It did *not* appear to be critical to Freud, who almost seems to have taken for granted that the constituent elements of the personality he was mapping in 1923 resided within, or were overseen by, an individual person who was different from *"his ego"*—something which belonged to that individual, was possessed by him or her. Thus he will say, for example, that "we have formed the idea that in each individual there is a coherent organization of mental processes; we call this his *ego*" (Freud, 1923, p. 17).

Adding to the conceptual indeterminacy regarding the status of the self vis-à-vis the ego, was it the same as or different from that ego, was Freud's (1923) additional assertion, in "The Ego and the Id," that the individual shall be looked upon as a "psychical id" (p. 24).

In fact, at a juncture comparatively late in his work, Freud (1930) seems rather unambiguously to equate the ego and the self. Thus, we note that within the context of a discussion of the individual's feeling of connection to the world around him, Freud (1930) observes that "normally, there is nothing of which we are more certain than the feeling of our self, of our own ego" (p. 65). In this phrase, "of our self, of our own ego," surely the comma reads "that is to say." Here at least, there is considerable clarity, the self and the ego are one and the same.

Finally, at least from the point of "Mourning and Melancholia" (1917), Freud's views began to take on a distinctly interpersonal hue, raising an entirely new, though certainly related, set of questions regarding the nature of self-identity. Indeed, as the shadow of the objective cast a new and formative light upon the subjective, it becomes clear that Freud (1917) is actually addressing the self as it is identified with the object. The ego as a defined structural entity actually will not make an appearance until "The Ego and the Id" (1923).

It is from this ambiguous Freudian notion of self, perhaps even from an ambiguous linguistic rendering of the term *self* from German to English, as Bettleheim (1982) has suggested, that the great diversity of analytic theories of self have emerged. For residing within the seminal essays of Freud's project are the kernels of the American analytic view of the self; the British view of identity formation; and the "radically orthodox" vision of Jacques Lacan. We shall look at each of these Freudian "offspring" in turn, and here begin with ego psychology.

Chapter 1
THE INTENTIONAL EGO OF HEINZ HARTMANN

In assigning pride of psychic place to the ego as a structure defined by its functions and known by a character which is both an outcome, a "precipitate," of "abandoned object-cathexes" (Freud, 1923, p. 29), and the influence of reality, some important alterations were made in the way psychoanalysis began to understand the self.

First, and perhaps foremost, the theoretical emphasis began to shift toward the formative impact of what is variously termed reality, the interpersonal or object world, and the formative influence of discrete early objects.

The ego began to be studied also in terms of its specific functions vis-à-vis the external world as well as sensations and perceptions arising internally. *Mastery* became an important accomplishment of the ego, as would the *toleration* of frustration, the *anticipation* of consequences, and the acquired ability to *delay* gratification. The latter entails the developed capacity to *censor* and *redirect* or sublimate originally antisocial proclivities toward libidinal or aggressive expression.

Clearly, the ego was becoming the agent of socialization and the pivotal work of Heinz Hartmann (1939) would lend decisive impetus to a theoretical "turn toward adaptation." Indeed the very notion that mental conflict is *the* source of individual development was modified to allow for the emergence of traits and capacities that could be conceived as arising without the need or presence of any conflict at all. Thus, "not every adaptation to the environment, or every learning and maturation process is a conflict" (Hartmann, 1939, p. 8). Critical areas of mastery and central tools of volitional activity, in short, a full array

21

of skills which define human agency and efficacy, were lifted from the realm of instinctual determinism, a psychoanalytic shibboleth after all, and placed within a newly created "conflict-free ego sphere." Thus, "I refer," Hartmann (1939) asserts, "to the development *outside of conflict* of perception, intention, object comprehension, thinking, language, recall-phenomena, productivity, [and] to the well-known phases of motor development, grasping, crawling, walking, and to the maturation and learning processes implicit in all these and many others" (p. 8).

This is a weighty list of functions which are now no longer necessarily the product of instinctual vagaries. It represents a sure and certain leave taking from a psychology of the id, but more importantly, it is, in fact, a radical departure from the intent of the analytic superseding of a structural psychology of the ego. The potential, and later actual, accretion of formative psychic powers to the structure of the ego is considerable, though not what Freud (1923) had considered.

In fact, with respect to the *person*, matters are quite the contrary. Thus, as we have noted, Freud (1923) says that, "we shall now look upon an individual as a *psychical id* ... " (p. 24; emphasis added). That is, the psychology of the individual is largely unconscious (the realm of the id) and libidinal; the ego being the conscious, perceiving arm of the id in its efforts to reach the external world. Indeed the ego is "a poor creature owing service to three masters and consequently menaced by three dangers: from the external world, from the libido of the id, and from the severity of the super-ego" (Freud, 1923, p. 56).

This is hardly the increasingly masterful ego depicted by Hartmann (1939), who was undoubtedly aware of the radical implications of his assertions. "I am not speaking," he assures us, "of a province of the mind, the development of which is in principle immune to conflicts, but rather of processes *in so far as*, in an individual, they remain empirically outside of the sphere of mental conflict" (p. 9).

Hartmann had indeed strengthened the ego beyond Freud's (1923) original formulations in his avowed effort to institute psychoanalysis as a "general psychology," and his work begs the interesting cultural question as to why he, more or less correctly, believed that a "masterful" ego, freed in significant part from the dark seductions of instinct, represented the key to "generalizing" psychoanalysis. For now we may perhaps leave this avenue of inquiry untroubled by our investigations, except to remark that a somewhat more competent horseman was that much more palatable to the empirically dominated American psychology, and psyche, recently emerging, itself a master, from the maelstrom of wartime irrationality.

More to the point in our investigation of the analytic concept of the self are some of Hartmann's writings subsequent to *Ego Psychology and the Problem of Adaptation* (1939), perhaps most particularly "Comments on the Psychoanalytic Theory of the Ego" (1950), in which he introduces the concept of the self within the context of his discussion of some inconsistencies presented by the problem of narcissism in the light of the structural theory. Just what were the theoretical difficulties that led Hartmann (1950) to introduce the concept of self at all as he moved to enhance the efficacy of the ego? As we have seen, the concept had not, after all, enjoyed theoretical clarity, let alone prominence, in Freud's own work. Why not bypass the notion all together?

The notion might well have been bypassed had it not been for the confounding problem of narcissism and the ambiguous meaning of the concept ego in Freud's earlier and "middle period" theorizing, prior to "The Ego and the Id" (1923). Indeed, Freud's assertions with respect to the ofttimes interchangeable "self-ego," admit of variable enough understandings of the concepts to create both inconsistencies in theory as well as opportunities for creative emendations. In tackling narcissism, Hartmann (1950) brilliantly managed to repair an instance of the former while simultaneously, in his introduction of the self, constructing the latter.

Subsequent chapters will illustrate how other schools of thought with respect to the self, such as the British object relations tradition and the French analytic conceptions, particularly of Lacan, drew creatively upon different aspects of Freud's work to develop their own distinct views of the self. The balance of this discussion will follow the self-concept as it entered into the American tradition of ego psychology as developed by Hartmann, elaborated by Jacobson and Mahler, and strengthened and enriched by Kernberg and, finally, departed from, in varying degrees, by Kohut.

The Ego's Strength

Though certainly aware of the conceptual ambiguities associated with Freud's development of the ego concept (see, for example, "The Development of the Ego Concept in Freud's Work," 1956) and its ofttimes easy interchangeability with the self concept, Hartmann (1950) does not hesitate to tell his readers clearly what the ego is; or, more precisely, what it is not.

It is not, Hartmann (1950) asserts, at all the same as the self. "Ego," he states, "is not synonymous with 'personality' or with 'individual'; it does not coincide with the 'subject' as opposed to the 'object' of experience; and it is by no means only the 'awareness' or the 'feeling' of one's own self. It is a substructure of personality and is defined by its functions" (p. 114).

There can be little doubt but that Hartmann here intends to distinguish the ego from the idea of one's own person. It is destined to be much more than, as he said, "only the 'awareness' . . . of one's own self." Ego is one of the three constituent elements of the psyche, indeed, in his view, the preeminent constituent, and as such demands a more complete understanding than it has hitherto been accorded.

That a psychology of the ego had not achieved its final form in Freud's work seemed clear to Hartmann (1950, 1956), whose impression it was that "Freud himself considered his formulations of that period [the 1920s] as a bold first inroad into a new territory rather than as a systematic presentation of ego psychology or as the last word on the structural aspects of personality" (1950, p. 114). Thus, quite correctly citing the unfinished nature of the Freudian text, Hartmann moved boldly, and in the service of the larger aim of instituting psychoanalysis as *the* general psychology, to strengthen and to expand the functional range of the ego. In the course of doing so we note, and will focus upon, the particular choice he made in accounting for the self, the traditional seat of personal agency, within the context of a transformed ego, now a *system* and the executant of that personal agency.

How then did Hartmann (1950, 1953) account for the self? What were the theoretical concerns that led him to do so, and what was his view of the nature of the ego and how it developed? A close reading of selected defining essays will shed important light on these and other issues surrounding the introduction into the American psychoanalytic tradition of this theoretically confounding concept.

One of the primary issues that led Hartmann (1950) to account for the self was, as we suggested earlier, narcissism and the question of ego cathexis. He was to make this accounting in a theoretically elegant manner. This paper was not, however, the first time that the self concept would be distinguished from that of the ego.

Indeed, in the course of an earlier essay, in which Hartmann, Kris, and Loewenstein (1946) set themselves the task of clarifying a number of key terms in the psychoanalytic literature, the self concept is rather sharply distinguished from that of the ego. Specifically, the authors are discussing the shifts in meaning which may occur when metaphor is employed in reference, for example, to psychic structure. They warn that structure may become misleadingly anthropomorphized, thereby endowing *systems* with qualities more aptly suited to persons.

Hartmann et al. (1946) illustrate the difficulty by drawing out the distinction they believe must be made between ego and self in order to eliminate the offending metaphorical distortions. Thus the authors refer to a sentence of Freud's in which they quote him as saying that "the Ego presents itself to the Superego as love object." The objection is the attribution of love relations between structural entities. Better, they maintain, to "replace the word 'ego' in Freud's text by the word 'self.' We do so since the ego is defined as part of the personality, and since Freud's use of the word is ambiguous. He uses 'ego' in reference to a psychic organization and to the whole person" (Hartmann et al., 1946, p. 16).

Such distinctions, in which the self is applied to one's own person, while the ego is reserved for the more circumscribed references to one of the substructures of personality, were to be greatly elaborated by Hartmann in future papers.

Although Hartmann's (1950) paper sets itself the relatively modest aim of discussing "a few aspects only" of ego psychology, it is, in fact, a far more sweeping position statement with respect to the leading role of the ego in the candidacy of psychoanalysis to become a general psychology. In order that psychoanalysis itself become a viable frontrunner it must, of course, appeal to its particular constituency, in this instance American practitioners of a pragmatic, functional, empirical, and, above all, purposive bent, firmly rooted in a strong medical heritage. Psychoanalysis had to be made recognizable to a predominant American preference for reality oriented and progressively "improving" (i.e., self-mastering) explanations of behavior, with a decided emphasis upon what is normal and normative in human expression.

Thus Hartmann (1950) informs his audience that there is indeed a trend within psychoanalysis toward an emphasis upon "a growing number of aspects of normal as well as pathological behavior . . . [as]

the techniques of adjustment to reality and of achievement . . . '' (p. 116), but that, at the same time, this trend ''should not be interpreted as a tendency away from the medical aspects of analysis or, for that matter, from its biological or physiological aspects'' (p. 117). On the contrary, psychoanalysis, by more vigorously pursuing an ego psychological line of investigation, which underscored the ego's capacity for adaptation, as well as its ''organizing'' and ''synthetic'' functions, had actually ''extended the sphere in which a meeting of analytic with physiological, especially brain-physiological, concepts may one day become possible'' (p. 117).

Hartmann's (1950) concern with methodological issues was of considerable import in establishing psychoanalysis as a respectable line of inquiry, for the manner in which it pursued its data and drew its conclusions would tell those who cared to listen whether this was ''serious'' (i.e., empirical, measurable and material) science or speculative tale spinning. An American psychological community dominated by the pragmatics of John Dewey was not likely to offer a warm reception to anything less. (To affirm that the ''objective'' yet retains dominance over the ''subjective'' as a respectable line of inquiry, one need but recall the theoretical tensions created by Kohut's bringing to prominence the latter as a method of psychoanalytic investigation; see, for example, Stolorow, Brandchaft, and Atwood [1987], who conceive of psychoanalysis in terms of an intersubjective approach.)

Thus, ''our hypotheses in this field [of ego development] rest on the solid grounds of manifold and verifiable findings of psychoanalytic data'' (Hartmann, 1950, p. 117).

These methodological concerns would etch the character of the ''American'' psychoanalytic ego as well as influence the (relatively minor) role that an independent self-concept would play in theory elaboration. For one may perhaps verify adaptation to reality, and measure one's increasing mastery of that reality; it was, and is, another matter entirely to assess the nature of self-feeling or to verify that one has psychological existence. While such phenomenal matters would be left untouched by mainstream inquiries, others became involved with them (see the discussion below of Federn, for example).

Methodological considerations aside, Hartmann's (1950) paper had two avowed aims which are of interest to this discussion: the problem of ego development and the question of ego cathexis, or what

Hartmann has characterized as "the many-faceted and still puzzling problem of narcissism" (p. 126).

The thrust of Hartmann's (1950) discussion of ego development centers around establishing a few key points, each of which is elaborated in the service of supporting the fundamental assertion that psychoanalysis is a verifiable, empirical science, rooted in biology and concerned with such matters as the genetic inheritance of predispositions for the adoption of particular defense mechanisms.

Hartmann (1950) begins his discussion of ego development by reasserting that the ego is more than the outcome of the influence of reality on the instinctual drives. In fact, in referring to his earlier work, Hartmann here notes that "we may speak of an autonomous factor in ego development" (p. 119), which, he suggests, may be understood as clusters of "inherited ego characteristics." That is to say, the ego is no longer to be understood as developing from the id: "I should rather say that both the ego and the id have developed, as products of differentiation, out of the matrix of animal instinct" (p. 120). Thus, while in substantial agreement with Freud that a formed entity, or structure, recognizable as ego does not exist from the outset, he believes genetically inherited "primordial functions" (such as perceptual and motor functions) which become an ego, do.

Hartmann (1950) then suggests, or more accurately offers as a hypothesis, that there is a "genetic correlation between individual differences in primary factors of this kind [i.e., responses to stimuli; styles for managing the postponement of drive discharge] and the later defense mechanisms" (p. 125), proposing that child analysts may wish to conduct longitudinal studies which would establish the conjectured connection. "I think," Hartmann allows, "that this hypothesis will prove to be accessible to direct verification or refutation" (p. 126). In other words, psychoanalytic conceptualizations are subject to the same rigors as other sciences and as likely to yield fruitful empirical findings.

Hartmann (1950) emphasizes that "it is indeed tempting to consider very early processes in the autonomous area as forestages of later defense against both inner and outer danger" (p. 125). I suggest that this temptation is so strong precisely because, again, it underscores that psychoanalysis is a product of acceptable biological determinants (in contradistinction to less acceptable origins for behavior, such as sexual drives). It also underscores that the ego is increasingly the seat of recognizable functions belonging to the conscious, rational self, such as cognition, perception, adaptation, and, perhaps above all, mastery, the traditional territory of behaviorists and learning theorists. The ego did not come into being as an arm of the unconscious, inarticulate, and hence unknowable id.

In consequence of Hartmann's sustained effort to "generalize" psychoanalysis, the ego became increasingly "biologized," both with respect to its genetic, nonconflictual (and thus that much less psychoanalytic) inheritance, and "sanitized" as regards its no longer libidinal ancestry. As well, the ego, at least with respect to its autonomous functions, will develop into an ego, become what it is to become, "as a result of experience (learning), [and] . . . also of maturation" (Hartmann, 1950, p. 121). That is, the ego is now, along with the influence of instinctual urges, equally the product of biology (i.e., maturation) and cognitive mastery (i.e., learning).

Hartmann (1950) calls upon Freud for the textual authority to make the theoretically innovative claim that significant aspects of ego (though not ego itself) were present at the creation, so to speak, and may rightfully assert an autonomous, nonlibidinal origin. Thus Hartmann (1950) refers to Freud's comment in "Analysis Terminable and Interminable" (1937) that "we have no reason to dispute the existence and importance of original, innate distinguishing characteristics of the ego . . . [and] each ego is endowed from the first with individual dispositions and trends . . . " (p. 240), as a strong indication that Freud had, as Hartmann (1950) asserted, "come to develop his theory in a direction which modifies his previous stand [with respect to the ego] . . . " (p. 120).

Indeed, Freud (1937) does indicate his belief that there are primary characteristics which belong to a nascent ego. However, what Hartmann (1950) is suggesting is that Freud's authority may be called upon in support of his (Hartmann's) contention that these characteristics are independent (i.e., autonomous) of the id and possess a "nonid" character; that they have emerged, as we have said, from a nonlibidinal source. This is not what Freud (1937) appears to mean, even in this late essay.

What Freud (1937) *does* say, and to which Hartmann (1950) also refers, is that:

> [W]hen we speak of an "archaic heritage" we are usually thinking only of the id . . . and assume that at the beginning of the

individual's life no ego is as yet in existence. But we shall not overlook the fact that *id and ego are originally one*; nor does it imply any mystical overvaluation of heredity if we think it credible that, even before the ego comes into existence, the lines of development . . . are already laid down for it [p. 240; emphasis added].

It seems accurate to say that Freud did not here intend to suggest an autonomous origin for these ego trends, but simply that these trends are present as forerunners of an as yet undeveloped ego, dormant within an id matrix. If the individual's "archaic heritage" is the id, and if "id and ego are originally one," then it is reasonable to say as well that ego devolved from this original heritage and that the "lines of development" that will become ego are laid down in, and are in their original character, of the id.

It does not seem entirely accurate to call upon Freudian authority in granting the ego considerable, though not entire, theoretical independence from the id. It does, however, tend to obscure the radical nature of Hartmann's addendum to the Freudian text. For where Freud (1937, 1940), it can be argued, maintained until the last that human nature, one's essential identity, was arcane and libidinal, Hartmann was re drawing that nature, employing a newly independent and masterly ego as the vehicle of an increasingly delibidinized, conflict-free image of selfhood. Thus, despite the fact that Hartmann (1950) would actually have the self-concept function as the carrier of libido being withdrawn from objects (i.e., to be the seat of narcissism), the ego, now more or less free of the libidinal burden, would increasingly come to signify the rational, desexualized self.

In his last published work, Freud (1940) says that "the core of our being . . . is formed by the obscure *id*, which has no direct communication with the external world . . . " (p. 198), and goes on to characterize that id, the core of being after all, as, among other things, obeying the "inexorable pleasure principle" (p. 198). In a most interesting comment, following immediately upon his characterization of the id as being in service to the pleasure principle, Freud (1940) suggests that to varying degrees, *all* agencies of the mind are so engaged. "But the id," Freud (1940) asserts, "is not alone. It seems that the activity of the other psychical agencies too is able *only to modify* the pleasure principle, but not to nullify it; and it remains a question of the highest theoretical importance, and one that has yet to be answered, when and

how it is ever possible for the pleasure principle to be overcome'' (p.
198; emphasis added). The ego, though owing its original impetus for
development, its raison d'etre, to the press of the external world, remains in its originary essence of the id. The psychoanalytic human
being is of this id, yet is constrained to form a defensive, and ofttimes
quite desirable, defensive shell in response to the pressures of the
outside world.

Hartmann, on the other hand, is fashioning a ''core being'' which
is, at least in part, said to arise on an equal footing with the id and to
form aspects of its protective nacre from substances *other than* the
libidinal or aggressive (e.g., one's presumably conflict-free genetic/
biological inheritance). Central portions of selfhood do not, in this
evolving view, owe their origin to the id. However, this should not be
construed to imply that drive theory had been thoroughly rejected,
either by Hartmann (1939, 1950) or the American tradition. On the
contrary, though subordinated to the ego, the id and the force of the
drives continued to play a role, albeit a modified one, in theorizing.

From the existing psychoanalytic view that maintained a person
(i.e., the personality) is a product of conflict and its idiosyncratic resolution; and Freud (1923, 1940) who had maintained that the driving
force (and the force of the drives) in human nature and behavior was
unconscious and libidinally motivated, Hartmann (1939, 1950) had
fashioned a rather different image of the individual as significantly
more rational, conscious, and, at least by biologic intention, designed
for a timed increase in mastery and self-control. He did this by desexu-
alizing significant aspects of ego, and emphasizing those functions
(such as perception, motor activity, and delay) which served what he
had referred to as autoplastic and alloplastic ends (i.e., effecting
changes in the self or the environment, respectively; see Hartmann
[1939]). An analytic notion of self as knowable and as coincident
in large part with what one *does*, was emerging from Hartmann's
constructions.

At the same time, Hartmann's commitment to the structural theory, and the prominence he attributed to the ego and its own intrasys-
temic complexity within that structure, led to an interesting, and
somewhat awkward, theoretical redistribution of conceptual priorities
such that the self was no longer the executant of personal agency. This
traditional function of selfhood would now also belong to the ego.

The Self in the Ego's World

What, then, prompted Hartmann to confront the hitherto silent ambiguity that had long existed among the concepts of self and ego? As we suggested earlier, it was the incommensurate equivalences that resulted from the application of the concept of narcissism within the light of the subsequent structural theory. Prior to 1923, narcissism had, as we have seen, been variously conceived as the libidinal cathexis of one's own self or of the ego without presenting much difficulty. After the introduction of the structural theory of the mind, however, it became a matter of considerable theoretical import just what was being cathected, for the integrity and theoretical consistency of the newly established structures was now involved.

Hartmann (1950) readily acknowledged that "in analysis a clear distinction between the terms ego, self, and personality is not always made" (p. 127) but asserts that now, in a "poststructural age," such distinctions had become essential. They are essential, that is, if one aims above all to preserve the structures created by Freud's (1923) "second theory" of the mind.

But what is it in the nature of the concept of narcissism that appears to threaten the consistency of the idea of the ego? And what is there about the ego itself that seems somehow incompatible with narcissism?

To begin with, the ego was now a system, one of three substructures of the mind; and the source of libido had been moved by Freud (1923) from the ego to the id. The relocation of the libidinal reservoir, depleting the ego of its own original supply, now made any libido which accrued to the ego by way of withdrawal from objects necessarily secondary in nature. Herein rests the difficulty, for libido originally attached to external objects (other persons) could not reasonably be understood to transfer cathexis to an *impersonal* structure. If libido is originally sent forth from the id to cathect satisfaction—producing persons in one's external world, and is withdrawn in the face of loss or significant disappointment, what can it mean to say that this libido, once adhering to another person, is now the property of an internal structure of the mind?

Hartmann (1950) did not think it meant anything promising for the concept of ego, for what can be done in the face of this inconsistency but to say either that the original libido actually cathects external systems or structures, a commensurate if manifestly impossible solution for a theory of human being, or that withdrawn libido cathects another person, in fact one's own person, one's self.

Now, the latter solution is eminently more appealing, for its humanity if nothing else, and to adopt it one must still, if the aim remains to retain the ego as a structure, take care just what role and functions this now clearly articulated target of narcissism, the self, is assigned. It is a slippery business for, as the seat of reclaimed libido, the self can easily retake the theoretical high ground, and in this way threaten to eclipse not only the ego but the structural theory itself. This threat looms large at least in part because the self remains a rather ubiquitous notion; not, as has been eternally true from a philosophical standpoint, "locatable." As such, the self is potentially discoverable anywhere, and Hartmann (1950) will, we shall see, say as much; though he will also say otherwise. What, in fact, *does* Hartmann (1950) say about this theoretical knot?

He says that the term *narcissism* has often been employed to refer to "two different sets of opposites" (p. 127) which confound clarity by being inappropriately "fused." Specifically, these opposites include the selfobject unit and the ego/id/superego equivalences; the latter possessing the character of an intersystemic relationship while the former betokens the (libidinal) ties among selves. Inconsistency rears its head when ego is imprecisely substituted for self in these equations.

Hartmann (1950) proposes this remedy: "the opposite of object cathexis [will] not [be] ego cathexis, but cathexis of one's own person, that is, self-cathexis . . . " (p. 127). Thus, as the cathexis of one's self, narcissism can no longer be said to belong to the ego, it is not, after all, what is now being cathected. Narcissism belongs instead to the self, wherever it may be "located." And indeed, "in speaking of self-cathexis we do not imply whether this cathexis is situated in the id, ego, or superego . . . [on the contrary] this formulation takes into account that we actually do find 'narcissism' in all three psychic systems . . . " (Hartmann, 1950, p. 127). This is commensurate with saying that the *self* may be "found" in all three systems. This statement is important because it opens the theoretical door to a notion of self as a kind of "movable feast," capable of discovery in *all* substructures of the mind and being a part of them. In making this assertion the self has been awarded the potential for conceptual supremacy. As well,

"in all of these cases," Hartmann (1950) says, "there is opposition
to (and reciprocity with) object cathexis" (p. 127).

Hartmann (1950) further amends the role of the self in narcissism
by editing traditional analytic language so that such well-known
phrases as ego libido take on new meaning. Thus:

> [I]n speaking of ego libido, what we ... mean is not that this
> form of energy cathects the ego, but that it cathects one's own
> person .... Also ... where we are used to saying "libido has
> been withdrawn into the ego" or "object cathexis has been re-
> placed by ego cathexis," what we actually should say is "with-
> drawal onto the self" in the first, and ... "by self-love" ... in
> the second case [Hartmann, 1950, pp. 127–128].

In these formulations the self was becoming the "object world's"
necessary other face; a conceptual Janus guarding the gates to a theoretical Pandora's box. Inside rests what Kohut (1977) would finally come
to call "a center of initiative and a recipient of impressions" (p. 99); or,
put another way, the predominant conceptual source of human being.

Although he surely did, as we shall see in following the concept
in Jacobson's (1964) work, for example, leave the door ajar for the
self concept to increasingly assert its presence, for now Hartmann
(1950) had rather different intentions. Indeed, he was seeking, by the
formulations outlined with respect to narcissism, to more certainly
secure the (structural) ego's ascendant position.

Thus, despite the absence of any (initial) implication in Hartmann's (1950) statement above that self-cathexis (i.e., narcissism) was
situated in any one particular substructure of the mind, he will nevertheless claim, in the sentence just following his discussion of the redefinition of terms herein quoted, that "if we want to point to the
theoretically and practically important part of *self-cathexis being localized in the system ego*, I would prefer not just to speak of 'narcissism'
but of narcissistic ego cathexis" (p. 128; emphasis added). Here the
self, cloaked though it is by the term *self-cathexis,* has been placed
under the purview of the ego. We have already seen how Hartmann
(1950) redefined narcissism to signify a cathexis of the self (or self
cathexis) in contradistinction to the cathexis of the ego, and now we
see that he has housed that self within the structure ego. Thus it turns
out, interestingly enough, that libido *does* return to the ego after all,
there is no departure from Freud here, but seeks out and attaches to

the newly established tenant therein, the self. Narcissism is indeed a cathexis of the self which occurs within the context of the ego. In the larger sense then it may accurately be referred to, familiarly enough, as a cathexis of the ego. Thus it is that Hartmann (1950) may express his "preference" for speaking of a "narcissistic ego cathexis." It is, mutatis mutandis, the analytic manner of depicting one's own person in an ego structural environment.

Though by no means here a "center of initiative," the self has become a certain recipient of the instinctual impress of returning libido. In consequence, the ego is freed to convert stores of instinctual energy into neutralized energy, largely because the self serves as a kind of lightning rod, drawing masses of libido upon itself, and thereby preventing the ego from becoming overwhelmed by the instinctual influx. The self may risk grandiosity, and other more severe forms of pathology (Hartmann, 1953), but as an encapsulated pocket of narcissism it allows the ego to perform other neutral functions. Thus Hartmann (1950) considers the amounts of energy the ego can neutralize as a sign of its overall strength, but adds that he "want[s] to mention, at least, the clinically well-established fact that the ego's capacity for neutralization is partly dependent on the degree of a more instinctual cathexis being vested in the self" (p. 129). Much of what the ego is able to do depends upon this ego-serving self functioning as a shunt for incoming libido.

Summary

Though there is no evidence to suggest that Hartmann intended to minimize, let alone ignore, the phenomenon that is the "awareness of one's own self," the assignment of the concept to a psychic location within the ego surely reversed the long standing Cartesian paradigm which places the idea of the self at the certain center of operation. Nonetheless, this "relocation" did not by any means close the book on the issue of the self vis-à-vis the ego. On the contrary, Hartmann's clear introduction of the concept raised more questions than it answered, for the functions being given to the ego by Hartmann, as well as by those who followed, began to sound more and more like the emoluments of the traditional self.

Hartmann's (1950, 1953) introduction of the self concept, as we have noted, was effected largely in response to the theoretical needs of the structural ego and his encompassing commitment to establishing psychoanalysis as a general psychology.

The discussion thus far has underscored that the self became a necessary component of the ego as a consequence of the inconsistency presented by equating object cathexis (the cathexis of a person) with that of ego cathexis (an impersonal structure). The self, as the psychically internal target of former object cathexes, served the useful function of establishing balanced and viable conceptual equations.

Making the self the recipient of withdrawn object cathexes did at least two important things: As the ego's reservoir for secondary (i.e., withdrawn) libido the self-concept freed the remainder of the ego to engage in energically neutralized activities. Thus, first, Hartmann (1950, 1953) constructed a self which may fairly be characterized as sexual and aggressive in nature (i.e., a libidinized self) while, second, he presented psychoanalysis (and perhaps most especially American psychoanalysis) with a structural theory of the mind characterized in large part by a neutral, rational, and, indeed, self mastering component.

We have seen as well that in making the self, in contradistinction to the ego, the container of narcissism, Hartmann (1953) was able to put forth a theoretically consistent explanation of schizophrenia as a particular instance of self pathology.

A further observation, I suggest, is that Hartmann (1950, 1953) has effected a division of labor such that the self concept contains the *contents* of personality (i.e., sexual-aggressive motives and conflicts; necessarily involving objects) while the ego is the *functional* arm of the psychic apparatus. Another way of putting this is that the ego is form, the self the substance of being; and that neither is viable without the other. The functional ego contains the self and functions on its behalf; while the self contains the contents whose absence would make functional capacity a hollow exercise. While Hartmann does not say so, he has, in my view, at least implied this fertile psychic partnership among self and ego. Indeed, he does comment that the ego's ability to perform one of its key functions (i.e., neutralization) is reliant upon the self fulfilling its role as the repository of sexualized (and aggressivized) energy. Thus, "I want to mention, at least," says Hartmann (1950), "the clinically well-established fact that the ego's capacity for neutralization is partly dependent on the degree of a more instinctual cathexis being vested in the self" (p. 129).

The nature of the ego's functions are interesting in themselves. For example, Hartmann (1939, 1950, 1952) asserts that the ego is the personality's seat of, among other things, *intentionality*, to name but one capacity whose character seems quite distinctly to suggest agency and "personhood" rather than structure.

Intentionality may be understood as one's capacity or ability to aim toward some particularly selected thing; to *choose* and express preference. How is it that such capacity may rest with the ego's function not the self's content? Many of the functions assigned to the ego bear this stamp of agency or direction which, as we have noted, traditionally suggests selfhood. And perhaps this may in part account for the definitional confusion that yet persists when speaking of ego and self. The capacities of ego do look awfully like what *people*, selves, do. Is there some viable way in which we may understand both the ego and the self as conceptual agents of the elusive essence of human identity?

Among the many fertile implications of Hartmann's work, I have chosen the following for particular emphasis:

1. Hartmann "located" the self concept within the structural ego, while at the same time asserting that the self could be found within all three substructures of the mind.

Thus we recall that in speaking of narcissism Hartmann (1950) declined to imply any particular "location" for the self, allowing that as the recipient of withdrawn object libido it may be situated in all three substructures of the mind. However, he also claimed that the self is to be understood as an entity, or more accurately an image, situated within the ego. In this way, Hartmann provided two very different avenues for theory to pursue in seeking the self concept, and we shall discuss both as they apply to the American as well as other major theoretical traditions.

Thus, the self can be portrayed, and theoretically developed, either as a mental representation created by, and housed within, the ego or, on the contrary, as a more dynamic concept, liable to turn up as an integral part of any or all substructures. The former notion of the self, we shall see, was largely adopted by the American tradition, while both the British and the French had less difficulty discussing the idea of self without establishing permanent residency within the ego.

2. The self is a product of the impersonal. While sexual and aggressive struggles remained a significant aspect of a psychoanalytic

conception of human being, it has been contained within a concept of self which, in its turn, is contained within the bounds of the neutral, rational ego. I suggest that this may also be expressed by saying that it is the impersonal which fosters the personal; that function creates the form and content of the self; or, finally, that it is the objective which contains and structures the subjective.

In other words, Hartmann's work suggests the further claim that the self is an internally established representation, a palpable and distinctly idiosyncratic experience of being created by and contained within the impersonal epigenesis of functional capacities. From the "emptiness" or "absence" of the psychic interior, images ("pictures") arise from the heat of functional interaction and establish internal "fullness" and "presence." This theme, of presence-absence, will be seen to play a significant role in the elaboration of the British and French theories of the self as well, though with a definite preference, particularly in the case of Lacan, for the "absent side" of the equation. In the chapters to follow we shall demonstrate how these rather abstract notions of presence and absence are made manifest in the interpersonal theories of self developed by prominent theorists of the American tradition, and how the concepts of self and object constancy contribute to our understanding of the subjective self as a product of the objective other.

3. A separate theory of self is contained within the ego theory. In making the self the recipient and container of libido, as well as the equational and interactional partner of the object, Hartmann laid the groundwork for a separate theory of selfobject relations. Indeed, Jacobson (1964) would entitle her most important work in this regard *The Self and the Object World*, while theories of the development of the self within, alongside of, and finally, supraordinate to the ego would all play a role in characterizing the American ego psychological tradition.

The Self and the Constant Object

As we have seen, Hartmann (1950, 1952, 1953) added theoretically ground breaking elements to a theory of the ego, making it the functional centerpiece of human development vis-à-vis both reality and the internal world of instinctual forces. We have also addressed the establishment by Hartmann (1950) of the self within the ego, specifically as an *image* within the ego.

In the following discussion we shall see that the ego is also the executant, and prime contributor, to the capacity of the self to develop a libidinal *constancy* with respect to its own self and to the external object. What is involved here is the ability to maintain the conviction of one's own sameness through time as well as to retain a consistent and mnemonically recognizable image of libidinally significant objects. We shall also further investigate the implications to an understanding of the self of the placement of the self-concept within a functional matrix (i.e., the ego).

Hartmann's (1952, 1953) placement, as we have suggested, both laid the groundwork for a study of self and object relations independent of ego functions, and left some thought-provoking implications about the interdependent nature of what I would call the self-ego matrix. Placing an image of the self within the ego, an image created by the ego, suggests that though it is the role of the self to build the mnemonic content of human affective life (ties with objects), the quality of such ties will remain dependent upon the functional efficacy of the ego. We shall have more to say about this later; first we need look at what Hartmann (1952, 1953) and others had to say on these and related matters.

Interestingly enough, it will prove more enlightening if we embark upon this aspect of our discussion by noting what, in fact, Hartmann (1952, 1953) did *not* say about the self, or more accurately, the self representation.

It will be recalled that in "Comments on the Psychoanalytic Theory of the Ego" (1950), Hartmann established the idea of the self as a representation contained within the ego and set it up in equational opposition to the object representation. However, two years later, in "The Mutual Influences in the Development of Ego and Id," in which Hartmann first mentions the term *object constancy*, he does not provide the conceptual equilibrium he had sought and achieved earlier in introducing the self concept to begin with. That is to say, there is no commensurate elaboration of an idea of *self* constancy nor will he consider the idea in his important paper of the following year, "On the Metapsychology of Schizophrenia," (1953). Let us review more closely just what was said, left unsaid, and where it led theoretically.

Mutual Influences

In many important respects Hartmann's overriding concern with enlarging the scope of psychoanalysis, employing a greatly strengthened and energically more neutralized ego concept, is reflected in his 1952 paper. Here, as elsewhere in his writings (e.g., 1939, 1950), Hartmann (1952) sets himself the aim of establishing that the ego–id relationship is a far more substantial and equally matched one than is represented by the characterization of the ego as "lead[ing] a shadowy existence" (p. 157), obscured by the instinctual press of the id. On the contrary, Hartmann (1952) asserts that "it is not always advisable to conceive of these relations between ego and id as if they were just two opposing camps" (p. 159). Rather, the ego is more productively conceived of as the id's structural coequal, representing the site of a host of mental functions comprising normal as well as possible pathological developments. Further, while it has long been theoretically known that the id exerts significant influence upon the ego, in the sense of the ofttimes caricatured "hapless horsemen" struggling to contain "superior" forces, Hartmann (1952) here emphasizes a different balance. It is a "balance," in fact, which is now tilted toward the ego, though the discussion will, as the title suggests, address the *mutual* influences of one structure upon the other.

Thus we read that in addition to being susceptible to the shaping influence of the id, the ego can, in its turn, exert its own modifying influences upon the id itself. By way of example, Hartmann (1952) notes that, vis-à-vis the id, "the ego can take a measure of influence by draining the instinctual energies of the id or damming them up" (p. 159). On the other hand, "the strength of the ego in its relationships with the id lies in finding ways that make discharge possible; or, in other cases, in imposing changes of aims, or of the modes of energy involved; [and] in the capacity to build countercathexes . . . " (p. 160). The ego–id relationship, in Hartmann's (1952) emerging psychology, has been transformed from one in which the structures of the mind, and hence the nature of "personhood," had been characterized by a dominant submissive quality to one of mutuality.

In keeping with his unifying theme, Hartmann (1952) introduces his more tightly focused discussion of ego development itself with the caveat that "to describe ego formation only in terms of its dependence on instinctual development results in an incomplete picture . . . " (p. 160). The picture is drawn closer to completion by the addition of considerations of the aggressive drive, of those aspects of ego which are "partly independent," and, for our purposes, of most significance,

the study of object relations. It is interesting to note that as the ''emotionally most relevant representatives'' of the external world, objects,
and the child's relations with them, may be productively studied for the
light they shed upon ''how ego–id relations develop in the individual's
interaction with the environment . . . [and therefore] I shall at this point
say a few words about those facets of object relations that seem relevant to our discussion'' (Hartmann, 1952, p. 161). Object relations are
by no means here a subject of study in and of themselves; on the
contrary, they represent but one important factor exerting a modifying
influence upon evolving structural entities, and it is for that reason that
they merit greater understanding. Indeed, Hartmann (1952) takes the
time to underscore the complexities of the correlations among ego
development and object relations, seeming to dismiss, and not without
irritation, those who would attribute more determinative influence than
is due to the object. Thus he asserts that ''the fact that the mother has
'rejected' her child in one way or another is frequently, in unilinear
causal relation and rather indiscriminately, made responsible for nearly
all varieties of later pathological developments and particularly of ego
disturbances . . . '' (p. 163).

The Constant Object

It is in this context that Hartmann (1952) would introduce the concept
of object constancy as he sought to clarify the role of the object in
ego–id relations. Thus, object relations will impact upon ego development, and, in turn, developing ego functions will direct the nature,
quality, and duration of object relations, so that there is a clear mutual
dependence of nature and nurture, so to speak, here as well. And object
constancy will play a significant role in making more emotionally
nuanced and enduring object relations possible. What did Hartmann
(1952) intend to convey by the concept which would be subsumed
under the broader conceptual category of object relations themselves?
That relational exchange with the object in a fully developed sense
cannot occur without first establishing the constant object.

   Hartmann (1952) draws the important distinction between ''the
object that exists only as long as it is need satisfying [and] that form
of satisfactory object relations that includes object constancy'' (p. 163).
In this way he suggests that the nature of the child's experience and

perception of the object will, or may, change over time. What accounts for the shift from "need satisfying" to "constant" object?

Nothing less than the functional capacity of the ego to neutralize stores of energy can explain the transition to constancy. "That is," Hartmann (1952) says, " 'satisfactory object relation' [sic] can only be assessed if we also consider what it means in terms of ego development" (p. 163). That is to say, the ego must be able to prepare the way for constancy; it cannot be achieved without the presence of such capacity as a functional part of the ego. Object constancy is first of all an indication of the ego's growing strength.

Now it will be recalled that in his earlier paper, "Comments on the Psychoanalytic Theory of the Ego" (1950), Hartmann defined narcissism as the libidinal cathexis of the self rather than the ego. He added parenthetically that "it might also be useful to apply the term *self-representation* as opposed to *object representation*" (p. 127; emphasis added), thus introducing these terms to denote images or pictures of the self as well as objects established within the ego. Hartmann (1952), it will be further recalled, defined the *self* as a term coincident in meaning to the expressions "self image" and "self representation," and interchangeable with them. In this way we see that the "object representation," coincident with the achievement of psychic constancy, is established alongside the "self representation" within the ego. It remains there, and acquires increasingly nuanced features because the ego is functionally able to maintain constancy, and "this constancy probably presupposes on the side of the ego a certain degree of neutralization of aggressive as well as libidinal energy . . . " (p. 163).

Two significant observations may be made here. First, Hartmann (1952) does not say constancy requires *complete* neutralization, only a *certain degree*. Thus we may extrapolate from that, as indeed later theorists would (perhaps especially Mahler), that constancy will include sustaining some libidinal cathexis of this psychic representation of the object. Another way of putting this is to say that libidinal (i.e., sexual) energy, a metaphor for human desire, attaches (i.e., cathects) to a representation, an image of *what is not*. For what is this representation of the object, but a picture, a sign, a *trace*, of what is not there?

Later in this discussion I will address this notion of object constancy as the conceptual expression of human desire bears kinship with Lacan's development of desire as the perpetual absence of fulfillment.

There are, of course, significant differences as well. Object constancy, in addition to speaking to desire, is also the manifestation via representational activity of desire's *fulfillment*, while Lacan will maintain that it is precisely the *lack* of fulfillment that defines desire and that it is such desire, in turn, that will define the self. I will address as well selected aspects of the British tradition (particularly clear in Bollas' work) that can serve as a conceptual bridge from desire to fulfillment (i.e., absence to presence) and offer an alternative way of viewing the self concept.

A second important observation, more closely tied to our immediate investigation, is that while Hartmann (1952) does introduce a notion of *object* constancy, he does not provide any discussion of what would seem to be its obvious conceptual partner, *self* constancy. This omission is left unaccounted for in his subsequent discussion of object constancy.

Contributions

The idea of the constant object reappears in Hartmann's (1953) "Contribution to the Metapsychology of Schizophrenia," where it plays a role in explaining aspects of the etiology of schizophrenia from an ego psychological point of view.

Acknowledging that Freud had understood psychosis largely in terms of conflicts and ensuing breaks with reality, which could be attributed to either the increased pressure of the drives or to specific features of reality, Hartmann (1953) sets himself the task of elucidating yet a third etiological factor "which will emphasize more strongly the role of the ego in the process" (p. 184). To a considerable extent, this is where object constancy will be discussed. Hartmann (1953) entertains a "broadening of the economic approach" to include not only quantities of energy, but "to include also the consideration of the different modes or forms of this energy . . . " (pp. 191–192). Together these two foci represent Hartmann's attempt to effect a coordination among the "instinctual and the ego aspects of the problem of psychosis" (p. 183).

In conjecturing that the ego may be the "weak link," failing to effectively mediate between reality and instinctual pressure, which in turn may lead to a break with reality (i.e., psychosis), Hartmann (1953) turns to object relations, and particularly their disturbance in infancy

and early childhood, as one possible source of explanation for schizophrenia. Thus he maintains that the failure of specific ego functions,
which under normative conditions provide the mechanisms for a functional exchange with reality, may account for the pathology. What are
those functions, and how does Hartmann (1953) understand the process
of psychological success or failure? The answer is in terms of the
structural theory of the ego, and, more specifically, in terms of his own
descriptive distinction between the ego and the self which is housed
within it.

In fact, this latter distinction is quite important, not only for the
argument at hand, but for future theoretical elaborations as well. For
in clearly asserting that the self and the ego are not the same entities,
Hartmann (1950, 1953) makes it feasible to speak, and construct theory, along two separate lines of development. Thus, in beginning his
discussion of some of the ego and object relations contributions to
schizophrenia, Hartmann (1953) says that there is "the developmental
description of object relation, on the one hand, and of the ego functions
involved, on the other . . . " (p. 187). These are clearly not the same
things, and can (and would) be developed as separate lines of study
by many in the American tradition, Kohut being perhaps the most
striking current example. Thus it is that Hartmann (1953) planted the
seeds of a psychology of the self as well as of the ego. We have yet
to satisfactorily integrate these twin disciplines.

Hartmann (1953) introduces a discussion of object relations in
order to illustrate the significant normative contribution that the ego
makes to such relations, and to the construction of an internal psychic
life. This point, in turn, is employed to assert that ego specific failures
in these respects can, in large part, account for schizophrenia. Object
relations failures are not the cause of psychotic process, they are the
manifestation of specific failures in the ego functions which enable
such relations in the first place.

Hartmann (1953) describes his view of the development of object
relations as consisting of two stages, alluded to in his earlier paper
(1952) as well, as the "relation to the need satisfying object and the
achievement of object constancy" (p. 187). And this development of
object relations contains in its turn two metapsychological concerns,
both of which arise in consideration of the second stage of this two-
part transition, namely the achievement of object constancy.

First, Hartmann (1953) asserts that ongoing relations with objects, even when satisfaction is not a pressing need, is possible because a certain degree of neutralization has taken place. Thus, object constancy is in considerable part attributable to the ego's capacity to redress the economic balance in favor of delibidinized (and deaggressivized) energy. Hartmann (1953) views this hypothesis as essential to his understanding of what occurs in schizophrenia, and will employ the economic explanation to link instinctual forces to ego functions in constructing his theoretical explanation of the condition. We shall review this position later, but before doing so I wish to look more closely at the second of Hartmann's (1953) metapsychological foci with respect to the attainment of the constant object, the genetic transition from psychic fusion toward increasingly sophisticated distinctions.

Here Hartmann (1953) conceives of an early stage in psychological being in which the infant is incapable of distinguishing between objects and his own actions toward those objects; and a later stage in which precisely such distinctions can be made. The former stage is associated with "magic action," in which the object is experienced simply as a "prolongation" of the infant's action; while the latter Hartmann (1953) says, in accord with Piaget (1952), represents an aspect of the "objectivation" of the relation, leading to a certain constancy of the object's mental representation. "Metapsychologically speaking . . . from then on there is a difference between the cathexis of an object directed ego function and the cathexis of an object representation" (Hartmann, 1953, p. 188). Here is the beginning of the inner psychic life; of the lifelong process of building, modifying, and, with varying degrees of stability, maintaining, internal representations of the object. Hartmann (1953) is quite clear in his assertion that the cathexis of the representation is a different matter entirely from the cathexis of the particular ego function which directs one's action toward the object. The individual child, in this process, is becoming aware that what he does and what he thinks and feels about what he does are indeed different matters.

This has particular bearing on Hartmann's (1953) understanding of psychosis as the breakdown of this distinction, resulting in a refusion of these normatively separate elements. Thus, the psychotic process is one in which, at least in part, the differences between one's own actions toward a reality-based object and one's mental representation of that object, are obscured. It is perhaps in this way that for the person suffering a psychosis, wishing *does* make it so.

We can now return to Hartmann's (1953) discussion of the economic feature of object constancy, seeking particularly to discern the implications for our understanding of the self concept, as well as to note how this metapsychological viewpoint impacted upon a grasp of schizophrenia.

Hartmann (1953) emphasizes that the various ego functions which are necessary to normal development and which are lost in schizophrenia, including most particularly (but not only) the ego's contribution to object relations, discussed above, become impaired or lost altogether in consequence of a failure in neutralization. It is the "sexualization or aggressivization of ego functions [which] leads to their disturbance" (Hartmann, 1953, p. 192).

Conversely put, Hartmann (1953) is actually saying that psychosis is more than Freud's (1911) original attribution of the process to a withdrawal of libido from objects into the self. Indeed, "hypercathexis of the self [i.e., narcissism], or of the ego functions, can hardly, by itself, be expected to account for the failure of the ego functions that we actually find impaired [in schizophrenia]" (Hartmann, 1953, p. 193). Narcissism may be a necessary explanatory condition, but it is not sufficient. For narcissism cannot account for those forms of self cathexis which do not involve a "sexual overestimation" of the self; nor can it answer for the distinction between the cathexis of self images and those of ego functions (the latter not being subject to *narcissistic* cathexis, which is, we recall, the libidinal cathexis only of the self, not of the ego or its functions). Finally, Hartmann (1953) notes that while characteristic ego functions (such as thinking and action) may be self directed, they may also be directed toward objects, and in the latter instance cathexis of these functions "does not mean increased interest in the self" (p. 193); that is, it does not mean narcissism. Libidinal cathexis of the self alone does not explain the ego impairments that accompany schizophrenia. What then does Hartmann (1953) propose?

We can do no better than to cite his own words at some length which, in the aggregate, have expanded Freud's (1911) statement regarding psychosis to include the ill-effects of nonneutralized libidinal energy:

> [T]he damaging effect of the withdrawal is due not only to the resulting hypercathexis of self (and ego functions) but also to the

fact that in this process they (also the object directed ego cathexes) are flooded with nonneutralized libido. Self-cathexis is sexualized, which leads to the "sexual overestimation" of the self, and so are at least part of the ego functions, which leads to functional trouble . . . [Hartmann, 1953, p. 193].

We have spent some extended time reviewing this important paper not so much for what were at the time theoretically innovative statements regarding psychosis, as for what Hartmann (1953) has said, and not said, about the self, as well as the closely related issues of the "internal world" and the role of the object.

First of all, it is clear that, taken together, Hartmann's (1953) comments regarding object constancy as the outcome of a cognitive transition to Piagetian "objectivization," made possible in consequence of the availability of neutral energy, reasserts his view that the ego and its functions make the self, and its relations with objects, possible. Constancy is an ego function after all and "the capacity for full object relations and for neutralization, and the resistivity against object loss and deneutralization are in part rooted in ego development" (Hartmann, 1953, p. 193). Normal object relations, Hartmann (1953) is saying, require functional ego capacity, including some sufficient quantity of neutral energy to maintain object relations. This view will be substantially turned about by Jacobson (1954) as an object relations theory begins to emerge from the Hartmannian background.

Second, as we have just suggested, Hartmann (1953) has, in pursuit of a theoretical explanation of schizophrenia in terms of the ego, laid the groundwork for what would become an American object relations school of thought. For it is here that he begins to outline how the internal object is established, within the ego, as a representational way of distinguishing outside from inside; reality from wish. The emphasis that Hartmann (1953) places upon the object in this paper is quite understandable, both in light of the distinctions, and equivalences, he drew earlier (1950) between the self and the object in narcissism, and in consideration of the fact that the attainment or loss of internal relations with the object had become a pivotal explanatory axis upon which his understanding of schizophrenia, particularly as a loss of ego function, turned. Placing the object representation within the ego makes it subject to the ego's functional efficacy; but it also, along with the already present self representation, sets the stage for a theory of the personality less and less in terms of the functions of the ego, and increasingly in terms of the contents of the internal representations. Ego functions themselves will come to rely upon the relationship to the internal representation and the quality of its constancy.

Finally, we cannot leave our discussion of object constancy without taking note of the curious omission from Hartmann's (1953) paper of any concomitant discussion of the self representation and, more to the point, of *self constancy*. Why is there no comparable effort here, as there was in his earlier work (1950), to establish conceptual equivalence? It was, after all, in that earlier work that Hartmann (1950) introduced the self as a representation within the ego. When, in this paper (1953), as well as in "The Mutual Influences" (1952), he introduced the notion of object constancy, why would he fail to bring a similar balance to this discussion by addressing self constancy?

In suggesting that the absence of a balancing discussion of self constancy presents a lack, the question reveals as much about the influence of hindsight as it may about any incompleteness in Hartmann's theoretical constructions. For the self concept was introduced, it seems to me, less for the sake of symmetry than for the purpose of retaining the original Freudian assertion that the ego is the seat of withdrawn object cathexes while, at the same time, advancing his own claim that the ego qua structure is not the target of libido. The self concept allowed Hartmann (1950) to remain theoretically aligned with the original assertions of "The Ego and the Id" (1923), while at the same time moving well beyond the initial, and comparatively modest, claims for the ego that Freud made in that work.

In other words, the self was introduced for its utility in promoting an ego increasingly free of libidinal constraints, and did not appear to merit any independent conceptual development, although such interest would, nearly concomitant to some of Hartmann's later work, be taken up by Jacobson (1954).

That the object *did* require further elaboration is a function of the explanatory role it was assigned in the etiology of schizophrenia. What, Hartmann (1953) asks, causes the confusion of reality and fantasy so apparent in schizophrenia? The reply elevates the object, among other factors, to causal status, for it is the failure to retain a consistently differentiated (i.e., constant) psychic image of the object that reinitiated a condition of selfobject fusion, or dedifferentiation. Thus it was that

Hartmann (1953) had to discuss the more normative evolvement of the object (i.e., object constancy).

The self required no such complimentary elaboration because there was no theoretical need to postulate its evolvement. It was enough that it was present as one aspect of the ego; in particular, that element which received withdrawn libidinal cathexes. The role it played in the schizophrenic process was to become one extended image with that of the object. It was the creation of the constant object that was seen as more important to the presence or absence of psychotic process. There was no pressing theoretical need to expound upon the self concept and, to the contrary, there may have been some perceived theoretical threat.

For to elevate the self to a causal status similar to that of the object imparts a weight to that concept which may have stretched the structural tolerance of the ego. Indeed, this is precisely what would happen as the self began to attract increased theoretical interest.

In concluding this aspect of our discussion of the emergence and evolution of the self concept in the American tradition, there are a number of significant summary statements which may be made with respect to the concept as Hartmann (1950, 1952, 1953) introduced and employed it.

Perhaps most notable among any set of closing comments is Hartmann's (1950) introduction of the self as a *representation* within the ego. As such, it may be said that the self is an idea or image created by the cognitive and perceptual functions of the ego in consequence of experiential contact with the world and with one's own body. It is to this idea that affective import is attached. Thus it is that the self is one of many functional productions of the ego, and clearly within the dominant purview of this substructure of the mind. The self is a dependent concept, reliant upon a substrate of ego capacities which antedate its own emergence and which play a significant role in shaping a knowledge of one's own person. Thus we may say that the self is a precipitate of the interaction of more elemental ego functions, as cognition and perception; the outcome of structure.

It may also be noted, in connection with Hartmann's (1950) having established the self as a representation, that in doing so he also *located* the self. Thus the concept, which in psychoanalytic thought prior to Hartmann, and most particularly as Freud himself employed it, was frequently interchangeable with the idea of ego at all levels of the latter concept's evolvement, now not only was subject to the direction of the ego, but was to be found within it as well.

Having said this, it is worth recalling that at the same time that he assigned the self an originary seat within the ego, Hartmann (1950) also asserted, in equating narcissism with the libidinal cathexis of the self, that narcissism, and hence the self, could be found "in all three psychic systems" (p. 127). Although most of Hartmann's own writing, as well as prominent theorists of the American tradition following his lead, would adopt the former stance in addressing the self concept, he nonetheless did also suggest the theoretical possibility of pursuing a notion of the self which is necessarily an aspect of all regions of the mind and not confined to any one in particular.

A second observation that may be made in concluding this aspect of our discussion is that for Hartmann (1950, 1952, 1953) the *self functions primarily as a libidinal lightning rod.* In taking returned object cathexis to itself the concept serves as a magnet within the ego, collecting the unpredictable and conflictual forces of libido in one narcissistic bundle, freeing the ego to employ neutral energy in its pursuit of harmonious, successful exchanges with the external world.

Finally, we note that overall the self concept appears to have been introduced by Hartmann (1950) not so much as an explanatory tool in furthering the understanding of the person or personal identity, as for its utility both in establishing internal consistency within Freud's (1914) dynamic of narcissism and in elevating the ego to the predominant position of executant of the mind. He apparently felt no theoretical need to pursue, as we have noted, any concomitant postulation of a self constancy to match the development of object constancy. For the latter served to advance his aim of explaining schizophrenia in terms of the ego without sacrificing Freud's (1914) narcissistic speculations. A notion of self constancy offered no comparable utility, for Hartmann's ego psychology was disinclined to pursue the more detailed questions of how development, particularly identity development, proceeds. As we have suggested earlier, introducing self constancy as an area meriting independent elaboration implies an equal theoretical footing for self valuation, which Hartmann seemed not to find necessary or desirable as he sought to secure the ego's structural dominance.

Hartmann's (1939, 1950, 1952, 1953) very fertile body of work generated many important theoretical statements addressing the persistently ambiguous ego–self relationship (e.g., Jacobson, 1954, 1964;

Spiegel, 1959; Sandler and Rosenblatt, 1962; Sandler, Holder, and Meers, 1963; Mahler, 1967) and the role this relationship has in the development of human identity. The American tradition became increasingly interested in pursuing questions of an interpersonal as well as, and in some instances rather than, a structural nature. Consequently, because the questions raised were designed to elicit more information about the contributions of significant other objects in the evolving life of the child, the self necessarily began to take on enhanced conceptual importance. For even as Hartmann (1950) had said, the equivalent partner of the object is not the ego, but the self. As the object grew in explanatory stature, so inevitably did the self.

Chapter 2
THE REPRESENTATIONAL SELF
OF LEO SPIEGEL

The conceptualization, even if in nascent form, of an internal world, which in some respects represents the events and significant objects of the external world, has been an increasingly important aspect of psychoanalysis, at least since Freud's (1917) early declaration that "the shadow of the object fell upon the ego . . . " (p. 249). Not only is this a concise recognition of the importance of the object, but an introduction to what would become a richly detailed and dynamic inner world.

In concert with his increasing acknowledgment of the formative impact of the object upon the elaboration of personality, Freud's (1920, 1923) theoretical formulations during the 1920s began to construct and refer to the mechanism of identification and, of course, the formation of the superego, both of which serve as analytic signposts to a complex psychic life. Indeed, we may say that Freud (1940) himself aptly characterizes the "internal world" (in a brief chapter of the same name in his posthumously published work) when he comments that "a portion of the external world has, at least partially, been abandoned as an object and has instead, by identification, been taken into the ego and thus become an integral part of the internal world" (p. 205). Thus here, as earlier in "The Ego and the Id," Freud (1940) dates the onset of the internal world as coincident with the consolidation of the superego, a consolidation made possible by employing the internalizing mechanism of identification.

From the sketchy suggestions of an internal world initially formulated by Freud (1917, 1920, 1923, 1940), a virtual explosion of theoretical construction has followed. The increased consideration given to

51

the nature of the internal world by psychoanalysis in conjunction with, and as a necessary conceptual companion to, an emphasis upon the impact of the external began, as we have seen, with Hartmann's (1950) introduction of the self. However, a preoccupation with interiority, and increasingly, with questions of subjectivity and the formation of the self, were by no means restricted to the American school of ego psychology. Such issues were, if anything, even more central to the concerns of the British and French psychoanalysts, whose work we shall review below. Here, however, we will focus upon the elaboration of the internal or representational world as it unfolded within the boundaries of an ego psychological point of view.

That the key word in this aspect of theory building was to be *representation* is of consequence to our argument that American (and British) theories of self are fundamentally theories of presence or, more accurately, demonstrations of the achievement of psychic coincidence. The word carries the implication that there is or was an actuality and that it can be had again.

A representational world is literally one in which things (people, events, experiences) which were palpable in one realm, the external, are made present again (i.e., *re*presented) in another. Now that other realm, the psychic interior, *is* only insofar as it is an imaged constellation of occurrences made coincident to and identical with the somatic interior (i.e., present), which sensate experience has differentiated from the exterior. The representational world is the psychic equivalent of an already encountered somatic reality and becomes the increasingly complex pictorial presentation of that reality as well as the reality which is outside the body.

The theoretical introduction of the representational world, which in many respects is a conceptual term equivalent in meaning to self representations, mental representations, and, as in the case of Spiegel's[1] (1959) important work, the self, led analytic theory in some unanticipated directions with regard to the self concept. Theory became increasingly taken with the "mutual influences" of the self and the ego, and in some cases, as we shall see, of the *prior* influence of the self representations upon the formation of the ego itself. What follows is a review of selected theoretical statements which have contributed

---

[1] References to Spiegel's ideas in this chapter are exclusively to his 1959 paper.

significantly to the conceptualization of the self, and psychic life generally, as a *re*presentation.

Spiegel's Self as Framework

Many of the issues alluded to above, and in previous chapters, as the
nature of the self vis-à-vis the ego, its relationship to the object, and
perhaps of most immediate relevance, its connection to the self representation, are taken up by Spiegel in his important if unexplored paper,
"The Self, the Sense of Self, and Perception."

In this paper Spiegel sets himself no less a task than offering a
reconceptualization of the self in terms of the more distinctly ego
psychological point of view of perception. His approach includes a
comparative discussion of the differences between self, self representation, and self feeling, highlighting some of the inconsistencies that
arise when theory is, paradoxically, strictly consistent.

Thus, Spiegel begins by noting that the very term *self representation* is predicated upon the prior assumption of an independent entity
called the self. Further, regardless of one's position on this point, all
theoreticians, he asserts, do agree that self representation refers to
images of the body. Thus, taken to its logical conclusion, the self
representation, as a representation of the self, requires one to concur
in the view that the self and the body are one and the same. This,
Spiegel notes, is internally consistent but "does violence" to the psychoanalytic project, which aims to describe its concepts in mental
terms. Thus, he concludes, it "seems quite difficult to maintain the
concept of an *independent* entity, the 'self,' which is mirrored in self-
representations" (p. 86; emphasis added).

If the self representation, as a collection of the various images of
the body, is not the same thing as the self, what is the self and how
is it distinguished from the object? Before responding to that query,
Spiegel first sets about tracing the evolution of the self representation
itself, as distinct from that of the object representation. How does *that*
take place?

Here the reader is reminded of the well-known phenomenon of
dual sensory perception, which refers to the fact that in touching one's
own body two sensations are experienced, from one's hand touching,
and from the part being touched. This sensation is not mirrored when

touching another, an experience in which there is but a single sensation. In this latter event, we know only what it felt like to touch (the other), but not what the other felt in being touched. Now this duality of sensation, as Hartmann (1950) has pointed out, does not extend to the interior of the body, where only single representations arise. Thus, knowledge of the interior, Spiegel reasons, derives from the press of instinctual stimuli failing to reach motor discharge. Self representations in and of themselves, are more or less organized collections of sensations attributable to one's own being, and distinguishable, by reason of sensual and perceptual experience, from the concomitant collection of sense data attributable to the object representation.

Spiegel concludes that it is "these principles, of duality of sensation and failure of motor discharge, [which] make of the totality of self-representations something more than a heterogeneous collection; they become an organization, they become a unity—the self" (p. 87). Here is a concept of the self as the outcome of the increased organization of mental representations, themselves reliant upon sensory experiences. The self is an organizational principle, derived from the prior mental representation of sensory activity and clearly *not* an independent entity.

In light of the persistent confusion of the term *self* as it is popularly used to denote one's total being, and the far more restricted technical usage in psychoanalysis to indicate narcissistic constellations in the mind, Spiegel proposes to use the word *person* to signify the total physical and mental individual, while reserving self "for the totality of self representations as opposed to object representations within *one* mind" (p. 87). The self, in this view, has clearly, and in line with Hartmann (1950), been held to an essentially passive position, dependent upon antecedent operations for its developed realization. What then, is self feeling? Are not *self* and *self feeling* coincident terms, denoting one and the same quality of me-ness? In Spiegel's conceptualization, the terms would indeed coincide if they were *person* and *person feeling,* for in such an instance we are referring to our total being and the feeling associated with it. The relationship between self and self feeling, however, is considerably more complex. Indeed, it will require Spiegel to construct a very interesting paradigm which offers a novel explanation of depersonalization while at the same time, and perhaps most significantly, introducing the idea of *self constancy* within the context of a new conceptualization of the self.

The Averaged Self

Drawing upon data from the field of perception, specifically the phenomena of the afterimage and its distinction from the primary percept, Spiegel sets about constructing a convincing analogous explanatory model to account for the steady, or not so steady, state of the self feeling.

The difference between the constancy of the primary percept and the more variable afterimage is attributable, Spiegel reports, to the fact that in the former case, wherein we are actually perceiving an object, that percept has the external world as its frame of reference and it is a reliable (i.e., constant) framework. On the other hand, the afterimage must depend upon the framework of the body to reproduce and sustain the image. This is a framework which, though functional, is far less steady for not having the invariable cues of the physical world to call upon.

Now, Spiegel reasons, internal mental states must, as do perceptions of the afterimage, also have some more or less reliable manner in which to be "seen" if chaos and discontinuity are to be avoided. Just as the perceptual afterimage has the body as a framework, the mental representations of particular physical and mental states, Spiegel posits, also have a framework to which such representations are referred and against which they may be assessed. "This framework is the self" (p. 96).

The self, we shall see, is here conceived as an internally constructed paradigm against which individual self representations are assessed for essential "recognizability." Further, once established, this self serves to provide the sense of continuity so intimately associated with self identity by referring otherwise intermittent and discontinuous mental representations to their place within the more extensive frame. Another way of expressing Spiegel's idea is to envision the self as a complex web of averaged self representations which, in its entirety, represents a fund of information against which subsequent single self representations may be "recognized" and hence understood as belonging to, but not the same as, the person. But how does this self as framework get constructed?

At the outset of mental life, Spiegel reasons, each discrete sensation, typically of bodily tension discharge states, leaves its own mental trace or representation. Initially, these events, such as thirst or hunger, are not mentally recognized as that which had occurred before. Instead, they are regularly *re*presented to the mind as separate mental images, and in this way account for the posited discontinuity and chaos of early mental life. After a time these individual representations are "pooled" into what Spiegel refers to as "an average representation which . . . now possess[es] permanence and continuity in time" (p. 96). These "averaged representations" now come to stand for the more general experience of thirst or hunger even if each discrete thirst or hunger experience varies slightly from the one before.

Self-Constancy

In like fashion, these "averaged representations" in turn "become interconnected and grow into a steady frame of reference to which we give the name of self" (Spiegel, p. 96). And as this self becomes increasingly weighty, the cathectic importance of any single, fleeting self representation is proportionately reduced. That is to say, the entire person is less and less subject to the disturbances of randomly represented images as she or he is increasingly able to understand and often anticipate them in terms of the steady presence of the frame.

Now, Spiegel tells us, the feeling of constancy associated with the self is attributable, among other factors, to the maintenance of a balanced ratio between the cathexis of individual representations, or small clusters of representations, and the entire self. In other words, the person must be able to focus upon new and perhaps idiosyncratic events, while at the same time sustaining a perpetual investment of the larger frame into which such events can be more or less comfortably assimilated. The person must simultaneously be able to cathect the particular and the general.

Such self constancy can be disturbed when there is a sharp disruption in the cathectic ratio such that the ego is temporarily (or more permanently) overwhelmed by increased amounts of instinctual cathexis (e.g., as in adolescence). An imbalance in favor of the discrete representation leads, Spiegel claims, to depersonalization experiences, or alterations in the self feeling. Conversely, we may say that self constancy is the normative outcome of the ego's capacity to sustain cathectic investment in the self as frame of reference, while yet diverting sufficient cathexis to mentally represent the discrete events of daily living.

It should be noted that, consistent with his avowed intent to conceptualize the self from an ego psychological standpoint, Spiegel attributes to the ego the functional responsibility for "pooling," or averaging, the discrete self representations, and for establishing connections among them to construct the self as a framework within the ego. There is no self that is not the product of the structure ego and may be considered an epiphenomenal product of the ego's capacity to organize and synthesize sense data into consistently recognizable, and hence *personally* meaningful occurrences.

Spiegel's conceptualization, building as it does upon Hartmann's (1950), represents a unique illustration of the construction of psychological presence in the mental representations comprising the self as framework from absence, or more strictly speaking, the absence of meaning that discontinuous and random assaults of sensate experience may be fairly deemed. For where there had been only the mental *trace* of a single event which could not be "refound," the ego establishes a construct within the mind that is available as a constant referent. Where there had only been brief moments of intense bodily sensation which left in their wake only the mental sign of what was absent, the ego erects a more or less permanent sign, a continual presence, in the form of the self. This sign, this referent, not only integrates separate representations, *it makes order of chaos and something of nothing*.

Sandler and Rosenblatt's Representational Expansion

Spiegel's hypothesis of the self as a massive framework of interconnected representations whose presence makes for *meaningful* experience, is echoed and amplified in the decisive formulations of Sandler and Rosenblatt (1962) in their important paper entitled "The Concept of the Representational World."

The concept was introduced in order to account for a number of observed difficulties in the course of their research on the Hampstead Index,[2] of which this paper is a partial report. The authors had observed that many of the therapists participating in the effort to place treatment material within the categories of the Index appeared disinclined to

---

[2]The Index was a plan to classify material from the Hampstead Clinic (see, for example, A. Freud [1959] and Sandler [1960]).

characterize the behavioral expressions of their child patients as manifestations of internal superego conflicts. On the contrary, most therapists preferred to classify material in object relational, particularly
transferential, terms. That is, Sandler and Rosenblatt (1962) concluded,
therapists were interpreting behavior in terms of the *external* rather
than the *internal*. This, the authors surmised, might well be the result of
the patient's having reexternalized what is actually an internal conflict,
leading the therapists "to see the material produced by the child more
clearly in terms of the externalized conflictual relationship rather than
the internal structural one . . . " (Sandler and Rosenblatt, 1962, p. 130).
This led to the hypothesis that the difficulty with regard to indexing
was arising in consequence of a lack of clarity with respect to terms
such as identification and introjection. It was in order to clarify issues
such as these surrounding the inner-outer dichotomy that the concept
of the representational world was here introduced.

In taking into account "our knowledge that perception of objects
in the external world cannot take place without the development . . . of
[a] set of representations . . . " (Sandler and Rosenblatt, 1962, p. 131)
of that world, the authors have clearly gone beyond the descriptive
accounts of the child's inner world that were then prevalent and which
may have taken their cue, as we suggested above, from Freud's (1940)
own account of this realm. For here Sandler and Rosenblatt (1962) put
forth the dynamic claim that a representational substrate must have
established a prior presence in order that the raw sensory data of the
external world be properly processed and organized into meaning. This
representational container, as it were, is the necessary causal agent, the
essential condition under which the child can construct a meaningful
understanding of the world and, as we shall see, create an idea of self.

Thus have Sandler and Rosenblatt (1962) themselves created the
notion that there is a dynamic, actively causal internal world, which
exists, indeed, which must exist, *prior to* the internalization of parental
norms and strictures which traditionally had marked not only the acquisition of the superego, but of the structured internal object as well.
And so it is, the authors assert, that "transferring the authority and
status of the love objects to the 'inner' world can only take place after
the child . . . has created stable object representations in his representational world" (p. 132). The more complex structural components of
the mind, we now see, are reliant upon the prior existence of a viable
set of internal representations. The prior arrival of the representational

world is an activity different in kind from the functional operations of the structure ego. How, in fact, do Sandler and Rosenblatt envision the relationship between the representational world and the ego itself?

Indeed, the authors believe that it is "important to delineate the relation between the representational world and the ego . . . ," and do so in asserting that "it is a function of the ego to construct a representational world from the original undifferentiated sensorium of the infant. This goes hand in hand with ego development, for the building up of representations is a *sine qua non* for ego development . . . " (p. 136). Now this is an interesting statement and appears to make two different claims with regard to the chronological sequence of events.

Sandler and Rosenblatt (1962) clearly assert that in this process of establishing the representational world "the ego is and remains the active agency" (p. 136), and that it is an ego function to engage in the construction of this inner world. In this the genesis as well as the function of the "representational world" bears kinship with Spiegel's (1959) elaboration of the self.

However, they have *also* said that the evolution of the representational world "goes hand in hand" with ego development (i.e., occurs *simultaneously*). Further, they seem to suggest, within the same statement, that ego development itself is dependent upon, and hence is, to a certain extent at any rate, *subsequent to*, the "building up of representations." We see from this somewhat detailed assessment that the struggle to retain the organizational primacy of the concept ego continues to manifest itself, while at the same time making room for a more distinctively *subjective* sense of interiority long associated with the phenomenology of the "I" experience.

We are reminded of observations made earlier, in connection with our discussion of Hartmann's (1950) introduction of the self as an entity within the ego, when we note Sandler and Rosenblatt's (1962) observation that "a specialized part of the representational world consists of symbols for things, activities, and relationships, and *provides the furniture for the ego function of thinking*" (p. 133; emphasis added). For here, as in Hartmann's (1950) work, we are struck by the fact that though structurally subsumed by the ego, the self, or the representational world, which includes the self representations, both serve as the necessary content of personhood, while the ego remains the indispensable container for and enabler of such content. Increasingly, the ego appears more and more to require the very representations it may create. At the same time, the suggestion is surely in the "air" here that these representations themselves are the more elemental constituents of the psyche and are responsible for, indeed are the sine qua non of, ego development itself.

In fact, it is well to recall that by the time Sandler and Rosenblatt (1962) were making these assertions, Edith Jacobson (1954) had already published her very influential paper, "The Self and the Object World," in which she had definitively asserted that "the meaning of the concepts self and self-representations, in distinction from the ego, become lucid when we remember that *the establishment of the system ego sets in with the discovery and growing distinction of the self and the object world*" (p. 85; emphasis added). The self and the object world, the interior–exterior divide, must be found before the ego can begin to be established. The implicit suggestion appears to be that the system ego is becoming the dependent variable.

Now what is the nature of this internal representational world that Sandler and Rosenblatt (1962) are constructing, and what has it to contribute to an evolving self concept? It is, the authors tell us, "more than object or thing representations . . . " (p. 133) and includes the body image, created from internally experienced sensations, as well as "affect representations," which are the psychic representations of the drives. This latter notion will later prove to be of considerable theoretical value to Kernberg (1975, 1976).

Interestingly, Sandler and Rosenblatt (1962) expand the idea of the body representation so that it is included within the more inclusive concept of *self* representation while playfully asserting that "the self-representation . . . is first and foremost a body representation" (pp. 133–134). However, the self representation, we shall see, is also "much more than a body representation" (p. 134).

All the Self's a Stage

Though initially deriving from bodily sensations of pleasure and unpleasure, the self representation comes to indicate a much wider constellation of elements which the person has perceived, consciously and unconsciously, as belonging to and characterizing his being in the world. Sandler and Rosenblatt (1962) underscore that the construction of the self representation is an outcome of ego functions, and is but one constituent feature of the more inclusive representational *world*.

Likening this representational world to a stage within a theater, the authors attribute to the ego all the silent service functions that a theater normally carries out in order to ensure the success of the performance. And all the representational world is a stage, upon which we may discover representations of significant objects playing supporting roles in the unfolding self representative drama.

Sandler and Rosenblatt (1962) aptly highlight, in their dramaturgical metaphor, the container–contained construct we have already noted in aspects of Hartmann's (1950) work as well and which, of course, Bion (1962) employed to such fertile ends, although with a somewhat different theoretical emphasis. Clearly, the authors here suggest, the "show" could not go on, the representational world could not be sustained, without the proper and regular functioning of the (theater) structure. Nonetheless, it is well to recall that, as Sandler and Rosenblatt (1962) themselves have said, and as their metaphor again clearly demonstrates, the play is the theater's raison d'etre; for without the play, the theater is "sound and fury" indeed.

Importantly, Sandler and Rosenblatt (1962) added significantly to the theoretical advancement of the self concept and, as had Spiegel, redressed somewhat the conceptual balance which Hartmann (1952, 1953) left askew when the idea of self constancy was not developed alongside that of object constancy. In referring to the self representation the authors clearly assert that "it has a status which parallels that of object representations . . . " (p. 134). The idea of the self is here, as it was, and would become elsewhere (e.g., notably Jacobson, 1954; Mahler, 1967) a concept which is being assigned attributes and features suggesting an increased impact upon the formation and character of personality. The self was not only moving to center stage, as it were, but there were signs that it might yet steal the theoretical show.

The certain theoretical expansion of the representational world contributed significantly to the increasingly prominent role of the self (i.e., the self representation) in post-Hartmannian as well as post-Freudian theory building. The self had become for Spiegel, as we have seen, an elaborate framework of generalized self representations to which all subsequent experiences are referred for assessment and integrative placement. For Sandler and Rosenblatt (1962) the representational world itself claimed a very similar organizing function, while the self is understood as an organized representation within that world, indicating the manner in which the individual perceives himself. In both cases the self is a construct created by the ego, but increasingly independent of it, and in neither case is the self coterminous with the person, as Hartmann (1950) had earlier suggested. A further contribution to the growing influence of the representational world, and the self within it, is the development of the "ideal self."

The Ideal Formulation

The concept, in direct comparison to that of the older, if variously conceived concept of the ego ideal, is drawn by Sandler, Holder, and Meers (1963). In this discussion the authors are led to the important if somewhat understated conclusion that "we *could not differentiate* an ego-ideal system or structure as functionally distinct from the ego and the superego" (Sandler et al., 1963, p. 150; emphasis added). They will, however, differentiate an ideal self, and place it within the representational world as one shape or form of the self representation.

"The Ego Ideal and the Ideal Self" (Sandler et al., 1963) is the outcome, as the paper before it, of the authors' ongoing efforts to classify case material within the Hampstead Index. Sandler et al. (1963) are led to formulate the concept of an ideal self in consequence of their having found it "impossible to distinguish sharply between the operation of an 'ego ideal' and the superego system" (p. 139), while at the same time observing many behaviors in their child patients which did relate to ideal formation. Thus if the psychic formulation of idealizations *is* taking place, but if it cannot, with any theoretical accuracy, be attributable to an agency (i.e., the ego ideal) which is consistently distinct from the superego, how can the idealizing processes be understood?

Following a brief but instructive review of the literature, including Freud's own statements regarding the ego ideal as well as post-Freudian explanations and emendations, Sandler et al. (1963) conclude, as we have noted, that "no precise agreement exists on what particular elements should be referred to as the ego ideal" (p. 150). Consequently, they suggest that the representational world be employed as the decisive explanatory concept in understanding the formation of the ideal. Thus, taking into account "the fact that the ideal self and object representations exist from early in development, well before the formation of the superego . . ." (Sandler et al., 1963, p. 151), it is more convenient to attribute idealizing functions to the representational constellations.

While not declaring the ego ideal obsolete, the authors do place the idealized *self* in a more elevated position. The concept of an idealized self has several advantages over its predecessor, including its definite location within the representational world, and its existence prior to the full consolidation of the superego, which explains the presence of idealizing activity before the appearance of that structure, to which Freud (1923) had married the ego ideal.

The ideal self, the authors go on to explain, is one of the manifestations that the self representation can adopt. That is, the ideal self is "that which, *at any moment*, is a desired shape of the self—the 'self-I-want-to-be' " (Sandler et al., 1963, p. 153; emphasis added). The ideal self, we see, is a variable construct, not given to fixed representation. Rather, it is subject to the assumption of many forms dependent, in turn, upon a number of largely economic influences.

This notion of the form or shape of the self representation, of which the ideal self is but one instance, is addressed by both Sandler and Rosenblatt (1962) and Sandler et al. (1963), and adds something to the concept of the self representation generally, as well as to the notion of an ideal self. It is, we read, a feature of the self representation that it "can assume a wide variety of shapes and forms, depending on the pressures of the id, the requirements of the external world, and the demands and standards of the introjects" (Sandler and Rosenblatt, 1962, p. 135). Similarly, Sandler et al. (1963) assert that the shape of self (or object) representation refers to "the particular form or character assumed by that representation at any given moment . . . " (pp. 151–152).

Thus not only the ideal self, but the self in *all* its representational manifestations, is a moment-to-moment affair, subject to the vagaries of instinctual pressure and cathectic allotment. The self representation may don a shape pleasing to the narcissistic interests of the person, or it may, in response to overwhelming unconscious wishes, involve attitudes which provoke the ego to erect defenses against its emergence.

While Sandler et al. (1963) do attribute a "stable core" of early identifications to the ideal self, the overriding impression is of its essential fluidity. Subject, as we have noted, to the vagaries of instinctual economics, we do not easily envision an ideal self which is continuous and selfsame, but rather as a series of photographs in search of a theme. Interestingly, that theme may reside in the authors' characterization of the ideal self as "an attempt to restore . . . the primary narcissistic state of the earliest weeks of life" (Sandler et al., 1963, p. 156). For that primary narcissistic state is a dedifferentiated condition, a time before knowledge of the other, when all was coincident with all. If the ideal self seeks to return to this state, to represent it, then perhaps we may detect the selfsame effort to reestablish a presence for the self, drawn from the past that has yet to pass. The ideal self may be understood, at least in part, as a representational effort to establish coincidence.

Summary

In concluding this aspect of our discussion we note the following with regard to the self concept as it emerges from the series of papers reviewed:

First, some comments regarding the important view of the self concept contained within Spiegel's (1959) paper. While never explicitly claiming the contrary, he opens his discussion by regretting the assumption of an independent self, which is contained within the term self *representation*. To represent, he reasonably comments, is to suggest there is some other thing which *is* in some other place. The nature of the construct Spiegel offers suggests his view that the self represents nothing, but rather *is* an outcome of the ego's work.

In going on to posit a self whose operational meaning is as a psychic framework constructed by the functions (especially perceptual and organizational) of the ego, Spiegel makes no claim for an *actual* self, instead referring to his *framework* as the self. The self representations which go into the collection that will become the framework are psychic depictions of *bodily* events, sensate experiences, and failures in the motor discharge of tension. We also recall that he made a clear distinction between the total mental and physical person and the self as a subdivision, within the ego, of that person. The self, we see, is a psychic phenomenon only, and is without its equivalent "presentation" in palpable reality.

Thus, in seeking to represent nothing, Spiegel has constructed a self concept whose function it is to create the psychic sensation of *something*—an originary presentation of continuity. It is a self which, in serving as an interconnected frame of "averaged" representations against which disparate and discontinuous single representations of bodily and external events may be recognized, effectively obscures the discontinuity that each psychic event suggests. His is a self which allows the events which occur to appear reliably real and present by serving as a kind of psychic screen upon which otherwise strange occurrences are seen to be familiar as they are successfully matched with similar configurations. Too many radically different experiences (i.e., "nonmatches") will shake the frame and leave the person complaining that he does not feel real, that is, events are *de*personalized, or no longer present to and coincident with the felt experience of self.

Thus we arrive at Spiegel's (1959) second important contribution. He has here also provided the first explicit statement regarding the nature of self constancy, relating it to the maintenance of a desirable balance between individual self representations and the more inclusive self as framework. His conceptualization of the constancy of the self goes a considerable distance toward explaining the phenomenology of disturbances in self feeling from a dynamic and essentially ego psychological point of view. Indeed, the very introduction of the self constancy concept provided a balance to Hartmann's (1950) earlier discussion of the importance of the constant object.

Sandler and Rosenblatt's (1962) paper, and Sandler et al. (1963), advance the notion of interiority considerably in their respective contributions. Here, an elaborate, complex inner world is posited in which increasing formative influence is assigned to the representations of self and objects. These representations have assumed a degree of chronological and determinative precedence over the more elaborate structures (i.e., the ego and superego) which, in their turn, are increasingly reliant upon the representations, both for their own unfolding and for their meaningful content.

Thus do Sandler and Rosenblatt (1962) attribute to the representational world as a whole antecedent organizing functions similar to Spiegel's (1959) self. And the variable shape or form attributed to the self, and the ideal self, by Sandler and Rosenblatt (1962) and Sandler et al. (1963) is also in accord with Spiegel's (1959) view of the original or regressive nature of psychic events. Indeed, it is his self as framework conceptualization which serves to mitigate against this variability.

It is, however, to the idea of chronological and determinative priority that we shall turn our focus. For it is in the view that the self and its world of objects is the formative bedrock upon which the structures of personality (i.e., the ego, the superego) shall stand, that contributed to the evolution of theory in the direction of the self concept. In order to see these developments in their clearest form, the following sections will review selected significant aspects of the work of Mahler (1958, 1963, 1967) and Jacobson (1954, 1964).

Chapter 3

THE INTERPERSONAL SELF OF EDITH JACOBSON AND MARGARET MAHLER

Both Mahler (1967) and Jacobson (1954, 1964) give more than a passing nod to the traditional analytic emphasis upon energic and structural influences in identity formation. However, the thrust of their work, though different in some significant respects from each other, shares a move from explanation, which drive and structure represent, to description. Both bodies of work seek to reconcile their observations in terms of established principles of metapsychology (e.g., economic, structural, and genetic axes of explanation).

Edith Jacobson's Self

Jacobson (1954) introduces her discussion of the self embedded within the larger context of a reconsideration, and eventual reformulation, of the energic aspects of the concepts of narcissism and masochism. Her understanding of the self will be directly tied to the meaning attributed to primary narcissism and primary masochism, conditions which exist prior to the child's discovery of self and others. What, Jacobson (1964) asks, can these concepts possibly refer to in the organization of a psyche which antedates the evolution of the structure ego and the consequent emergence within that ego of self representations?

We recall Hartmann's (1950) related discussion of this issue, in which he reconceptualized narcissism as the cathexis not of the ego but of the self representation within the ego. Hartmann's (1950) formulations, however, were referring to secondary narcissism within a more structured psyche, while Jacobson (1964) is here addressing the role

of *primary* narcissism in a far more primitive arrangement, in which
there is as yet no awareness of self. As we shall see, the absence of
awareness of self will not preclude the presence of some rudimentary
form of self, not unrelated to Hoffer's (1950) notion of the body ego.

In seeking to reconcile Freud's (1923, 1924) somewhat ambiguous statements with respect to primary narcissism and primary masochism (and perhaps especially the associated activity of the postulated
death instinct), referring as they do to discharge upon a self which is
as yet unstructured, Jacobson (1964) posits a Hartmannlike "undifferentiated 'psychosomatic' matrix" (p. 6) which contains both (narcissistically characterized) libido and the energy of the destructive instinct,
for which, Freud (1940) noted, there is no comparable descriptive
term. Jacobson's (1964) undifferentiated matrix is not the same as
Hartmann's (1939, 1950, 1952); rather, it is its economic equivalent.
That is, while Hartmann's (1950) undifferentiated matrix describes the
common *structural* source of both the ego and the id, Jacobson's
(1964) matrix addresses the fused, essentially valence neutral, *economic* state of instinctual energy prior to bifurcation into libidinal and
aggressive tendencies.

In postulating an undifferentiated drive energy state, Jacobson
(1964) is able to "dispose of the concept of primary masochism, i.e.,
of Freud's death instinct" (p. 15) by hypothesizing that what is being
discharged is simple drive energy, in its original state devoid of aggressive (and libidinal) character. In this way Jacobson (1964) does away
with the need to explain the puzzling original investment of the self
with the destructive forces of aggression in the service of a primary
death instinct. But does not the same undifferentiated matrix which
defuses primary masochism also eliminate the need for a primary narcissism?

Indeed, in her initial version of "The Self and the Object World"
(1954) Jacobson did assert that, should her notion of an undifferentiated energy mass prove valid, it would "compel us to dispose of the
concepts not only of primary masochism but also of primary narcissism" (p. 83). However, by the time she revised this work, Jacobson
(1964) came to believe that narcissism ought to be retained, as it was
still useful as a term to describe the infantile state in which the only
awareness is of one's bodily tension and relief. Importantly, and consistent with the valence neutral demands of her postulated paradigm,

Jacobson (1964) is careful to underscore that the term *primary narcissism* "bears no reference to energic and structural differentiation and the corresponding establishment and cathexis of self and object representations" (pp. 15–16). Such references are strictly reserved for secondary narcissism. Now it is within the parameters of her discussion of the nature of this early economic distribution within the psyche that Jacobson (1954, 1964) introduces the self.

Distinguishing drive discharge to the "inside" from that to the "outside," Jacobson (1964) reasons that the early infantile state is likely to be characterized by a pronounced cathectic tilt toward body organs (i.e., the "inside") over drive investment of the "periphery," that is, the perceptual and motor apparatus. Thus, at the outset a "continuous, 'silent' discharge of small amounts of psychic energy may occur . . . mainly through 'inside' physiological channels" (Jacobson, 1964, p. 8). It is precisely this "inside space" that constitutes the self. It is a physiological self, a body self, comprised of the sensations experienced when undifferentiated drive energy is discharged inward. It is Jacobson's (1964) "*primal psychophysiological self*" (p. 6), characterizing the origins of self as it is correlated with a particular psychoeconomic state of energic fusion. Further, we see in the "primal psychophysiological self" the assertion that, as Jacobson (1964) herself claims, "psychic life *originates* in physiological processes which are independent of external sensory stimulations" (p. 11; emphasis added).

Thus does Jacobson (1964) assert that psyche is the offspring of soma; the person a product of the impersonal. Here we note the origin of the self in the body, much in the manner of Hoffer (1950) when he asserts that "the self emerges as a function of the interaction between inner drive (stimulation) and the apparatus (bodily organs like the mouth) through which the drive acts" (p. 23).

In an important footnote to the introduction of the "primal psychophysiological self," Jacobson (1964) underscores that she is adhering to Hartmann's (1950) conceptualization of the self as "referring to the whole person of an individual" (p. 6n). Jacobson (1964) goes on to say that for the sake of clarity she will, when speaking of the self, qualify the term with such modifiers as *physical* or *psychic* or indeed *psychophysiological,* for " 'self' is an auxiliary descriptive term, which points to the person as a subject in distinction from the surrounding world of objects" (Jacobson, 1964, p. 6n).

Thus, the "primal psychophysiological self" is but one of many facets of the whole person, both psychic and somatic, for which the term *self* is to be employed. The psychophysiological self is perhaps the first of these manifestations, but by no means the only one. Self is both a compound referent, speaking to the "manyness" of the person, and the semantic indicator of his or her ultimate "oneness" (i.e., the entire, complete, and *"whole* person of an individual"*).

Despite tying the initial manifestation of the self to the sensate impact of drive forces, Jacobson (1964) actually devotes much of her discussion to the idea of the self as a *representation* within an aspect of the mind. A representation which is comprised of endopsychic images of the bodily and mental self. In this, she is a leading post-Hartmannian influence upon theory construction as it turned toward the representational, and we have already seen the fertile, and increasingly drive-distant direction that such theory was taking in the hands of Spiegel, and Sandler and Rosenblatt (1962), for example.

Thus, Jacobson's (1954, 1964) effort to marry the self, at least in its embryonic form, to the drives, seems more an effort to remain within the bounds of orthodoxy than a commitment to the roots of personal identity and selfhood as residing within the essentially somatic pursuit of drive gratification. Indeed, as we have noted, the first stirrings of self are within a *neutral* drive matrix and thus may be said to be tied to a general bodily "energy" rather than a particular valence of drive.

On the contrary, we shall see that not only does the self largely emerge as a function of the representation of its interactions with objects, but that it is the very dawning of the awareness of one's own self that triggers the development of psychic structure.

Indeed, the ego is now at least as influenced by the self as it enters awareness, as the self is shaped by the evolving ego structure. Jacobson's (1954, 1964) development of the self rests upon the antecedent discovery of the object world; the not-me having to be found before the me can be known. The "self" and the "object world" must also have been "discovered" for the ego to get started. Thus both the self and the ego are reliant upon finding the object world, while for the ego to begin its development the prior distinction between that object world and self must take place. Jacobson (1964) says that "the establishment of the system ego sets in with the discovery of the object world and the growing distinction between it and one's own physical and mental self'' (p. 19).

Now the ego is reliant for its structuralization upon the prior discovery of the external, but as Jacobson (1964) here clearly asserts, that is not the end of it. The ego also requires that there be a "growing distinction" made between that object world and "one's own physical and mental self." Without the distinct awareness of me/not-me there can be no ego. Structuralization cannot proceed, nay it cannot begin, if this distinction is not made. Further, if it is to be made at all, we must concede the inevitable antecedent presence of some notion of self, no matter how rudimentary, which makes the distinction. And we must note as well the almost casual manner in which such statements contain the acknowledgment that self and ego are not the same entity.

Lest there be any doubt, Jacobson (1964), elaborating somewhat on Hartmann's (1950) original distinction of the self representation *within* the ego, clearly states that much conceptual ambiguity can be attributed to the absence of clarity among the terms. She notes "the lack of distinction between the ego, which represents a structural mental system, the self . . . and the self representations" (Jacobson, 1964, pp. 18–19). In this we see that Jacobson (1964) is making no metapsychological claim for the self. On the contrary, it is the ego which represents a *structural* system; while the self is an "auxiliary *descriptive* term . . . " (Jacobson, 1964, p. 6n; emphasis added).

Jacobson (1964) goes on to note that it is the distinction between the object world and one's own physical and mental self that clarifies "the meaning of the concepts of the self and self representations, as distinct from that of the ego . . . " (p. 19). Clearly, self and ego are not the same; and it becomes equally clear, we see, that Jacobson (1964) maintains the chronological coequivalence, if not primacy, of the self concept in laying the psychic groundwork for the ego.

Indeed, there is reason to believe that Jacobson (1964) envisioned the self-*representation* as distinct from the self as a descriptive term for the "person as subject" as a kind of supraordinate structure which, in the course of development, comes to subsume the ego within which it began. Thus we note her commentary on this point, made in a discussion of the formation of a "realistic image of the self." Such an image, Jacobson (1964) asserts, will more or less accurately reflect "the potentialities and abilities, the assets and the limits of our *bodily and mental self.*" While the bodily self will consist of anatomy, appearance, and physiology, the mental self is, on the other hand, comprised of "our ego, our conscious and preconscious feelings and thoughts, wishes, impulses and attitudes . . . [and] since ego ideal and superego are part of our mental self, such an image must also correctly depict our preconscious and conscious ideals . . . " (p. 22). Jacobson (1964) here appears to be pointing in the direction of an overarching "mental self" (presumably the mental self representation) which comes to both supersede and include the ego, the ego ideal, and the superego. Thus, the notion of a supraordinate self which, we shall see, is quite unambiguously adopted by Kernberg (1982a), may trace its roots to Jacobson's (1964) earlier suppositions.

The ego begins to develop as the object world is discovered to be separate from the self. That discovery, in turn, is contingent upon the construction of endopsychic self and object representations of the "actual" self and world. That is to say, the ego dates its own beginnings to the psychic representations of the self and object, and it is to these same self and object representations that the continued structuralization (i.e., increased complexity of mental life) of the ego may be attributed. And this construction of self and object representations, Jacobson (1964) tells us, is the outcome of "ever-increasing memory traces of pleasurable and unpleasurable instinctual, emotional, ideational, and functional experiences and of perceptions with which they become associated, [from which] images of the love objects as well as those of the bodily and psychic self emerge" (p. 19).

Now Jacobson (1964) takes a moment to define her conceptualization of the self representation, and in reviewing that understanding here we shall be rewarded with an interesting insight into the nature of what the self is and what it can possibly know.

We come to know ourselves, to construct our self (and object) representations, Jacobson (1964) asserts, in two distinct ways. First, by a "direct awareness of our inner experiences" (p. 20), as sensations and functions of the body and the thoughts and emotions internally generated. Second, we arrive at a degree of self knowledge by viewing ourselves as objects; that is, by achieving a (more or less) detached stance vis-à-vis our own activities.

Jacobson (1964) is presenting some interesting notions here. She tells us that we know that we are, and come to recognize who we are, by the internal images, or "pictures," we draw; and that we do this "drawing" both in subjective and objective hues.

Let us briefly consider our first observation that self knowledge is a matter of the self representations which evolve. It seems to me that Jacobson (1964) here suggests that a self is indeed a psychic construction; the epiphenomenal outcome of a biological substrate whose psychic potential is actualized in contact with the objective. The self, in other words, begins as a silent inner space in which physiological processes make themselves felt but not known; the self *becomes* as that inner psychic space is filled with the autonomously elaborated perceptions of both our own internal experiences and our subjectively colored visions of the "actual" object world. Jacobson's (1964) self, not unlike Spiegel's (1959), is a psychological construction resulting from, paradoxically, a self constructed or "autoinitiated" paradigm in which random sensations and inchoate external stimuli are endowed with (personal) meaning by way of a set of more or less idiosyncratic pictorial representations.

Self, as we have noted, begins as a body self. Built upon the mnemonic traces of a host of sensations generated by "autoerotic and . . . beginning functional activities . . . and of playful general body investigation . . . " (Jacobson, 1964, p. 20), the first images of self are, indeed, bodily. At the outset, these representations are hardly stable or continuous, but rather, Jacobson (1964) posits, a "constantly changing series of self images which reflect mainly the incessant fluctuations of the primitive mental state" (p. 20). Thus, a "sense of continuity over time" that may fairly characterize what is meant by self, is fashioned and refashioned, growing in complexity, as the subjective interacts with the objective.

Jacobson's (1954, 1964) work is often, and rightly, understood as an important conceptual moment in which analytic notions of self, and psychic structure formation, took a decisive turn toward the interpersonal, the "object world." It will, I suggest, prove instructive to review some of the implications of her understanding of the nature of the objective and what that may say about the self.

Jacobson (1964) makes the apparent but important observation that one's ability to be objective is limited at best, since such an ability rests in the necessarily circumscribed capacity for self detachment. This being so, Jacobson (1964) adds that "the self representations will never be strictly 'conceptual' . . . [rather] they remain under the influence of our subjective emotional experiences . . . " (p. 20). Our efforts at "objective" (i.e., indirect, nonsubjective, and detached) perception and contemplation of our selves are always "contaminated" by the inevitable presence of the subjective. In other words, not only is the "world-in-itself" largely inaccessible to purely objective knowledge, but, most significantly, one's knowledge of self is the product of subjective (i.e., internally generated) affective events.

The self, though it comes to self-recognition in the process of distinguishing the object world, the not-me, and though it requires the objective in order to become a psychological, that is a self-aware, being, it does so by making a particular use of the objective. The interpersonal world, to be "useful" as the agent sine qua non of selfhood, requires its own reformulation. The objective is passed through the necessarily subjective perceptual and emotional filters of intrapsychic experience to emerge as self knowledge. Perhaps another way of saying this is that we can only know ourselves by "translating" all not-me into the subjective language of me. Precisely because it is even more difficult to achieve detachment from one's self than from the other, the self representations "remain under the influence of our subjective emotional experiences even more than the object representations" (Jacobson, 1964, p. 20).

This notion, that the self remains tethered to and shaped by the influence of the subjective, sounds less extraordinary when viewed, inescapably, with the hindsight provided by the work of Heinz Kohut (1971, 1977, 1984) and those, such as Stolorow and Atwood (1979), Stolorow and Lachmann (1980), and Stolorow, Brandchaft and Atwood (1987), for example, who elaborated the intersubjective notion of selfhood. Thus, while Jacobson (1964) does not herself make such extensive claims, her early observations nonetheless serve as suggestive analytic forerunners of the idea of an objectively inaccessible self; a self knowable only, or very largely, in the context of one's essentially idiosyncratic experiences.

In briefly summarizing Jacobson's (1954, 1964) commentary upon the self, there are a number of items which merit emphasis. First, we would note that though the concept of "primary narcissism" is reintroduced in Jacobson's (1964) revised work, it is employed in a strictly circumscribed manner, referring only to the awareness of experiences of tension and discharge. Importantly, this conceptualization of primary narcissism connotes that period prior to the development of self and object images. No psychological self exists at this stage, though an undifferentiated "primal psychophysiological self," lacking in self-awareness, does. Thus Jacobson (1964) posits a very early self, though one lacking in those psychological attributes that allow for the distinction between itself and all else. Thus, *there is a very early concept of self, much before ego structuralization has begun.*

Second, Jacobson (1964) attributes the source of the two distinct drive valences to an originally undifferentiated psychic energy mass which is stimulated to differentiate under the influence of the external. In the process she makes a decisive theoretical move in the direction of the formative influence of the object world in determining the character of personality, and the formation of the self. *The differentiated drives themselves are established under the impact of extrapsychic forces.*

A third observation we would reiterate here is that the ego begins to develop as the self and object world are distinguished; and the self and object world themselves are distinguished as memory traces and perceptions are built into increasingly consolidated self and object representations. *The internal self representation is the necessary precondition, triggering the structuralization of the ego.* Nonetheless, despite some indication that Jacobson (1964) did consider the self as eventually becoming supraordinate to the ego, she made no metapsychological claims for the self. She adhered instead to the Hartmannian notion of the self as a descriptive for the whole person, the representation of which is housed within the ego structure.

Finally, we make mention again here, and will return to it in our concluding remarks to this section, that Jacobson's (1964) conceptualization of the self representation suggests that there is an inevitable veil between the object world "in itself" and our subjective psychic representations of that world. This veil is constructed of our necessarily emotionally colored experiences of self and object. *The self is inevitably and necessarily separated from the world in which it must find itself.*

Margaret Mahler's Developed Self

Perhaps one of the major difficulties with the concept of self in analytic theory, most particularly after 1923, is that it contains the implication of structure. To speak of a *self* is, often, to suggest *functionality*, and this, in turn, presents a theoretical threat to the conceptual preeminence of the ego. *Identity*, on the other hand, is a term more suggestive of process, of experience and becoming, than of direction, molding, and formative impact. Thus, as a concept in the passive voice, identity has had a more successful conceptual career. For example, the contributions of Erik Erikson (e.g., 1950, 1968), whose work turns upon the concept of identity, and more specifically, *ego* identity, has been well received and comfortably integrated within the body of analytic ego psychology, even if less often called upon in the current literature than was true at midcentury.

At least since Hartmann (1950) gave voice to the issue with respect to narcissism the analytic community has returned to and grappled with the concept of the self. It has sought some viable manner in which to account for the interplay of subjective and objective that explains the universally expressed and simultaneously idiosyncratic sense of I.

Mahler's work (e.g., 1958, 1963, 1967; Mahler, Pine, and Bergman, 1975; Mahler and McDevitt, 1982) is fully cognizant of this orthodox sensitivity to the functional preeminence of the ego, particularly at the time she was elaborating her central themes. As we shall see, her work will produce a concept of the self that emphasizes process and development rather than function and structure, while yet suggesting an increasingly prominent determinative role for the concept.

Setting out from the view that "a universal truth of human existence" is the "lifelong, albeit diminishing, emotional dependence [of the child] on the mother" (Mahler, 1963, p. 3), Mahler's work has proposed to investigate how it is, under what set of circumstances, that the human infant emerges, or may fail to emerge, as a separate individual being. Mahler (1963), as is relatively well known, attributes significant formative powers, in preparing the groundwork for self-identity, to the impact of the earliest months of the infant's life, when the species specific prolonged dependency is at its height. Thus Mahler (1963) asserts, "I believe it is from the symbiotic phase of the mother-infant dual unity that those experiential precursors of individual beginnings are derived . . . " (p. 3).

From this belief Mahler (1963) derives two "cardinal hypotheses," both of which originate in her important early work with psychotic children (e.g., 1952, 1958; Mahler and Elkish, 1953; Mahler and Gosliner, 1955) which constitute the guiding assumptions of her extended observations of the process she entitled, at the suggestion of Dr. Annemarie Weil, "separation-individuation."

The first of these cardinal hypotheses proposes to explain childhood psychosis as a failure of emotional development to keep pace with the biologically predetermined evolution of the ego apparatus. That is, while inborn constitutional factors unfold in a timely fashion, making it biologically and physically possible for the child to function in an increasingly independent manner, psychological maturation has lagged significantly, thus making the necessity for such functioning an occasion for profound panic accompanied by a psychotic denial of the biological fact of separation. Thus, the disjunction between normative biological and delayed psychological maturation may be held accountable for "symbiotic childhood psychosis," (see, for example, Mahler, 1963, 1967; Mahler and LaPerriere, 1965).

The second major hypothesis, to a large degree the obverse of the first, asserts that for a "sense of identity" to develop and be sustained, the child must, as a "crucial prerequisite," enjoy a "normal separation-individuation" (Mahler, 1963, p. 5). That is to say, the child must have been able to, first, engage himself, attach to the mother, and then, somewhat later, *differentiate* from the psychological state of symbiosis and move progressively toward separate functioning.

Derived from her observation that psychotic children have lost, or have failed to achieve, a sense of personal identity, Mahler (1958) reasoned that, consequently, "these children do not attain the separation-individuation phase which is the first level of the normal child's subjective, but all-important, sense of individual entity and identity" (p. 173). This second hypothesis suggests that identity is a matter of successfully achieving the milestones associated with progressively separated and individuated psychological functioning. Indeed, as Mahler and Gosliner (1955) unequivocally state, "the aim and successful outcome of this individuation process is a stable image of the self" (p. 111).

From these two hypotheses, which inform Mahler's work nearly from the outset, we see that her claim for personal identity, one's sense of self, of being a distinct person, rests upon the conception of two developmental tracks, the biological and the psychological, which normatively but not necessarily coincide to produce a fully functional self. It is, as her hypotheses suggest, and subsequent observational data appear to support, possible to develop requisite ego apparatuses, which at least since Hartmann (1939) are understood to develop as part of one's genetic, conflict-free inheritance, and still fail to achieve one's self. The ego can develop without generating a stable sense of self.

Though now a commonplace in most analytic exchanges, the notion that the physical arrival of a child was *not* the entire story, was surely breaking new ground when Mahler (1972) suggested that "the biological birth of the human infant and the psychological birth of the individual are not coincident in time. The former is a dramatic and readily observable, well circumscribed event; the latter, a slowly unfolding intrapsychic process" (p. 120). Now, not only was Mahler (1972) suggesting that the child enters the world in some profound, and characteristically human sense incomplete, but the potential to become a fully human being (in possession of a sense of self) requires a second birth, which is by no means as readily achieved as the first.

What is the origin of that sense of self? How, psychologically, is it constituted? It will be recalled that the second of Mahler's (1963) major hypotheses asserts that the elaboration of a sense of identity is attributable to a successful separation-individuation phase and that, conversely, symbiotic psychosis is the outcome of a "lack of differentiation between the self and the nonself" (p. 5). Thus we may say that self, here employed interchangeably with identity, is a product of differentiation. The self is all that is not nonself, and the infant first becomes acquainted with this dichotomy through the body.

Much as Jacobson (1954, 1964), Spiegel (1959), and Hartmann (1939, 1950) had, Mahler (1963) also reaches back to the Freudian heritage, paraphrasing the well-known claim to assert that the self is first and foremost a body self. Equally in accord with her analytic colleagues, Mahler (1963, 1967; Mahler and LaPerriere, 1965) will, as well, conceptualize that body self as a *representation*.

The earliest sense of self derives, Mahler (1952, 1958; Mahler and Gosliner, 1955) says, from those sensations, most especially enteroceptive–proprioceptive in nature, which comprise the first representations of what will somewhat later yield individual identity. Following Schilder (1935) among others, Mahler (1952) asserts that the essence of ego development resides in the early differentiation of an image of the body, a psychic representation of the body, which constitutes the earliest knowledge of the self. The body self is a psychic composite, a translation of the accumulated experiences of being touched, of undergoing temperature changes, and of nursing, for example, into a pictorial representation of what belongs to one's own being and self and is identical with it.

Mahler (1958) makes an important further distinction with respect to the formation of the earliest self representations, suggesting that particular kinds of stimulation are responsible for nascent forms of identity, while others more directly impact upon object discrimination. Thus:

> [P]roprioceptive inner stimuli, as well as contact perceptions . . . [and] kinesthetic experiences . . . contribute much more importantly and immediately to the *core of our feeling of identity* to our body image, than the later maturing distance—perceptive–visual and auditory images. The latter contribute primarily and most importantly to the recognition of and distinction from the object world [Mahler, p. 174; emphasis added].

In other words, some aspects of biophysiological experience contribute to individuation while other aspects provide the ground for separation. Put otherwise, Mahler (1958, 1963, 1967) seems to suggest, it is indeed the constitutionally determined development of those autonomous, "conflict-free" ego functions, as visual and auditory capacity, which are necessary preconditions for psychological separation; while those factors which constitute the proprioceptive perceptions, and prepare the ground for self-identity, occur, as we have noted, in the psychologically undifferentiated state which Mahler (1967) has termed *absolute narcissism*. The self, albeit in a nascent, dedifferentiated state, here appears to antedate the ego.

Some important observations may be made regarding this distinction. First, Mahler (1958) clearly suggests that both the sense of identity *and* the recognition of objects arise from the body, the first source of psychological information. In the eternal conundrum of mind-body, the latter here surely gives rise to, indeed, rouses from dormancy, the henceforth formidable agency of the former.

Second, conceding bodily primacy, we yet may recognize that even as the body produces its most decidedly internal sensations (i.e., the enteroceptive-proprioceptive), or what Spitz (1965) has termed *coenesthetic receptivity* to refer to these preperceptual sensations, many are stimulated by the presence of an external agent. That is, a goodly proportion of the kinesthetic experiences an infant has are associated with nursing and its attendant ministrations, as are, of course, the many "contact perceptions" of early infancy. Nevertheless, this level of awareness, a proprioceptive awareness, is, as we have noted, largely associated with an *absolute* primary narcissism or "normal autism." At this very early period of extrauterine life, Mahler (1967) posits, there is no infantile awareness of the world outside. Thus we reiterate that the first stirrings of identity are prior to awareness of the other, though the other is, in part, responsible for rousing the formative inner stimuli.

Third, we observe that it is "later maturing" distance perceptive and auditory images which form the necessary foundation for becoming first "dimly," and than increasingly more surely, aware of the object world, that is, of the nonself. The ability to discriminate what is nonself is, much as we noted that it is for Jacobson (1954, 1964), an absolutely necessary condition of finding what *is* self.

But in this context we emphasize that this discovery of the object world is subsequent to (i.e., is "later maturing" than) the sensations which suggest, by their profound "innerness," that they are indeed "identical" to, coincident with, "me-ness." Mahler (1967) rather unequivocally attests to the primary formative import of the idiosyncratic proprioceptive "knowledge" of universal biology in claiming that "the infant's inner sensations form the *core* of the self. They seem to remain the central, the crystallization point of the 'feeling of self,' around which a 'sense of identity' will become established" (p. 80). The self, though hardly cognizant, begins to evolve in consequence of the biophysiological activity of the body, from which one's first "inner life" may be said to derive. This depiction of the essential, or "core" self, bears a conceptual relationship to Winnicott's (1960b) "true" and "false" self dichotomy; particularly in the implication contained in both that there *is* an irreducible, essential self.

Nonetheless, Mahler (1958, 1963, 1967) also surely emphasizes that the meaningful elaboration of identity rests in the successful recognition of separateness. Now, in order that this move toward separation take place, a prior *cathectic shift* from proprioceptive to sensory perception, mediated by the "symbiotic mother," must first occur. Later, we shall note, Mahler (1967) outlines a "second massive shift of cathexis" from the symbiotic unity to the autonomous apparatuses.

It is this first shift, however, which amounts to a "transfer of power" from the inside, and its proprioceptive language, to the outside, and the language of vision, of hearing, of the sensorium altogether, which constitutes a major step in self development. Indeed, "we know now that this major shift of cathexis is an essential prerequisite of body ego formation" (Mahler, 1967, p. 80).

The Representation of Self

Mahler (1958, 1963, 1967), as Jacobson (1954, 1964) and Hartmann (1950) before her, attributes the arrival of self, or perhaps more accurately, of self-awareness, to the moment when formerly disparate "memory islands" come together to establish a representation or image of the body. Now, in accord with Hartmann's (1950) original formulation, Mahler (1958, 1963, 1967) appears to place the representation of the self *within* the ego, thereby asserting the primacy of the latter, the origin of which is also attributable to the body. Once the images are "deposited," as an inherent part of a successfully established symbiotic matrix, these "representations of the body that are contained in the rudimentary ego mediate between inner and outer perceptions" (Mahler, 1967, p. 80).

We note in this statement of Mahler's two ideas of significance. First, that the representations are here assigned a *functional* status. From the moment of their arrival they henceforth serve as the instrumentality of differentiation allowing the infant to distinguish what is, and what is not, the self.

As well, we note a curiosity in this statement. Mahler (1967) tells the reader that the representations of the body are "contained in the rudimentary ego," thus suggesting that such an ego has prior existence. However, just before this statement, Mahler (1967) had said that in accordance with the pleasure pain sequences, "demarcation of representations of the body ego within the symbiotic matrix takes place" (p. 80).

What is meant by "body ego"? If Mahler (1967) is referring to a structural entity, distinct from the self, then it is difficult to reconcile how it may be that early representations of the body can be contained in this ego which itself is just being demarcated.

Where are the representations of the body ego being deposited, if not in the ego? Mahler (1967) here seems to suggest, in fact says, that such representations are being elaborated "within the symbiotic matrix" itself. Indeed, in so saying, it becomes possible to think of this matrix as a kind of interpersonal structure, the optimal maintenance of which serves as the cradle of the ego. For if representations of the body ego are being demarcated within the symbiotic unity, it follows that the body ego is being intrapsychically formed within this matrix, that it does not yet exist, and that the mother–infant dual unity is responsible for its successful formation. Put more succinctly, we may here note Mahler's (1967) implication that psychic structure itself is the outcome of a prior condition of psychological symbiosis. In fact, there is more than implication in Mahler's (1967) view of the symbiotic matrix. "It is," she asserts, "within this matrix of physiological and sociobiological dependency on the mother that there takes place the structural differentiation that leads to the individual's organization for adaptation: the ego" (Mahler, 1967, p. 79). Prior to ego, and reliant upon it for its own elaboration, is the interpersonal matrix which gives rise to intrapsychic structure.

Indeed, as we have noted, it is within this unity that, by way of any number of proprioceptive stimuli, particularly of a kinesthetic nature, the infant becomes tentatively acquainted with his own me-ness; it is within this unity that the first images of this nascent identity, expressed as body ego, are contained. And this early acquaintance with self, as we have seen, antedates the ego which, theory would hold, is the "rightful" container of such psychic representations. Identity begins here and the ego begins here. A close reading appears to suggest that chronology favors self identity, albeit rudimentary and lacking knowledge of itself.

Mahler, like many theorists grappling with the ego–self dichotomy in a postego structural era, retains a degree of semantic ambiguity when employing the terms *self* and *ego*. Thus, for example, Mahler (1972) makes an interesting comment which underscores the difficulties that may accompany the ego–self contest.

In discussing the initiation of the differentiation subphase, Mahler (1972) asserts that "during the symbiotic months, through the activity of the *pre-ego* . . . the young infant has familiarized himself with the mothering half of his symbiotic self" (p. 121; emphasis added). Now to what does this "pre-ego" refer? It is clearly not ego, but is not necessarily a "forerunner" either. It seems to refer, of course, to a chronological demarcation, antedating the ego. But it also suggests a *functional entity* which predates the ego. For Mahler (1972) speaks of the formative impact of the *"activity"* of this pre-ego, so we may note that it is an entity which acts; indeed it acts to cause the infant to distinguish the object world, in the person of the "symbiotic mother," an achievement of momentous psychological import. Thus we see that here Mahler (1972) attributes the beginnings of separation, the very act of which differentiates self from nonself, to an undefined pre-ego, while earlier she seemed to suggest that separation came in consequence of the distance-perceptive autonomous activities of the ego itself, such as vision and hearing.

This apparent lack of precision among the terms *self* and *ego* is symptomatic of a long-standing struggle to reconcile form and function, content and container, within the American tradition of ego psychological theorizing. For while the ego has been understood, at least since Hartmann (1950), as "a substructure of personality . . . defined by its functions" (p. 114), it lacked those characteristics of subjectivity which define the more palpable, phenomenological sense of being that one tends to refer to as "my self."

Yet no credible psychological theory could, nor aimed to, dispense with some explanation of the nature and origins of the self. As we have already noted, the concern with orthodoxy propelled many theorists to seek to distinguish among the concepts in order that the self not preempt the ego's functional structural status, but yet stand as the explanation for the consistent feeling of one's own "individual entity" as well as fragmenting disturbances in that feeling.

Perhaps this concern with differentiating among the concepts is nowhere more clearly presented than in Mahler and McDevitt's 1982 paper entitled "Thoughts on the Emergence of the Sense of Self with Particular Emphasis on the Body Self." This is an important statement in which the authors reassert the "Mahlerian" view that the self emerges, and is first recognized, as a bodily self. Indeed, "we want to stress," say Mahler and McDevitt (1982), that "at this very earliest developmental stage, proprioception, *with minimal influence from sensory inputs*, conveys the first glimmerings of a primitive core of a body self" (p. 829; emphasis added). Thus, we note again, that the self, or more properly the *sense* of self, originates in the workings of the biophysiological substrate. The first sense of self derives from sensations arising within the infant's body.

This paper also makes clear, however, the kind of distinction that Mahler's (1958, 1963, 1972) work has drawn all along. It is of considerable significance that this paper purports to address the emerging *sense* of self, not *a* self. For while the latter carries structural connotations (i.e., that some thing or entity emerges) the former speaks more certainly to a feeling, or an experience. By all accounts, the sense of self is a descriptive term, indicative of process and carries little or no metapsychological implications with regard to structure, the untroubled domain of the ego. Indeed, although the authors do not focus upon this point in the paper, they allude to it at the outset and conclude their discussion with the disclaimer that "all inferences contained in our paper about the emergence of the sense of self were made from the point of view of the central organizing, integrating, and synthesizing institution of the mind, the ego. We agree with other authors that the developing sense of self has both experiential and structural aspects" (Mahler and McDevitt, 1982, p. 845).

There can be little doubt but that the authors here wish to impress upon the reader that the ego remains the source of essential functional capacities, the absence of which effectively blocks the sense of self from emerging at all. Further, that the authors are in accord that the self has *both* an experiential and a structural aspect actually asserts more than it may at first appear. While seeming to concede the obvious, Mahler is here claiming as a legitimate realm of analytic study, the subjective phenomena associated with the acquisition of a more or less certain awareness that leads the child to "know" that "I am I." For theory as it addressed the self concept in the post-1923 era had not placed any particular emphasis upon the experiential aspects of the self. Hartmann's (1939, 1950) work, as we have seen, was virtually silent with respect to the issues of self awareness, self constancy, and other associated phenomena of subjectivity.

Where, for example, Hartmann (1939) spoke of the "average expectable environment" and "adaptation" in objective, essentially biological terms, Mahler (1966) particularized, and thereby lent subjective import to the concepts by understanding them to refer to a highly intimate, uniquely human symbiosis. Thus "the infant's environment consists at first of the mother-infant dual unit . . . [and] adaptation may be regarded as beginning with the infant's fitting into his symbiotic environment" (p. 60).

Of course Jacobson (1954, 1964) was also quite alert to the impact of the subjective, and we have noted in some detail her assertion that the self representations inescapably "remain under the influence of our subjective emotional experiences'' (1964, p. 20) and in this way circumscribe the impact of the objective. But it was Mahler (1958, 1963, 1967, 1972; Mahler and McDevitt, 1982) who, paradoxically, by way of an objective methodology, elevated the role of the ''phenomenological self.'' This particular methodology has yielded some interesting findings vis-à-vis the subjective aspects of self, which bear, as we have seen, a provocative conceptual kinship to the earlier, and differentially drawn, inquiries of Paul Federn (e.g., 1926, 1928b, 1932).

Thus we see that Mahler's effort (1958, 1963, 1967, 1972; Mahler and McDevitt, 1982) is well within that tradition which seeks to acknowledge the ego's unassailable theoretical position, but is at the same time an important thrust in the direction of the ''experiencing,'' ''feeling,'' ''subjective,'' and somewhat later ''intersubjective,'' self. That there is some terminological ambiguity is, it would seem, an unavoidable byproduct of the attempt to retain the traditional viewpoint of *self as ego*, as structure, while increasingly elaborating a vision of the self as the outcome of experiential events, particularly those generated by the ''other.'' So, for example, we have seen that at one point the representations themselves are given functional responsibility for allowing the infant to distinguish ''inner'' from ''outer,'' while at another it is the functions of the ego itself (e.g., vision, hearing) which make such differentiation possible. Finally, we note what seems to us to be Mahler and McDevitt's (1982) effort to ''rationalize'' the ambiguous Freudian inheritance when they observe that ''in his 1923 paper Freud stated that the ego—*we believe he meant the self*—'is first and foremost a bodily ego' '' (p. 829; emphasis added).[1]

Although Freud (1923) was indeed addressing, just prior to that oft-quoted phrase, the dual nature of touch perception as it relates to ''a *person's own* body'' (p. 25), and in this way may well have been thinking of subjective events, within the larger context of ''The Ego and the Id,'' the aim was surely to establish the origins and functions of the *ego*. The Freudian intent, of course, remains, as ever, available to a certain interpretive dynamism, while Mahler and McDevitt (1982) have been quite explicit in asserting that, at least in this one context, self can, and would be, substituted for ego.

---

[1]Freud's (1923) ''oft-quoted phrase'' is actually somewhat different in two different locations. On page 27 he says that ego ''is first and foremost a *body*-ego,'' and on page 26 he says ''*bodily*-ego.'' I have used the former, Mahler and McDevitt (1982) the latter.

Nowhere, then, is the self concept unambiguously given structural functional capabilities; indeed, by suggesting that the self contains both structural and experiential aspects, Mahler and McDevitt (1982) contribute to the maintenance of the theoretical, and probably artificial, distinction between feeling, experience, and structure. As we shall see, Kernberg (1982a) will dispense with this distinction. In addition to asserting no structural functional attributes for the self, Mahler (1963, 1967; Mahler and McDevitt, 1982) also makes no claim for the conceptual ascendancy of the self, but the suggestion of such things is increasingly discernible as the meaning and import of the concept unfolds.

In sum, we may say that the thrust of Mahler's theoretical statement (1958, 1963, 1972; Mahler and McDevitt, 1982) asserts that the self emerges as the result of a specific set of developing events. The self is not so much a formative entity as it is an outcome of processes both biological and interpersonal. Thus, the self is in part the result of crucial cathectic shifts from the inner to the outer world, moving the infant from autism to symbiotic "dual unity." Within that unity the active drawing out of the infant by the mother will serve to stimulate development of those perceptual functions which allow for the awareness of separate identity. Meanwhile, and this is an important point, that which is "the self" in a psychostructural sense, is coming together in the form of early internal images of the body either within the ego or as precursors of the ego itself, for this remains somewhat unclear. This latter point is of particular interest because despite the popular view that Mahler's, Jacobson's, and perhaps even Hartmann's theories represent interpersonal views of the self, and they do to a large extent, they remain, in their essence, *intrapsychic* explanations of the self. For to the extent that the self *is*, it is an *image*, a picture internally maintained which seeks to "cohere" those islands of sensate experience which seem to connote what is me and what is not.

A Mediated Self

The concept of representation provokes some interesting questions, as well as observations, about the kind of self which is being drawn. What is the purpose of the representation? What is its role?

Spiegel (1959), and Sandler and Rosenblatt (1962), alongside Hartmann (1950), Jacobson, (1954, 1964), and Mahler (1958, 1963,

1967, 1972; Mahler and McDevitt, 1982), all lend significant weight to a theoretical movement which literally, in developing its representational theme, *envisions* the self. That is, we see that the self has become, above all, an *idea*, a visual reinterpretation, of otherwise unknowable experiences. Much as Spiegel (1959) has suggested, the self is a psychologically constructed framework which mediates otherwise inchoate events, rendering them "recognizable" insofar as they conform to the elemental requirements of this frame. We have noted that there is some variable degree of cloudiness with respect to where this self is to be "located," but there is virtual unanimity that it is a *representation*.

We have observed that while the body appears to be the original source of those stimuli which give rise to a self, they do so only in "imaged" fashion. The self is not a palpable entity, but rather an intangible product of *imag*ination. And yet it is by way of this self concept that the world of reality and the "inner life" are discerned. The self quite actually serves to *represent* the world, and one's own sense of being, to the would-be knower.

All the theorists reviewed thus far, regardless of other variations, conceive of the self as the descriptive which is applied to that aspect of being which feels, which experiences, which is the seat of the subjective sense of I. While requiring the apparatus of the ego in order to approach the world and knowledge of it, such as cognitive, sensory, and motile skills, it is not the ego, but the self representation, which serves as the source of knowledge of the world and of one's own person.

In conceiving of the self as a representation there is the certain implication that what one is able to know of the world, and of one's person, is not the actual world in itself, nor even one's own actual being, in itself. Rather, what one is able to know, this view suggests, is necessarily mediated; sifted through a prefigured net, we think here of Spiegel's (1959) framework, for example, so that the nature of our knowing is already more or less precast by the shape and nature of the first representations.

The self as representation is, in some significant respects, similar to the Kantian notion that the thing-in-itself can never be known directly, but only as it is grasped by already present "preconceptions." While "representational theorists" clearly do not claim that such representational conceptions are, so to speak, "hardwired" in, they do imply that once established, they henceforth assume a like role. Thus we recall Mahler's (1967) assertion regarding the consolidation of the representations that "from now on, representations . . . mediate between inner and outer perceptions" (p. 80).

We refer once again to Spiegel's (1959) elaboration, recalling that he too constructed a paradigmatic frame of reference against which disparate representations of self and other could be assessed. His frame, in common with Mahler's (1967) notion, as well as that of Sandler and Rosenblatt (1962) and other theorists reviewed here, also served to mediate single events, measuring them against a set of already established and "averaged" representations. Thus, what is known of the world and of one's own person is known by virtue of the particular kind of "fit" that obtains between raw experience and the frame. Self, in this view, *is* the frame.

Finally, in making the claim that the self as representation is a statement regarding the inevitable distance, or gap, between what "is" and what can be known, we may fruitfully recall Jacobson's (1964) observations with respect to this very issue.

Briefly, we reiterate her main point in this regard, that though one of the primary sources of the image of self derives from the effort to view our mental and physical self as an object (i.e., in an objective manner) we can never fully escape the subjective frame from which we are bound to perceive. For Jacobson (1964) as well, the objective can only be known as it is mediated by the inevitably misshapen forms of the subjective. Thus, "we must consider that our view of the world, and especially of the animate object world, handicapped as it is by the insufficiency of human perception, easily permits distortions . . . " (Jacobson, 1964, p. 22).

The point I wish to underscore here is that in conceiving of the self as a representation, these theorists have offered up a profound contributory statement with respect to the analytic understanding of the self, and how personal knowledge may be constructed, which has not been sufficiently emphasized heretofore. For as the vehicle through which the world and one's own essential biopsychological being may be grasped, the self as representation implicitly claims both that there is an ineluctable gap between what "is" and what we can know of it; and, at the same time, that the representational understanding of self stands as a conceptual bridge across that otherwise yawning space. We shall have occasion to return to this important contribution, but first we shall pursue our rereading of analytic statements regarding the evolution of the self in analytic theory.

In what follows we trace the concept of self in selected aspects of the work of Kernberg (1975, 1976, 1982a,b) and Kohut (1971, 1977, 1984), noting that in these works the themes and struggles of the American tradition are, to a very significant extent, though eventually from very different vantage points, resolved in favor of the conceptual ascendancy of the self.

Chapter 4

THE ASCENDANT SELF OF OTTO KERNBERG
AND HEINZ KOHUT

The work of Kernberg (1975, 1976, 1980, 1982a,b) and Kohut (1971, 1977, 1984) differs in many significant respects, most notably for our purposes as regards the origin, role, and analytic meaning of the self. However, in one overriding instance they share an important conceptual link. Both Kernberg and Kohut, even as they diverge in their analytic visions, create a concept of the self which is unambiguously in the theoretical ascendant.

While, as we shall see, Kohut (1971, 1977, 1984) will eventually craft a self concept which owes little to the more traditional sources of analytic explanation, Kernberg (1976, 1982a,b) will fashion a view of the self which appears to arise almost seamlessly from all that had gone before, but is nonetheless a "radical" departure as well. The theoretical elaborations of both theorists reflect, in a sense, the "return of the repressed," in that each finally makes manifest the latent preoccupation with subjectivity, experience, and identity (i.e., with the self) that we have observed in earlier works in the American tradition.

Kernberg's Supraordinate Self

We have noted on several occasions in the course of our discussion thus far the problematic raised by a self concept embedded within a body of theory that expresses itself primarily in terms of an ego-structural conception of the mind. Thus we have seen Hartmann (1950) introduce the self as a representation within the ego, only to observe

91

that the concept remained largely in the backwaters of theoretical consideration while he elaborated upon the structural and functional components of the ego. And we have seen his intellectual inheritors, Jacobson (1954, 1964) and Mahler (1955, 1958, 1967; Mahler et al., 1975; Mahler and McDevitt, 1982) chief among them, retrieve the concept, positing an intrapsychic "representational world" in which the concept of self came increasingly to explain our own sense of being. In other words, Hartmann's (1950) heirs developed the descriptive, phenomenological aspects of self which he abjured. However, neither Jacobson (1954) nor Mahler (1955, 1958, 1967; Mahler et al., 1975; Mahler and McDevitt, 1982), not to mention Spiegel (1959) and the other "theorists of representation," ever made any metapsychological claims for the self. Such claims awaited the "radically integrative" work of Otto Kernberg (1975, 1976, 1980, 1982a,b,).

There will be no effort within the parameters of this discussion to be inclusive with respect to Kernberg's vast opus. Rather, we shall focus upon his significant contribution to the understanding of the role and meaning of the self concept in analytic object relations theory. In the course of such a review we will necessarily touch upon other aspects of his work, particularly some proposed modifications in the dual instinct theory, but this will be incidental to the primary aim of elucidating Kernberg's (1976, 1980, 1982a,b) enlarged view of the self.

"I think," Kernberg (1976) has remarked, that "the structuralization of internalized object relations constitutes a major determinant of the overall structures of the mind" (p. 110). Here, perhaps for the first time, is the unambiguous assertion that "overall structures of the mind," which must surely refer to ego, id, and superego, are determined in large, in *"major,"* part by the psychic representations (i.e., the internalizations) of relations with environmental objects. The ego itself is derived from these internal manifestations.

Thus, from relatively early in the development of his theoretical views, Kernberg (1976) would maintain, much as Jacobson (1964) and Mahler (1967; Mahler et al., 1975) had, that the psychic elaboration of the mind (i.e., *structure*) was dependent in significant and formative ways upon the prior attainment of internal representations. Indeed, ego was not the first structure of the mind. Instead, *"the first intrapsychic structure is a fused representation of self and object* that develops gradually under the impact of the relationship between mother and infant" (Kernberg, 1980, p. 25; emphasis added). Now, it is within the parameters of this revised view of the elaboration of psychic structure that the self comes to be defined.

In a paper entitled "Self, Ego, Affects, and Drives" Kernberg (1982a) offers a succinct overview of his conceptualization of the self and its relation to the ego within the context of his particular understanding of the structural theory. What was that understanding, and how did it impact upon his eventual redefinition of the self?

Kernberg (1982a) begins his discussion by acknowledging the long-standing definitional cloudiness among the terms *ego* and *self*, noting that they have often been used interchangeably, while at other times have been assigned more precise distinctions. Suggesting, much as Bettleheim (1982) had, that the semantic history of *Das Ich* is one of questionable translation and the ensuing elaborations made upon such translation, Kernberg (1982a) maintains that Freud used the word *Ich* to suggest both psychic structure *and* personal agency. Thus, "Freud never separated what we think of as the metapsychological ego from the experiencing self" (Kernberg, 1982a, p. 894). This has left the meaning of the term open; ego need not, in fact, Kernberg (1982a) argues, does not, refer only to structure, but to experience as well.

Much as we have noted earlier in this discussion, Kernberg (1982a) reminds the reader that Freud (1923) provides two distinct ways of understanding the ego within the defining text of the structural theory itself. He recalls that while the ego is described, in "The Ego and the Id," as having its roots in the id—indeed is but a surface precipitate of that id—and being dependent upon perceptual consciousness, Freud (1923) also offers a second statement concerning the derivation of the ego. The ego, we remember, is also a "precipitate of abandoned object-cathexes" (p. 29). The ego is a structural entity whose essential character is that of mnemonic container for relational experience.

Kernberg (1982a) argues that the Freudian ambiguity is to be applauded as an intentional effort to leave the ego and the self forever linked as two terminological aspects of one phenomenon. In this way, Kernberg (1982a) employs the textual authority of the structural theory itself to assert the legitimacy of his expanded definition of the self. Thus the ego, in Kernberg's (1982a) reading, contains these two meanings: (1) A *structure* which differentiates from the id, or the originally undifferentiated id-ego matrix, and crystallizes around the perception

consciousness system, and (2) a *subjective* byproduct of the internalization of psychic representations of instinctually cathected objects.

Having established the groundwork, Kernberg (1982a) proposes
to employ the term *self* in a manner explicitly at variance with what
has gone before. Quite in keeping with his view of the intentional
ambiguity of the structural theory of the psyche, Kernberg (1982a)
regrets what he refers to as the "fateful separation" imposed upon the
concepts of ego and self by the Hartmannian (1950) initiative, suggesting that "this separation unnecessarily complicated conceptualiz-
ing the relations between 'impersonal' ego functions, subjectivity, and
character structure" (p. 898). To repair the rent Kernberg (1982a)
proposes to "eliminate from further consideration" any use of the
term *self* in Hartmann's traditional opposition to object. To retain this
equivalence, Kernberg (1982a) maintains, is to foster a view of the
self as an essentially "psychosocial" entity, obfuscating the distinctions among psychoanalytic and sociological viewpoints. Thus, "insofar as *the self as person* is a psychological, behavioral, and interactional
entity, I suggest replacing 'self' with 'character' " (Kernberg, 1982a,
p. 900; emphasis added). The concept of self, we shall see, is going
to be a wholly intrapsychic entity, the formative impact of the actual
caregiving external object(s) notwithstanding.

Having dispensed with the psychosocial connotations of the term,
Kernberg (1982a) proposes reserving its use to indicate "the sum total
of self-representations in intimate connection with the sum total of
object representations" (p. 900). In asserting that the self is to be
understood in terms of the libidinal, and aggressive, investment of the
representation, Kernberg (1982a) draws heavily upon the theoretical
assertions of Jacobson (1964) and Mahler et al. (1975), whose work,
he suggests, is a "contemporary elaboration of the dual aspects of
Freud's *Ich*" (p. 900). Nonetheless, it is Kernberg (1982a) who actually maps the theoretical territory, employing as his "true north" both
Jacobson's (1964) idea that the origin of the ego is tied to the initially
fused self and object images, and the developmental data derived from
Mahler et al.'s (1975) direct observation of infants and children, to
elaborate his own developmental schemata of the self. A schemata
which, he argues, is contained within the dual meaning of *Ich* in
Freud's (1923) structural statement.

The self will develop in consequence of the evolution of internalized self and object representations, themselves subject to a particular

developmental pattern which Kernberg (1976) keys to Mahler's phases (1967; Mahler and Gosliner, 1955) and Jacobson's object world (1954, 1964). Kernberg (1976) attributes considerable formative influence to these internalized object relationship units, suggesting that they represent the "subsystems on the basis of which both drives and the overall psychic structures of ego, superego, and id are organized . . . " (p. 85). Internalized object relations units are the building blocks of the psyche.

Indeed, Kernberg's (1976) developmental framework is designed to suggest exactly that the complex structures of the mind evolve through a series of stages in which an initially fused selfobject unit, linked by an affect disposition, is gradually transformed into separated, affectively integrated, internal representations of the self and of the object. While Kernberg (1976) is not quite as explicit in his earlier formulation, it is still clear enough that his developmental schema as constructed in *Object Relations Theory and Clinical Psychoanalysis*, is primarily addressing the elaboration of a *self* system rather than the ego.

To wit, we see that his framework culminates in a fourth stage, "characterized by the integration of libidinally invested and aggressively invested self-representations into the *definite self system*" (Kernberg, 1976, p. 67; emphasis added), while somewhat in the nature of a footnote, Kernberg (1976) adds that the "ego, superego, and id, as definite, overall intrapsychic structures, are consolidated in this phase" (p. 67). Again, in the stage just proceeding this one, in which self representations and object representations are differentiated from each other, Kernberg (1976) notes that it is this "differentiation of self and object components [that] determines, jointly with the development of cognitive processes, the establishment of stable ego boundaries" (p. 64).

Thus we note that the various migrations of the internal object relations units in Kernberg's (1976) developmental framework recount a journey from autistic dedifferentiation to what is characterized as the ultimate achievement of "higher level intrapsychic object relations-derived structures" (p. 67). These "higher level" structures, as we have noted, do indeed include the ego, superego, and id, but the key term here is *object relations-derived*, for it is not until this culminating point in the elaboration of internalized object relations that the ego, superego, and id are themselves finally consolidated. They are more in the nature of outcomes than organizers. Thus, for example, Kernberg

(1976) proposes, in discussing this final stage of internal psychic development, that "insofar as the operation of repression from now on separates id from ego, one might say that the id as a psychic structure comes into existence *only at this point*" (p. 69; emphasis added).

As we have seen, it was somewhat later that Kernberg (1982a) more certainly embraced the self-ego ambiguity, employing it to buttress his now quite explicit assertion that it is the self that is the supraordinate psychic structure, evolving from the consolidation of internalized self and object representations, and subsuming other functions of the ego. Thus Kernberg (1982a) defines a self that is the "supraordinate organizer of key ego functions such as reality testing, [and] ego synthesis" (p. 914), and represents the theoretical embodiment of what he understands to be the originally dual nature of the Freudian *Ich*.

Kernberg's (1976, 1982a) model of the mind, then, rests upon the defining influence of the internalized object relations unit, and culminates in the establishment of an all-inclusive self system. "The self as a *psychic structure*," Kernberg asserts (1982a), "originates from both libidinally and aggressively invested self-representations. It is, in short, an ego function and structure that evolves gradually from the integration of its component self-representations into a *supraordinate structure that incorporates other ego functions*" (p. 905; emphasis added).

The Self as Subject

We have seen Kernberg (1976) marry the fate of the self concept (i.e., its emergence, character and stability), to the establishment of the internalized object relations unit. And we have noted as well that the eventual consolidation of the self relies, in this view, entirely upon the normative—or pathological—development toward integration of these units. Kernberg (1976, 1982a) clearly maintains that the self is a developmental concept, subject to the vicissitudes attendant upon the establishment of internalized object relations, and destined to become, under optimal circumstances, the structural and organizational center of the psyche. But what is the "substance" of this self? How may we characterize the essential threads which hold this concept together?

In a telling, if lesser known, paper entitled "The Dynamic Unconscious and the Self," Kernberg (1982b) reasserts his view of the self as the end product of a staged and epigenetic unfolding of intrapsychic events, but here ties its development to the progressive elaboration of consciousness. By the conclusion of our review of Kernberg's (1982b) argument we shall see that he is asserting no less than the conceptual equivalence of self with consciousness. An important correlative conclusion to be drawn from this paper is that the *un*conscious (i.e., the id) is itself structured, in contradistinction to the more traditional characterization of the id as a "seething cauldron" of primary process chaos, and becomes so, as we noted earlier, rather late in the development of intrapsychic life. The weight of our discussion, however, shall rest in an exploration of Kernberg's (1982b) view of the nature of consciousness in its phased unfolding, for herein rests a developmental history of the self, and an important formulation of the eternal conundrum of mindbody.

Kernberg (1982b) initiates his inquiry into the nature of consciousness by noting that one may observe, in severe character pathology, that the "contents of the id appear in consciousness in split-off or mutually dissociated ego states" (p. 5). That which belongs to the id is not always or only characterized by being in a state of unconsciousness and, in fact, Kernberg (1982b) suggests that "the quality of being dynamically unconscious may be less central in the origin and functioning of the id than we used to think" (p. 5). Both the quality of being unconscious, and the integration of the ego, Kernberg (1982b) hypothesizes, are subject to a "developmental history." This is, in fact, a rather bold reformulation of traditional analytic understanding, in which Kernberg (1982b) is suggesting that the state of (dynamic) unconsciousness must evolve, that it is not there from the outset. Now, it was just these observations that led Kernberg (1982b) to develop his paper around an exploration of the nature of early consciousness and how it may develop and give rise to a dynamic unconscious. Most especially important for our inquiry into the nature of the self concept, we shall see that Kernberg's (1982b) self is indissolubly linked to, indeed is indistinguishable from, the quality of consciousness as here defined. What then, is Kernberg's (1982b) understanding of consciousness? What are the stages he posits, and how does this relate to the emergence of the self?

To begin, consciousness "implies a subjective state" which "involves awareness of one's awareness, or self-awareness" (Kernberg,

1982b, p. 7). Consciousness means the capacity for subjective experience, coupled with the knowledge that the experience is subjective. Consciousness is, at least in goodly portion, the quality of being subjective. Incorporating neuropsychological views which understand the nature of affect itself as subjective, Kernberg (1982b) moves to claim that subjectivity, in the form of affective pleasure and pain, is present from birth. The infant is a conscious, because subjective, being from the outset. Thus Kernberg (1982b) suggests that "subjectivity . . . can be assumed to constitute the first stage of consciousness and, by the same token the *first stage of development of the self*" (p. 8; emphasis added). The self begins, we see, simultaneously with the emergence of subjective experience which in turn seems to be an essential aspect of the neuropsychological equipment of the infant (Stern, 1985).

And so it is that Kernberg (1982b) suggests that "affective subjectivity, *the primordial experience of self*" (p. 8; emphasis added), is a first psychic organizer, serving to integrate perceptions, behaviors, and interactions as they are experienced, gathering them in the form of what Kernberg (1982b) refers to as "affective memory," or an "assembly of memory structures." We should underscore here, yet again, that the self, although without self-awareness, is present in the rudimentary form of affective subjectivity. The self is present from the beginning and the self is *subjective* from the very beginning. We shall see that the ego, id, and superego do not make their appearance as defined structures until well into the elaboration of this subjective self.

In this first stage of consciousness, then, there is an experiencing, or feeling I which has no awareness of itself as the experiencer. Further, during this early period the affective memory, under the influence of peak affective states (of intense pleasure or displeasure), may initiate early symbolic activity. That is to say, one aspect or element of the affective experience comes to stand for (i.e., to *represent*) the full experience.

Peak affective states transform affective subjectivity (i.e., the primitive self experience) into mental activity with symbolic functions, which are made manifest as fused selfobject representations. The selfobject images constitute the first psychic evidence of the (intrapsychic) self. Here Kernberg (1982b) suggests, much as earlier theorists who posited a bodily beginning for the psyche (e.g., Schilder, 1935; Hoffer, 1950; Jacobson, 1954; Mahler, 1967), that the self originates in subjective experiences of pleasure and pain.

Kernberg (1982b) suggests that it is during this first stage that the early internal images gradually separate into distinct layers, differentially characterized by the quality of affective state associated with their formation. Thus, "a deep layer of fantastic imagery" (Kernberg, 1982b, p. 10) emerges in coincidence with moments of considerable affective intensity (i.e., *peak* moments) while a more surface layer condenses around periods of affective calm. In this latter state of "ordinary wakefulness" the infant engages in perceptual explorations which produce more cognitively realistic imagery. I think it is clear that what Kernberg (1982b) is suggesting is the primordial stages of id and ego development, both of which are now reliant upon object stimulated affective states. This initial stage of consciousness then, gives rise to the first self experiences, and the early structural forerunners of the id and ego, each of which is interactively dependent upon the presence of the other and all of which evolve under the impact of subjectivity.

A second stage in the development of consciousness is characterized by what Kernberg (1982b) has described as a greater degree of proprioceptive stability under varying conditions of interaction with the object. That is, the infant begins to grasp that both "good" and "bad" experiences maintain properties in common, that both pleasure and pain share certain sensoriperceptive and proprioceptive elements; and that both experiences seem to come from the same place. The infant begins to recognize that two different subjective states of affect emanate from one center. It is this discovery of a "common thread" among seemingly disparate affective moments which, Kernberg (1982b) posits, "leads the infant to assign it a 'seat of consciousness,' in short, self-awareness" (pp. 10–11). Here, primitive affective subjectivity is transformed, under interactive impact, into an awareness of self which is correlated with the increasingly differentiated representations of self and object.

Finally, a third stage of consciousness, coincident with the end of Mahler et al.'s (1975) rapprochement period, is achieved when " 'good' and 'bad' self representations built up under opposite affective conditions are integrated into a *global concept of the self*' (p. 11, emphasis added). Once the object representations are similarly integrated, complete consciousness—i.e., a "full continuity of self-awareness" (Kernberg, 1982b, p. 11)—is realized. It is at this juncture, when contradictory features of one's own being as well as those of others can, so to speak, be held in the mind at one time, that "the self as a 'categorical' concept, the self as postulated by the philosophers as well as observed in the psychoanalytic exploration of neurotic and normal persons, comes into full existence" (Kernberg, 1982b, p. 11). Thus, in the developmental movement from an initial state of affective subjectivity, through the realization of self-awareness, culminating in the consolidation of contradictory states, the "intrapsychic *structure of the self*" (Kernberg, 1982b, p. 11; emphasis added) is achieved.

Now, during this final stage in the development of consciousness Kernberg (1982b) postulates the more complex structuralization of the mind, which will include the traditional analytic entities. First, this is the phase in which the "consolidation of the self" (p. 11) occurs and, as we have noted, this consolidation depends upon the successful integration of contradictory self and object representations. This having been accomplished, the mechanism of "ego splitting" is then able to be replaced by repression which, in its turn, "leads to the formation of the dynamic unconscious in a broad sense, and to the id as an organized mental structure in a narrower one" (Kernberg, 1982b, p. 12). In other words, the id as one of the three essential structures of the psychoanalytic mind is, as we have noted, reliant upon the consolidation of the self structure for its emergence. And the contents of this id structure are the "unacceptable states of *self*-awareness" (p. 12) as well as other affective states formed under the sign of frustration or displeasure. The contents of the id are discarded early states of subjectivity. The id is a reservoir of affect, not of drives; a container for psychological states, not biophysiological ones.

Now, "the integration of the ego," Kernberg (1982b) advises the reader, "includes, in addition to the *integration of the self*, the consolidation of integrated object representations . . . the ego also *incorporates* perceptive, cognitive, and psychomotor functions" (Kernberg, 1982b, p. 12; emphases added). We note that while the ego incorporates Hartmann's (1939) traditional trio of functions, its own integration is reliant upon an antecedent consolidation of the self. Kernberg's (1982a) definition, cited earlier, of the self as a "*supraordinate structure* that incorporates other ego functions" (p. 905), is recalled.

A brief semantic side trip may serve to highlight how Kernberg's (1982b) own tendency toward terminological indeterminacy may obscure the conceptual ascendancy of the self in his elaboration of theory. Thus we recall that in his discussion of ego splitting Kernberg (1982b) "adds" that "the original lack of integration of contradictory ego/id

states (contradictory peak affective subjectivity) is gradually transformed into an active mechanism of ego splitting . . . '' (pp. 11–12).
Now what I wish to emphasize in this context is the interchangeability
established among ''ego/id states'' and ''peak affective subjectivity.''
It will be recalled that we earlier noted Kernberg's (1982b) understanding that affective subjectivity constituted ''the first stage of development of the self'' (p. 8). Now if affective subjectivity connotes both
ego/id states and the early self, we are permitted to acknowledge the
necessary equivalence of ego/id states and the early self. The constellation of contradictory ego/id states *is* the self. And, as we have repeatedly underscored, as this early self passes through the stages which
Kernberg (1976, 1982a,b) variously refers to as the ''development of
internalized object relations,'' ''development of self,'' or the ''stages
of consciousness,'' it is the intrapsychic establishment of the self, reliant upon the integration of internalized object units, which will ultimately allow for the structural emergence of the ego itself (as well as
the id and the superego).

By way of conclusion we would draw particular attention to a
number of important implications teased from this selective review of
Kernberg's (1976, 1982a,b) theoretical elaboration of the self concept.

First, we note that Kernberg's (1976, 1982a,b) self, like those of
his theoretical predecessors herein discussed, is a self of representation.
Indeed, the fully realized self is the outcome of an increasingly complex and finally consolidated constellation of internally established self
and object images representing and ''picturing'' one's (idea) of one's
self, and others, to one's self. The self is not a palpable entity, but
rather an intrapsychic precipitate of affect-based experience.

Second, and very much tied to the notion of the self as representation, is the appearance together of self and symbolic activity. We recall
that Kernberg (1982b) establishes a coincidence, in the first stage in
the development of consciousness, among the emerging feeling of I
and the initiation of symbolic thinking. The self begins to emerge
insofar as peak affective states of subjectivity are transformed into
mental activity by way of the symbol. And symbolic function is, Kernberg (1982b) reminds us, ''an active representation of an entire sequence by one element of it'' (p. 9). Thus, when a single aspect of an
entire series of subjective affective states can ''stand for'' (i.e., *represent*) that entire series, we may say that a nascent self is present. This
self is a thoroughly mental phenomenon, an intrapsychic representation

of affective states; at first rather undifferentiated and without awareness, later fully consolidated and differentiated, but owing its presence
to the symbol which stands for the already completed experience.

In this way the self may be understood as a sign, an "assembly of
memory structures," representing "all that was," and as an organizing
principle, indeed a framework in Spiegel's (1959) sense, signaling
the proper placement of new experiences within the constellation of
affective memory. The self stands between the remembered, and hence
no longer present, affect and the anticipated, and hence *not yet* present,
event as the symbol of what was and what may be. The self is a link
between absences; a momentary presence, binding conceptions of past
to expectations of future, and it is this mental capacity to unite these
primary absences that renders the sense of continuity, identity and
"sameness over time." We shall have occasion to return to this important idea of the self as a present link, after we have explored the
significant implications of the French and British schools of analytic
thought with regard to the self.

Third, we reiterate briefly what we have been underscoring all
along in our discussion of Kernberg's (1976, 1982a,b) work, to wit
the "ever-widening scope" of subjectivity. We have seen that the self
derives from subjective experience and is sustained by it. We noted
that consciousness is subjective awareness of self and that the only
fashion in which the objective world itself can be known is by way of
assimilation into subjectivity.

Thus finally, we are led to observe that despite Hartmann's best
efforts to "generalize" psychoanalysis by objectifying its conceptualizations, and elevating the structure ego to executive status, Kernberg
(1976, 1982a,b), on the shoulders of those who had gone before, has
reclaimed a place of prominence for the subjective experience of self,
so long a shibboleth of psychological understanding. And he derives
theoretical legitimacy for such claims by a reliance upon the same text
from which Hartmann (1939, 1950) drew his conclusions. Thus, "The
Ego and the Id" (1923) remains the orthodox source of an essentially
impersonal, Hartmannian objectivity, but has, we have seen, also
served as the fount from which Kernberg (1982a) could draw support
for his view that any separation of the structural from the experiential
was artificial. Indeed, it is one of the distinguishing marks of Kernberg's (1976, 1982a,b) work that he reunited these aspects under one

conceptual roof, thus establishing the self as an ascendant center of subjectivity.

Such ascendancy, we shall observe, is also the hallmark of the work of Kohut (1971, 1977, 1984), whose self psychology is very much characterized by the primacy of the subjectively experienced center of initiative that is, in this view, the self.

Kohut's Center of Initiative

The nature of the methodological claims as well as the theoretical data derived thereby, both of which are subsumed under the rubric of self psychology, have presented the American psychoanalytic tradition with the kinds of challenges to fundamental assumptions most often associated with the upheavals in the British Psycho-Analytical Society during the "controversial discussions" of the 1940s. For the differences among self psychology and the tradition of American ego psychological object relations theories with respect to the origin, functions, aims, and essential character of the self are considerable.

We have noted, in discussing a selected number of American ego psychological object relations theorists, that many of the positions adopted contained some ambiguity with regard to the origins and meaning of the self concept, but open divisions and significant departures were assiduously avoided—albeit with varying degrees of success. However, the assertions put forth by Kohut (1959, 1971, 1977, 1980, 1984) and his adherents, particularly in their more fully elaborated form after the appearance of *The Restoration of the Self* (1977), made manifest the latent struggle with subjectivity, both as a core experience of being and the defining methodology of psychological investigation. What then are some of the points of departure that may be identified between the self psychologists and the ego psychologists?

The question may be responded to by identifying at least three distinct areas in which the differences between self psychologists and ego psychologists are definitional. These include points of variance in methodological, metapsychological, and developmental concerns, each of which will serve as an organizational cornerstone of our discussion of Kohut's (1959, 1971, 1977, 1980, 1984) important theoretical advance of the self concept. We shall note, in the course of our investigation, that at the center of Kohut's (1977, 1984) work, contained within his conceptualization of the self, is a very different overall view of the nature of human being, one that strikes at the essence of the analytic paradigm.

Developmental Issues

It is perhaps unimportant with which of the three concerns we begin our discussion as, in keeping with the principle of equifinality, we will arrive, at last, at the selfsame place, for at the core of all of Kohut's (1959, 1971, 1980 1977, 1984) work is his increasingly firm commitment to the executive centrality of the self within the psychic system. Nonetheless, we begin with a discussion of developmental issues because such an initial focus will highlight not only Kohut's (1977, 1980, 1984) view of the origin and development of the self, but of the self psychological view of the essential nature of humankind as well.

Thus, an important distinction between the representational–developmental theorists of the ego psychological tradition and the self psychologists rests in their differing views of development, particularly the manner in which it is depicted to culminate. The ego psychologists, most notably Jacobson (1964), Mahler et al. (1975), and Kernberg (1976, 1982a,b), all have proposed developmental schema in which the endpoint is the achievement of some form of psychological independence from the originally sustaining object. The very name *separation-individuation,* for example, clearly suggests this thrust, and concepts such as self and object constancy surely at least imply that selfhood coincides with the achievement of intrapsychic independence.

The essence of the ego psychological object relations view, then, is that one's basic sense of love, confirmation, and support are internally derived; and that the capacity, conversely, to sustain loss, failure, and abandonment is closely correlated with the quality and complexity of one's internal world. Health, or pathology, in this view, is largely a matter of internal resources; of being able to draw from one's own stockpile. This developmental position may perhaps be likened to an analytic version of the "bootstrap" view in social welfare. While we begin by importing some "goods and services," ultimate success will depend upon learning to "fish for ourselves." Perhaps Kernberg (1976) best expresses this when he notes that "clinical observation shows how much trust in one's self and one's goodness is based upon the confirmation of love *from internalized good objects*'' p. 73; emphasis added).

On the other hand, the contrasting view of self psychology is clearly highlighted in Kohut's (1984) definition of the "sustaining effect'' of the selfobject thus: "throughout his life a person will experience himself as a cohesive harmonious firm unit . . . as long as . . . he experiences certain representatives of his human surroundings as joyfully responding to him, as available to him as sources of idealized strength'' (p. 52). In this view, the human need for the *actual* object changes only in character, not in kind. Thus, for example, one may select friends or lovers on the basis of resonances from earlier experiences with objects, or one may demonstrate a preference for one or another type of cultural experience for the reverberations of satisfaction or exultation they may bring, but one will always require "the presence of a milieu of responsive selfobjects as a necessary precondition of psychological life'' (Kohut, 1980, p. 481).

Thus, from a self psychological viewpoint, a competent self is *not* coterminous with independence—neither intrapsychic nor actual. The mark of maturity is not independence, but a mature dependence. Indeed, "self psychology does not see the essence of man's development as a move from dependence to independence, from merger to autonomy . . . [but rather] from the point of view of man's abiding need for selfobjects throughout the whole span of his life'' (Kohut, 1980, p. 479). For the self psychologist the need (for the other) is not, and cannot be, relinquished. Instead, dependence upon the other itself moves through developmental stages from an archaic total dependence toward an evolved and selective reliance. The posited end, in this view, ought not to be, indeed, cannot be the relinquishment of dependence, but rather its evolution in the direction of the resonant acceptance of increasingly complex others, who are able to provide the particular levels of support to the self which may be needed across the life-span and which characterize the human condition. The self psychological position maintains that it is in the nature of human beings to need the other and to be responded to by the other. How may we characterize the Kohutian self concept, and what is the proposed course of its development?

In discussing Kohut's (1971, 1977) formulation it is important to note whether one is addressing the self prior to or subsequent to its "restoration.'' For, as we shall highlight here, the self which antedates

Kohut's (1977) statement in *The Restoration of the Self* bears only incidental kinship to the concept which emerges subsequently. In the former instance we are still discussing a self which is a component of the ego, whereas by his second formulation Kohut (1977) introduces the idea of a psychology of the self in a "broad" sense, defined as "a psychology in which the self is seen as the center of the psychological universe" (p. xv). Henceforth, Kohut (1977, 1980, 1984) would, with increasingly less ambiguity, adopt this position for what he believed to be its significantly greater explanatory power in the face of the psychological data. In both instances, however, Kohut (1971, 1977) was seeking one overarching goal, which for our purposes may be thought of as the explication of the emergence of a cohesive self which, in any case, is a developmental achievement.

The Self in the Narrow Sense

The Analysis of the Self (1971), it is important to note, is subtitled, *A Systematic Approach to the Psychoanalytic Treatment of Narcissistic Personality Disorders*, and indeed, the primary goal of this work is the introduction of some technical innovations with respect to the clinical management of certain "narcissistic phenomena." It is not, at least manifestly, a theoretical proposal for the reformulation of the self concept, but a rather more circumscribed exploration of the contributions of narcissistic elements to the eventual health or pathology of the individual.

It is in the course of his genetic investigation of such narcissistic phenomena, however, that Kohut (1971) will outline a developmental schema which does begin to shift theoretical attention toward the self as the source of psychic health and pathology, although Kohut will insist upon limiting that role to the narcissistic disorders only. Thus, while "the subject matter of this monograph is the study of certain transference or transference like phenomena in the psychoanalysis of narcissistic personalities" (Kohut, 1971, p. 1), it will nonetheless present a cautiously new conception of the self, its evolution toward cohesion, and the defining impact such cohesion, or its absence, has upon the traditional apparatus of the mind.

Kohut's (1971) conceptual starting point, much as it was for Jacobson (1954, 1964) and Mahler (1967; Mahler et al., 1975), for example, is Hartmann's (1950) introduction of the self as the recipient of withdrawn object libido, or narcissistic libido. Now, interestingly, Kohut (1971) refers to this introduction of Hartmann's as ''a deceptively simple but pioneering and decisive advance in psychoanalytic *metapsychology*'' (p. xiii; emphasis added). It is perhaps more accurate to claim that Hartmann's (1950) assertions with respect to the self prepared the foundation for what, in fact, would be Kohut's (1977) revision of the metapsychology (and, as we have seen, Kernberg's as well); but to claim that Hartmann (1950) intended such an ''advance'' is probably more than his formulations will bear. We recall that the self in Hartmann's (1950) conception was a content of the ego whose primary function was to draw narcissistic libido to itself. It did not present a conceptual alternative, or addition, to the traditional structural axis of the metapsychological triumvirate of id, *ego*, and superego. However, to imply such textual authority does suggest the direction in which Kohut's work (1971, 1977) was tending.

Accepting Hartmann's tenet that there is an intimate relationship between narcissism and the self nonetheless does not then exclude object relationships from the realm of narcissistic experience. Indeed, Kohut (1971) asserts that ''some of the most intense narcissistic experiences relate to objects'' (p. xiv), but objects of a particular nature. Thus we note that Kohut (1971) here introduces a distinction among kinds of objects, to wit those which are employed ''in the service of the self and of the maintenance of its instinctual investment'' and those which ''are themselves experienced as *part of the self*'' (p. xiv; emphasis added). The latter he terms *selfobjects* and it is to these, we observe, that Kohut (1971) attributes formative influence in the evolution and support of the self.

Thus, we begin by noting that Kohut (1971) here introduces a new formulation: an object, the selfobject, qualitatively different from the object of instinctual gratification which is specifically tied to the antecedent development of the cohesive self. There is, in this view, no longer a unitary object, serving the distinctly instinctual purpose, but objects, some of which serve the traditional psychoanalytic function, others of which serve to craft the self. We note as well that Kohut (1971) is suggesting, and indeed does so quite clearly in this work, that there is a developmental line which traces the evolution of the self, and which is quite apart from the construction of the functioning ego and necessary to it.

We observe here as well that in *The Analysis of the Self,* Kohut (1971) posited a division of libido which in turn would allow him to formulate what amounted to a separate and nonconflictual origin for the self. Thus Kohut (1971) proposes an alternate manner by which to understand the qualitative nature of instinctual investment such that it is no longer defined in terms of its target (i.e., the object or the subject [the self] at which it may be aimed) but rather, by the particular *charge* the libido carries. That is, whether libido is *instinctually* or *narcissistically* charged. This reformulation, itself "deceptively simple," represents a radical redefinition of libido.

It has been a fundamental tenet of psychoanalytic thought, after all, that libido is *always* instinctual, whether object or self directed; while different in aim, it is never different in kind. Here, however, Kohut (1971) asserts that, indeed, libido is of two different kinds, both of which may be employed toward objects and toward the self. Making this assertion clearly opens the way for subsequent claims for qualitatively different *levels of experience*, to wit, instinctual and narcissistic; both of which, in turn, are subject to normal or pathological development. And further, the one line of development, the object instinctual, requires the prior efficacious establishment of the other line (i.e., the narcissistic) resulting in the cohesive self. Kohut (1971), we see, has introduced two new formulations, that of the selfobject and that of narcissistic libido. Let us see how he relates the two to produce his theoretically innovative concept of the self.

What Kohut (1971) proposes is that narcissistic libido cathects objects and in doing so necessarily experiences them as selfobjects; that is, objects that are experiential extensions of one's own being and which in this way represent an attenuated form of narcissistic self cathexis. It is the function of these selfobjects to serve both as a "mirror" of the infant's own postulated grandiosity, and as a source of idealization when his or her own grandiosity is no longer entirely sustainable. A self emerges from the interaction with parental figures (selfobjects), and the relative health or pathology of this self will rest in the quality of these relationships rather than in the gratification or frustration of instinctual tensions.

Thus, at the outset of development Kohut (1971), much as had Mahler (1967), and indeed, Freud (1914), posits an initial condition of autoeroticism, which, he suggests, corresponds to the "stage of the fragmented self." Cohesion is a process which begins with, and is sustained by, the mother's total, joyful, involvement with the infant, reflecting her absolute sense of that child's perfection. Ultimately, and necessarily, such perfection, "narcissistic equilibrium," will tarnish when confronted with the series of relatively minor maternal "failures" which inevitably occur. Maternal perfection is replaced, Kohut (1971) asserts, by "establishing a grandiose and exhibitionistic image of the self: *the grandiose self*," while at the same time also "reassigning" the "previous perfection to an admired, omnipotent (transitional) self-object: the *idealized parent image*" (p. 25). In the course of normative development, the grandiosity of the earlier phase gives way, via empathic mirroring and idealization of the other, to a "healthy narcissism" in which a cohesive self possesses, and is prepared to pursue, a range of ambitions which are both defined and modified by a set of values and ideals (Kohut, 1971).

In addition to the concepts of *selfobject* and *narcissistic libido*, Kohut (1971) here introduces yet a third formulation, intended to explain the establishment of psychic structure. *Transmuting internalization*, we shall see, is designed to account for structure and, when normatively achieved, to explain the qualitative and chronological distinction among "archaic" and "true" objects.

Thus, according to Kohut's (1971) formulation, psychic structures are the outcome of the "gradual decathexis of the narcissistically experienced archaic object" (p. 51). That is, a partialized withdrawal of cathexis from selected aspects of the selfobject occurs in the wake of one inevitable disappointment after another; and, importantly, in order that structure is formed, there must be "a depersonalizing of the introjected aspects of the image of the object, mainly in the form of a shift of emphasis from the total human context of the personality of the object to certain of its specific functions" (Kohut, 1971, p. 50). That is to say, the initially subjective, narcissistic experience of the (archaic) object is "transmuted" into impersonal (i.e., depersonalized) psychological structures. Now, Kohut (1971) informs, these psychological structures "continue to perform the *drive-regulating, integrating, and adaptive functions* which had previously been performed by the (external) object" (p. 51; emphasis added). Here, we deduce by the functions attributed, that the ego emerges; that structure is the result of depersonalizing, removing the personal, while retaining, and claiming for the self, the impersonal.

Thus we note that psychic structure, specifically the ego structure, is the developmental precipitate of predictive experiences of narcissistic imperfection by early objects. The grandiose self, in the course of coping with disappointments, creates structure, and in the process transforms itself. What began as a subjective, personal experience of one's own grandiose perfection, via the self's extension in the form of the selfobject, becomes an objective, impersonal structure. It may be said that rather than dispense with the *functions* performed by the selfobject, the self dispenses with the disappointing *personal* aspects of that object instead. In this way the self retains, in "transmuted" form, the skills for mastery, a narcissistic victory in itself, and expels the "injurious" aspects associated with the actual object's failure.

An important consequence of successful internal transmutations is the developmentally achieved capacity to relate to the "true" or "mature" object. As the personal aspects of the archaic selfobject are relinquished, and the functional aspects transformed into structure, the true object, that is the object which is "loved and hated by a psyche that has separated itself from the archaic objects" (Kohut, 1971, p. 51), is realized. This is the object which is cathected with object libido and with whom, to begin, the child may enter into oedipal relationships.

Importantly, we underscore Kohut's (1971) suggestion that for true object relationships to be possible, the "transmuted self," the self which has evolved from an archaic to a cohesive condition, must emerge first. Thus, oedipal relationships, and the conflicts attendant upon such relationships, cannot transpire unless a cohesive, unitary self, which is capable of such interaction, is already present. *A self structure is a prior condition* of oedipal struggles and all subsequent object relations. Indeed, Kohut (1971) says quite certainly that "the experience of a unitary self . . . is an important *precondition* for a cohesively functioning ego [and] . . . the absence of such a cathexis tends to lead to disordered ego functions" (p. 132; emphasis added).

Kohut (1971) goes to some lengths, both at the outset of this work and directly within the context of the just cited assertion, to establish "conceptual clarification" between "the cohesion of the patient's self image" and "the unity and cohesion of the patient's ego and its functions" (p. 132). He notes that the two represent different levels of abstraction, the idea of the "self being nearer to introspective or empathic observation; that of the ego being further from it" (p. 132).

That he seeks to make this distinction as he is defining the self is significant in two important ways.

First, in suggesting that the self and the ego exist on different planes of abstraction it is possible to argue for their conceptual coexistence. The self may be seen as an experience-near formulation, access to which is afforded by empathic introspection. The ego is seen as an experience-distant postulate, representing in its particular constellation of functions, one aspect of the mental apparatus of the mind. The one need not "threaten" the other, for each is assigned a different "psychic territory." The self concept operates within the narcissistic line of development and with narcissistic libido, while the ego, although reliant, as we have seen, upon a preexistent and cohesive self, operates largely along object-instinctual lines.

Second, underscoring the qualitatively different levels of abstraction attendant upon the two concepts, when combined with Kohut's (1971) assertion that the self is a "precondition" of a cohesively functioning ego, suggests an interesting theoretical situation. In considering that the self is an experience-near, subjective concept, palpable knowledge of which is only available via the subjective method of empathic introspection; and considering that its establishment *precedes* the ego, we are led to observe that Kohut (1971) is at least implying that the psyche in all its subsequent elaborations can attribute its origins to subjective experience. Kohut (1971), we suggest, is moving toward a rather similar set of conclusions regarding the self and the nature of the mind that we observed in reviewing Kernberg's (1976, 1982a,b) position. Both, we see, have gravitated in the direction of an experience-near, subjectively colored concept of self which plays a chronologically antecedent role in the elaboration of the psyche.

Nonetheless, while Kohut (1971) certainly formulates a self which is of considerable influence, it is still, at this stage of theory development, conceptualized in essentially orthodox, Hartmannian terms. "The self then," Kohut (1971) here asserts, "quite analogous to the representations of objects, *is a content of the mental apparatus*, but is not one of its constituents, i.e., not one of the agencies of the mind" (p. xv; emphasis added). That is, the self is a component of one of the agencies of the mind, the ego, and does not, itself, constitute such an agency. Far more extensive claims for the self will, we shall see, be made for the "restored" self.

The Self in the Broad Sense

In embarking upon a discussion of Kohut's (1977) later view of the self concept, it is interesting to begin with a brief consideration of the very title by which he introduces his reformulations. For to claim of his work that it is a commentary upon the restoration, that is, the reinstatement or reestablishment, of the self, is surely to imply the return to an earlier condition, prior to the "dethronement" of the self. The suggestion, if not the outright assertion, is that the self concept *once was* of central theoretical significance and is in this work of Kohut's being restored to that center. It is certainly the case that in this work, and those which follow it, Kohut (1980, 1984) has clearly elevated the self to a supraordinate position akin, in its central role if not its origins, to Kernberg's (1976, 1982a,b) formulations. How has the concept of the self been altered in this second elaboration?

Our review of post-Freudian, post-Hartmannian theorizing suggests a general trend toward the discovery, or more accurately, the postulation, of an independent variable capable of accounting for the functioning of psychic structures.

For example, we note Hartmann's (1939, 1952) introduction of the notion of autonomous elements of the ego which, in addition to instinct and reality, may be called upon to explain ego development. Thus, Hartmann (1952) says that "those inborn characteristics of the ego and their maturation would be a *third force* that acts upon ego development . . . [and] they enter this development as an independent variable" (pp. 169–170; emphasis added). For a host of reasons, some of which had to do, as we have noted, with "generalizing" psychoanalysis, Hartmann (1939, 1952) sought in the particular elements he selected, "inborn characteristics," a general biological variable. But the move to seek a source of explanation other than that bequeathed by the Freudian heritage (of drives and the modifying impact of reality upon their gratification) suggests at least a latent restlessness with respect to the psychological data. Although not the case with Hartmann (1939, 1950, 1952), we have observed that theory subsequent to his contributions became increasingly preoccupied with providing some hypotheses regarding the distinctly psychological phenomenon of the chronological experience of being; that is, the apparently distinctly human sense of past and of future which frame any given moment in time.

Thus we have seen Spiegel (1959) construct a self concept which does not emerge from other psychic structures, but is itself an organizing principle. Here the *self framework* serves as an independent variable, able to account for the functioning of other structures, and to explain aspects of ontogenic chronology as, in part, a matter of recognizing patterns within the framework.

Finally, by way of example, we recall Kernberg's (1976, 1982a,b) introduction of the self and object representation, linked by affect, which is seen to serve as an independent explanatory variable. Here, the affect-bound internal representation not only accounted for a stable, self-knowledgeable, self-perceiving self, but for the subsequent development of the ego, the id, and the superego as well as the drives themselves (Kernberg, 1976).

This "third force," whether as autonomous elements of the ego, or as the idea of a representation, either of self as a "pooled" or averaged set of images or as an initially fused selfobject conception, sought to provide an explanation for a more fundamental constellation of psychological experiences. An explanation was sought that was capable of addressing the indisputable psychological awareness of one's own being. Increasingly, such explanations moved, with varying degrees of ambiguity, toward the subjective, and more often called upon the self as the sought after and theoretically viable "third force."

With the introduction of *The Restoration of the Self* Kohut (1977) took a rather decisive step in the direction of the self as the determining variable in psychic life, and subjectivity as the defining quality not only of the self, but of the science, or psychology, of the self. Let us see what it is Kohut (1977) claimed for this self, and for the methodology that provides access to it.

Kohut (1977) proposes that "we learn to think alternatingly, or even simultaneously, in terms of two theoretical frameworks" (p. xv). In the one, which he referred to as the "psychology of the self in the broader sense," the self is understood "as the center of the psychological universe," while in the other "the self is seen as a content of a mental apparatus" (p. xv). Thus, while by no means seeking to disclaim the positions adopted in *The Analysis of the Self* (1971), Kohut (1977) is clear that *The Restoration of the Self* is dedicated to the theoretical elaboration of the concept in the broadest sense yet outlined in the American tradition. He presents the self as a metapsychological challenge to the traditional analytic alignment of structures, as well as articulating a methodological blueprint which promised the only access available to the (psychological) self.

Whereas *The Analysis of the Self* set out to establish the viability of treating what Kohut (1971) had termed the "narcissistic personality disorders," *The Restoration of the Self* (1977) would maintain that the clinical data argued for a new set of explanatory principles which would *complement* classical theory. Thus, as "a center of initiative and a recipient of impressions" (Kohut, 1977, p. 99), the self is, in its Kohutian reformulation, assigned *functional* responsibilities. It is no longer a Hartmannian representation within the ego, but, as we shall see, a cohesive executive structure, present in some form from the very outset of life.

While it perhaps remains an open question to what extent the self concept as elaborated by Kernberg (1976, 1982a,b), for example, may be assigned a functional role, there is little doubt that this is the case for Kohut (1977, 1980, 1984). Thus, on the one hand, we recall that Kernberg (1982a,b) did define the self as a supraordinate structure which incorporated other ego functions, and so, presumably, had some functional role. However, on the other hand, we note that a characteristic component of a representation is, necessarily, that it is *non*functional; or, perhaps more accurately, that the only function of a representation is to indicate, or "stand for," some other element or constellation of elements. In itself, it does not *do* anything. This latter, as we have seen, largely characterizes the position of "representational theorists," such as Spiegel (1959), and Sandler and Rosenblatt (1962), for example.

Kohut (1977, 1984), however, now leaves little question but that the self does carry functional responsibilities. Indeed, we have already noted that Kohut (1977) has defined the self as a "center of initiative," and we add here that he has now also redefined his entire explanatory system, his psychology, more broadly as one "that puts the *self at the center*" (p. xv; emphasis added).

Thus, we note that one of the points at which the two American traditions addressing the self concept differ is in the explicit assertion by the self psychologists of the central, *functional role of the self*. And even in this we have noted that Kernberg's (1982b) later formulations have indeed been fairly explicit with regard to the position of the self in the psychic scheme of things. Somewhat later Kohut (1980) will emphasize a further distinction between his self concept and those "ego psychologists of the New York school" by clearly asserting that while "Hartmann's hypotheses still concerned an apparatus, i.e., the mental apparatus, and not a self . . . it is psychoanalytic self psychology which has hypothesized the existence of a *core self*" (p. 544; emphasis added). Clearly, Kohut (1977, 1980, 1984) is taking or, perhaps more accurately from his viewpoint, "restoring" the self both to the front and the center of theory.

Rather than embark upon a comprehensive review of *The Restoration of the Self*, we shall cull a few defining points around which to organize Kohut's (1977) evolving formulation of the self concept. Among these we shall highlight first Kohut's (1977) assertion that there is a self from the very outset, and, second, that this self has a particular developed nature, as a bipolar construction. Third, we will explore the empathic–introspective methodology which Kohut (1959, 1977) brings to the study of the self, emphasizing in particular his assertion that this method of data collection provides the only genuinely *psychological* access to the psychological phenomena of the self. We shall maintain that it is this methodology, as much as anything else, which has made manifest the otherwise largely latent substrate of subjectivity which has characterized most of the analytic contributions of the American school to the theory of the self. Finally, we shall briefly address Kohut's (1977, 1984) interesting formulation of "tragic man," particularly as it may fruitfully lead us into our discussion of the British, and perhaps especially, the French, analytic conceptions of the self.

We begin by observing that Kohut (1977) maintains that it is the self which is ultimately responsible for the overall functioning of the psyche, in healthy or pathological manifestations, and that the drive–structure model is an adequate explanatory model only in the presence of a cohesive, stable self. So long, Kohut (1977) argues, as a healthy self participates in both drive and defense maneuvers, it will remain a kind of deus ex machina, silently managing the "subordinate contents" of the mind. So long as the self does not actively factor into the psychological equation, due to its stable participation in all aspects of the mind, the drive–defense, structural model will serve to account for the clinical data.

Thus, "if the self is healthy, firmly coherent, and of normal strength, then it will not spontaneously become the focus of our empathic (or introspective) attention; our attention will not be claimed by

the encompassing supraordinated configuration that is in balance, but
by those of its *subordinated contents* (narcissistic aims, drive aims,
defenses, conflicts) that are not'' (Kohut, 1977, p. 97; emphases
added). We underscore that here the self is rather unambiguously
viewed as an all embracing, executive psychological entity, responsible
for the management and functioning of all aspects of the psyche (i.e.,
of its "subordinate" contents).

"I will not hide my belief," Kohut (1977) avows, even in granting
(circumscribed) explanatory value to the structural model, "that in the
long run a psychology of the self will prove to be not only valuable
but indispensable even with regard to the areas where the psychology
of drives and defenses now does the job" (p. 98). If there are even
greater psychological insights to be gained, more to be known about
mental life, then it is to the self that analytic theory must turn. Indeed,
Kohut (1977) reasons, this turn toward the self concept is entirely
reasonable, for from the very outset the human infant is responded to
"as if" she or he already had such a self.

Thus, by way of legitimizing the claims to primacy for the self
within the psyche, and for the self psychology whose purpose it is to
study the origin, development, aims, and components of this self, Kohut (1977) posits the presence of a self, albeit rudimentary in nature,
from very earliest infancy. It is a self which, he suggests, may attribute
its origin to that moment in time when "the baby's innate potentialities
and the self-object's expectations with regard to the baby converge"
(Kohut, 1977, p. 99).

This is not, Kohut (1977) emphasizes, much as we noted that
Kernberg (1982b) had underscored, a self that possesses reflective
awareness of itself. In fact, it is a self that exists insofar as it is "fused
via mutual empathy with an environment that does experience him as
already possessing a self" (p. 99). That is to say, the process that
initiates the self begins with the first glimpse the mother has of her
child, and proceeds henceforth as a series of interactions between them
in which, by way of selective responsiveness to some aspects of the
child's potential and not others, the *nuclear self* is formed.

In this way, Kohut (1977) argues for a self present *in statu nas-
cendi* from the beginning of life. This is not an actual self, but rather
a *virtual* self which "must be described in terms of tensions . . . not
in terms of verbalizable fantasies" (p. 101). Again we note the similarity to Kernberg's (1982b) formulation of an early self, lacking in

awareness, but associated with states of tension (i.e., with affective states of pain or pleasure; with subjectivity).

Interestingly, it is a self which bears some resemblance to Fairbairn's (1952b) unitary ego in that Kohut's (1977) self also begins as a totality, particularly in its "perfect fusion" with the selfobject, an actual extension, after all, of the virtual self. This self seeks, and thrives upon, the responses of its environment. It is only when confronted with intensely disruptive "failures" on the part of environmental selfobjects that the self becomes subject to disintegrative manifestations, as sexually and aggressively isolated fragments of behavior.

Kohut (1977) here stakes a claim for the early, original presence of the self, much before psychic structure in its traditional configuration can be said to exist. He argues for the viability of this claim in part based on the observation that the responsive environment of selfobjects responds to the infant ab initio as a "self," and in this way, precisely in consequence of this welcoming anticipation, marries the *expectation* of selfhood to the *potential* for selfhood, thus effecting an actual self. It is not only that the infant is responded to "as if" he were a self, but that potentialities of the baby and expectations regarding the baby converge. A self emerges, in the Kohutian view, when what is possible is also what is expected; for when, conversely, what is hoped for, is also what is possible, there rests realization. In the mix of potential with expectation we observe the union of the biological and the psychological. We note further, that the birth of the psychological in the neonate, the subjective experience of one's own being, rests, quite literally, in the waiting arms of already established subjectivities. In the selective responses of the selfobjects to some of the infant's displayed potentials and not to others, the self acquires its unique attributes, its distinctive coloration; the self becomes its own particular I.

Kohut (1977) delineates in a more specific manner a rather more general conceptualization of the self, here articulated as the *bipolar self*. We shall observe, as we proceed with our description, that this self, in its origins and its mature configuration, bears considerable similarity to the developmental scheme which Kohut (1971) had already offered in his earlier work. The essential difference here is the unambiguous priority assigned to the self.

To begin, Kohut (1977) advises that the "primary psychological configurations" in the life of the infant and child are not drives, which only make themselves manifest "as disintegration products when the self is unsupported'' (p. 171). Instead, we note that the two essential psychological functions, themselves subject to disintegration, are a healthy *self-assertiveness* vis-à-vis the selfobject, which reflects the child's perceived perfection or grandiosity, and a healthy *admiration* for selfobjects whom the child invests with idealized capacities and qualities.

Normatively, Kohut (1977) suggests, ''the bulk of nuclear grandiosity consolidates into *nuclear* ambitions in early childhood . . . and the bulk of *nuclear* idealized goal structures are acquired in later childhood'' (p. 179). These constellations of ambitions derived from archaic grandiosity on the one hand, and goals derived from primitive idealization on the other, become the two poles of the nuclear self. Their particular character, their makeup, is determined by the ongoing process of ''inclusion-exclusion'' by which certain infantile proclivities are responded to and others are left to atrophy.

Even after these basic constellations are in place, the actual establishment of the self, and its ultimate cohesive character, are yet in the balance and will finally be decided, Kohut suggests, by the outcome of yet a second set of processes. These processes, specifically, may be understood as compensatory in nature. Thus, if the child was not able to establish a firm grandiose–exhibitionist pole of experience, she or he may yet have the opportunity to enjoy idealizing opportunities and, in this way, the second formative pole of the self may serve to offset the weakness of the first. Of course, the process may take a reverse turn as well. The first pole of experience might well have been firmly established, while the second found little or no response. In this latter case, then, the ambitions might well come to support, even to create, the ideals. As we shall see, it is the particular relationship thus established between the two poles, and the ongoing exchange among these constellations, that will define the actual experience of the self.

Thus, Kohut (1977) suggests that the subjective sense of sameness or continuity throughout life that one comes to recognize as one's self, ''does not emanate solely from the abiding *content* of the constituents of the nuclear self and from the *activities* that are established as a result of their pressure and guidance, but also from the abiding specific *relationship* in which the constituents of the self stand to each other'' (pp. 179–180).

What is of deciding impact in the formation of the continuous self is the presence of a particular alignment of the core elements of this self; the manner in which ambitions and goals fit with each other. Kohut (1977) has expressed this relationship as a "tension arc," by which he intends to indicate the "abiding flow of actual psychological activity that establishes itself between the two poles of the self" (p. 180), suggesting thereby that the self is characterized in far greater part by process than by product.

The ultimate fate of the Kohutian self rests not so much with the particular ambitions which drive one, nor with the goals by which one is led, but rather, with the invariant process of exchange between these two constellations. "It may ultimately be," Kohut (1977) muses, "not the content of the nuclear self, but the unchanging specificity of the self-expressive, creative tensions that point toward the future which tells us that our transient individuality also possesses a significance that extends beyond the borders of our life" (p. 182). It would seem that Kohut (1977) is here suggesting that it matters less, within limits, what specific events went into the makeup of one's ambitions, or determined one's ideals, than that such ambitions and goals establish some ongoing, and perpetual, working relationship which enables a self to move through time (i.e., by pursuing those ambitions, modified by particular ideals).

The sense of sameness over time that is subjectively experienced as self is very much a matter of the way in which one comes to define the world and act in it (via ideals and ambitions). It is not what one strives for, but *how* one does so that speaks to the felt sense of cohesion and continuous chronological recognition reaching from the past into the future, that defines the presence of self.

In concluding this aspect of our discussion we observe that, as has been discussed in considerable detail elsewhere (Greenberg and Mitchell, 1983; Eagle, 1984), Kohut (1971, 1977, 1984) continued to struggle with the total abandonment of the drive theory and, particularly relevant for our purposes, some, if not the central, role for the ego. Nonetheless, Kohut (1971, 1977, 1980, 1984) has moved quite decisively to place the self, and more precisely the palpable, experiential, subjective sense of self, at the center of theoretical considerations of the mind, assigning it defining influence as an originary source of personal experience.

Perhaps Kohut's (1959, 1977, 1984) commitment to a subjectively derived self as the central organizer of the psyche is nowhere more certainly foreshadowed than in the particular methodology he has adopted. For it is via the *empathic–introspective* mode that we observe Kohut's (1959) rather early preference for the experience-near tools of phenomenological inquiry and a proclivity for discovering, thereby, clinical data which he did not find satisfactorily explained by structural concepts. At this rather early stage of his theorizing, however, Kohut had not yet proposed the self as the primary explanatory centerpiece that it would later become.

Indeed, his paper, "Introspection, Empathy and Psychoanalysis" (1959) is, overall, an assertion regarding the relationship between a particular mode of inquiry and the theory which is elaborated in consequence. As such, this paper represents an important statement with respect to what constitutes psychological data gathering as well as setting the foundation for concepts yet to be developed. A review of this paper will reveal the considerable extent to which the "psychology of the self in the broader sense" owes its origins to the mode of inquiry outlined therein, for the introspective–empathic mode will "discover" some few data of psychological life which are not subject to further reduction; aspects of the psyche, knowable only via this mode of inquiry, that are the essence of what can be known of the psychological experience. Among such data, although not claimed in this paper, will be the self.

Psychological Essentials

Kohut's 1959 paper, as we have suggested, is a statement concerning the relationship between the mode of inquiry and the theory which emerges from such inquiries. Kohut here asserts that the defining method of psychology, which, after all, is largely about the understanding of the inner world, is introspection and empathy (the latter being defined as "vicarious introspection").

Thus, one's thoughts, feelings, and wishes, for example, are not knowable through the sensory organs. They cannot be seen, touched, smelled, or heard, and so cannot claim any observable physical existence. Yet, despite the absence of a palpable reality, such experience is nonetheless real. By what means, then, can we know the inner life?

Kohut asserts that psychological phenomena can be observed as they occur in *time*, at the very moment we are feeling something, recalling a past thought, or contemplating a future wish. And this "observation" is accomplished by a particular method of looking inward which is characteristic of the psychological, which is here referred to as introspection, and, when used in the service of gaining knowledge of another's inner state, empathy. In fact, Kohut (1959) asserts, we can only call a datum of experience psychological if it is accessible via introspection and empathy. Thus, "the mere fact that we see a pattern of movements leading to a specific end does not, by itself, define a psychological act" (p. 461). Instead, in psychoanalysis, as in all psychological data gathering, "the final and decisive observational act . . . is introspective or empathic" (p. 463).

In introducing this method of psychoanalytic inquiry Kohut sought the Freudian imprimateur, much as Kernberg (1982a,b) had in calling upon the structural theory in developing his view of the self. Kohut does so by suggesting that historically a considerable body of psychoanalytic knowledge has, in fact, been derived from the introspective method. By way of supporting evidence, Kohut (1959) cites *The Interpretation of Dreams* (1900), which was built upon the data of Freud's own introspective journey. Not only have a large number of clinical facts been amassed in this self-analytic fashion, but it is also the method by which the analysand seeks to gain access to his or her inner life within the treatment setting. Kohut (1959) is, of course, suggesting in this way, that at its core, psychoanalysis has relied upon, and may rightly be characterized by, this mode of inquiry.

Although introspection and empathy play a key role in all psychological inquiry, Kohut (1959) claims that psychoanalysis, particularly via the early discoveries of Freud and Breuer, pioneered the *scientific* use of these tools. Kohut (1959) himself underscores the scientific aspect of the contribution, more likely than not to highlight the "rational" and downplay the "mystical" connotations frequently associated with not readily quantifiable methods such as introspection and empathy.

In support of his claim Kohut (1959) cites both free association and the analysis of resistances as "specific refinements of introspection" (p. 464). Thus, while these two techniques indeed typify psychoanalytic observation, they are particular instances of the more general introspective method. With the aid of free association, for example, access is gained to what had previously been an unknown aspect of inner experience (i.e., the unconscious). But free association is nonetheless a psychoanalytic expression of introspection.

Having established introspection and empathy as the "essential constituents of psychoanalytic fact finding" (p. 465) Kohut (1959) introduces the main focus of this paper, which is to demonstrate that the observational tools employed will both "define the contents and the limits of the observed field" (p. 465). That is to say, introspection and empathy, as the observational tools of psychoanalysis, will determine what the proper subject matter (i.e., contents) of psychoanalysis is, and the extent to which a datum may be reduced, its psychological essence circumscribed (i.e., the limits imposed upon the observable field by the tools). This is of considerable importance to a full understanding of Kohut's (1959, 1971, 1977, 1984) development of the self, both in its particular nature and in its eventual centrality. What introspection and empathy cannot further resolve to yet more basic constituents are taken in themselves to be essential psychic configurations. It is at the point at which the method itself can uncover no other elements of psychological influence that psychological inquiry may be said to have reached the "essence" of its investigations. In this way, "the limits of psychoanalysis are given by the limits of potential introspection and empathy" (Kohut, 1959, p. 481). Psychoanalytic discovery may go as far as an introspective and empathically able person may take it.

The foundation of the science, Kohut (1959) thus seems to suggest, rests with the scientific observer, for introspection and empathy are tools which vary with their "users." They are, in a sense, chameleonlike functions, possessing the breadth of scope and adopting the depth of insight of the person who employs them. Introspection will allow one to see as far as one is able, and what one will see cannot be precisely measured against what the other may see.

Now, surely the Western tradition of science, emphasizing as it does the empirical–rational method, has had a rather skittish attitude toward the ultimate reliability, and reality, of data obtained by subjective methods, such as introspection or empathy. Kohut (1959) suggests that while this reluctance may in part be attributable to sociocultural factors, as for example, a general distrust of the nonquantifiable as "mystical," he suggests that "perhaps the dread that causes the defensive neglect of . . . introspection . . . is the fear of helplessness" (Kohut, 1959, p. 465).

It is in the nature of introspection, Kohut (1959) notes, to require the suspension of activity. The method itself may only be operationalized or, so to speak, "put into action," insofar as the person who employs the method is able temporarily to forfeit action. This, Kohut (1959) proposes, challenges the (perhaps particularly Western) propensity for *behavioral*, in contradistinction to *contemplative*, modes of being.

Along these lines Kohut (1959) offers a more strictly psychoanalytic explanation for the reluctance to acknowledge the central role of introspection and empathy. As we have implied, the introspective method, much as psychoanalysis itself, necessarily places the participant in a passive, inactive role. Kohut (1959) suggests that the discomfort, even dread, engendered by the passive position may be attributable to the idea that "introspection seems to oppose the direction of the current by which we achieve tension relief . . . [and raises] a fear, in other words, of the prolonged reversal of the flow of energy through introspection" (p. 466). Tension, drive pressure, seeks discharge. Introspection, on the other hand, demands delay which, in its turn, produces significant discomfort.

We have already noted that the Kohutian self would become *the* "center of initiative." In reviewing Kohut's (1959) assertions in this early paper, we discern the conceptual roots of that self as the understandable outcome of the method. For, as we have discussed above, the introspective–empathic mode seeks, as other methods in other scientific endeavors, to resolve observed phenomena to their underlying components. The method aims to arrive at the *essential* element(s) of psychological experience, that is, those which cannot, by the methods appropriate to psychological inquiry, further reduce the material obtained. Thus, the purpose which the method is designed to fulfill is the discovery of basic, not further reducible, constituents of the psyche. We shall see that the Kohutian formulation of the self as such a "center of initiative" is a direct outcome of this method of inquiry.

Kohut (1959) reviews a number of primary psychoanalytic concepts, including endopsychic conflict, sexuality, the notion of drives generally, and the idea of transference, in the light of the particular methodology. We shall not attempt an exhaustive review of his findings with regard to all of these, save to say that by applying the introspective–empathic mode of inquiry Kohut seeks to illustrate the changed understanding thus obtained. By way of example, however, we shall note Kohut's comments upon the (altered) sense in which transference is understood when the introspective method is employed.

Kohut (1959) observes that the nonintrospective historical method of data gathering does not permit an adequate distinction between those factors in one's past which impacted upon the growth of psychic structure and the persistent influence of elements from the past which are continuing to affect behavior in the present (i.e., the repressed unconscious). The historical method does not tell the analyst which factors, particular object choices, went into the construction of the psyche and which continue in an unintegrated fashion to shape current behavior. However, Kohut (1959) goes on, "scientific introspection" will allow for a differentiation among those "object choices patterned after childhood models . . . and true transferences" (p. 472). This differentiation is discerned because the "true transferences," Kohut (1959) asserts, "can be dissolved by persistent introspection; the former [i.e., object choices based on childhood models], however, reside outside the sphere of structural conflict and are not directly affected by psychoanalytic introspection" (p. 472). A particularly important assertion is underscored here. We note that Kohut is already suggesting that structural conflict is subject to further reduction; that is, such conflict is not the basic psychological constituent, but a manifestation of another, more elemental, psychological "fact." Conversely, he asserts that those elements outside of conflict are not directly affected by psychoanalytic introspection: that is, they cannot be further reduced. The specific point to be abstracted here seems to be an early statement by Kohut (1959) regarding the psychologically essential nature of initial, nonconflictual object choices; that is, such object choices, later to be known as selfobjects, are basic elements of the psyche, discovered via the introspective mode of inquiry.

A second, more general point refers to the nature of the methodology itself. We note here, as we have implied earlier, that Kohut (1959) understands the function of the introspective–empathic mode to aid in the discovery of the essential elements of the psyche by resolving to the bare essentials all psychological data. Thus, by employing this method in this manner, the psychological theorist generally, and the psychoanalytic theorist in particular, derives the building blocks of his explanation of the workings of the mind. And indeed, it is precisely via this method that, over the span of his work, Kohut (e.g., 1959, 1971, 1977, 1984) "discovers" and formulates the self as the irreducible central concept of the psyche.

In fact, Kohut (1959) begins the effort in this paper by raising two interesting and characteristic problems long associated with the self concept: the problem of free will (versus psychoanalytic determinism) and the related phenomenon of the "I experience." Framing the inquiry within the parameters of the introspective–empathic method of obtaining data, Kohut (1959) formulates the question thus: "we can observe in ourselves the ability to choose and to decide—can further introspection . . . resolve this ability into underlying components?" (p. 481). In other words, can the experience of making a choice be reduced to more basic psychological configurations, as the psychoanalytic concepts of, for example, compulsion or narcissism? Kohut unequivocally replies that "the answer is no, despite the emphasis that psychoanalysis puts on unconscious motivation and rationalization; for all that the persistent recovery of unconscious motivations and of rationalizations leads to is, under favorable circumstances, a wider and more vivid experience of freedom" (p. 481). That is to say, persistent application of the introspective method will, on the contrary, reduce unconscious motivations and rationalizations to the more basic issue of freedom of choice.

Now, Kohut (1959) reminds the reader that every science has its natural limits, "determined approximately by the limits of its basic tool of observation" (p. 481). Psychoanalysis recognizes that introspection, in the particular form of free association or resistance analysis, and in conformity with the law of psychic determinism, is potentially able to uncover more basic motives for the decisions and "free" choices we make. However, psychoanalysis must also recognize the limits beyond which it cannot go, given the current method (of introspection) at its disposal. Thus, psychoanalytically, we acknowledge these "introspectively irreducible facts of observation" by, for example, the application of the basic term *drive* to those introspectively derived experiences of "compelling inner forces."

By the same token, Kohut here argues, psychoanalysis must also recognize the "introspectively irreducible fact" of other experiences as well. Thus, in connection with the problem of free choice, Kohut maintains that just such an "irreducible fact" is the "experience of an active 'I'," whether merged with the undischarged drive or apart from it in a self-observational mode. "What we experience as freedom of choice, as decision, and the like, is an expression of the fact that the I experience and a core of activities emanating from it cannot at present be divided into further components by the introspective method'' (1959, p. 482). The I is where we arrive at the irreducible end of introspection. Though not yet close to claiming the ascendancy of the self in psychic life, we do note that Kohut has, in placing the I experience alongside the drive as an irreducible fact of psychic life, established a conceptual equivalency among the two that would reassert itself, as we have already seen, in *The Analysis of the Self* (1971) and in the formulation of a psychology of the self in the narrow and the broad sense that characterized *The Restoration of the Self* (1977). In fact, in that work Kohut would return to the issue of free will, finding it far less intractable in the light of his more current formulations.

Thus, Kohut (1977) later reasserts his abiding commitment to introspection and empathy as the observational tools which define the psychological field, and to his view that psychoanalytic depth psychology ''*is* the dimension of reality that is perceived via introspection and empathy'' (p. 244). He reaffirms as well his certainty that choice, free will, and decision—precisely because they can be accessed by introspection and empathy—''were legitimate inhabitants of the psychological aspects of reality which are the domain of the depth psychologist'' (p. 244).

Despite this avowed psychological legitimacy, and despite his conviction that the classical formulation of the mind as a mental apparatus could not adequately accommodate these irreducible facts of psychic life, Kohut (1977) ''could find no place,'' at the time of ''Introspection, Empathy, and Psychoanalysis'' (1959), ''for the psychological activities that go by the name of choice, decision, and free will'' (p. 244). By the time of *The Restoration of the Self* (1977) that place would unambiguously be the self.

Thus, Kohut (1977) would now maintain that while ''mental apparatus psychology,'' directed by the laws of psychic determinism, could account for ''a great deal,'' it could not account for all introspectively derived data. ''It is equally true,'' Kohut (1977) asserts, ''that there are some phenomena that require for their explanation the positing of a psychic configuration—the self—that *whatever the history of its formation*, has become a center of initiative: a unit that tries to follow its own course'' (pp. 244–245). We see that the self, irrespective of the forces which may have contributed to its final configuration, is, in and of itself, that irreducible and *essential* psychological unit to which decision and freedom of choice are themselves resolvable. And that the self is arrived at by introspection forever characterizes the concept as subjective in character; for it is only observable when the subject "looks inside" (i.e., introspects) or when the outside other attempts to vicariously look inside the other via the empathic mode of inquiry.

The method, we see, has indeed determined the theory. It is a method which suggests that the self is only knowable insofar as it is made psychologically "observable" (i.e., conscious) via introspection. It is not that Kohut (1959) disavows the unconscious; but rather, as psychoanalysis in general implies, that the unconscious is only knowable insofar as it is made conscious. Kernberg (1982b), we have noted, established a similar equivalence among the self and consciousness. In this limited sense at least, there is a certain kinship among Kohut's (1959) methodology and aspects of phenomenological inquiry. For both would seek to describe what is observed, and both would reach back to Kant in asserting that all that we may know of any aspect of reality is that which appears to consciousness. Thus, while there is no reason to assert that Kohut (1959) is making the additional Kantian claim to the existence of a reality beyond what is presented to appearance (i.e., the "thing-in-itself" or *noumenon*) he is suggesting that all we may have access to in the realm of the psychological is that which one becomes conscious of, or the *phenomenon*. This is a notion common to the "representational theorists" as well, and will be discussed at somewhat greater length in the concluding remarks to this section.

The Nature of Man in the Broader Sense

It is, as we have noted, in *The Restoration of the Self* that Kohut (1977) clearly depicts a self concept which occupies the theoretical center of his overall conceptualization of the nature of the psyche and its evolution toward healthy, or pathological, functioning. It is from this commitment to the centrality of the self that the notion of "tragic man" emerges, for we "look at the self as the center of Tragic Man" (Kohut, 1977, p. 207).

In this way we understand that tragic man is the anthropomorphic translation of Kohut's (1977) psychology of the self in the broader sense; a psychology among whose avowed purposes it is to take as its object of study the self, and which "examines its genesis and development of its constituents, in health and disease" (Kohut, 1977, p. xv).

Now, it is well known that Kohut (1977) introduced "tragic man" alongside of "guilty man," the latter concept being associated with the psychology of the self in the narrow sense, in which the self is a constituent element of the mental apparatus (i.e., the ego). We shall not explore the nature of "guilty man," except to comment in passing that the concept represents those aspects of humankind that suffer the discomforts attendant upon the psychic wars (i.e., the structural conflicts) of id, ego, and superego. Tragic man, however, speaks directly to the essence of those psychological battles which characterize the self.

What is the nature, the psychic composition, of tragic man? To ask this question is, at the same time, equivalent to inquiring after the purview of Kohut's (1977) (broader) psychology itself. We see that the psychology of the self is designed to account for, as the particular concept of the self was introduced to explain, a set of psychological disturbances which were not, in Kohut's (1977) view, adequately addressed by the formulations belonging to "mental apparatus psychology." Among such disturbances, Kohut (1977) includes the *fragmented* self and the *depleted* self; "in short, the psychic disturbances and struggles of Tragic Man" (Kohut, 1977, p. 243).

Now, the pursuits, the very challenges, to "tragic man," are to be "located" along that arc of tension which Kohut (1977) proposed to join the poles of nuclear ambitions and nuclear goals. Failures in the pursuit of ambitions and goals will yield fragmentation or depletion, that is, tragic consequences. Tragic man, we cannot fail to observe, is here seen to be coincident with the bipolar self. Tragic man *is* the self and is thus, in the "broader (sociocultural) sense," as the self is in the "broader psychological sense," a supraordinate formulation; an overriding view of the essential nature of humankind residing in the struggles surrounding "integrity," and "wholeness," rather than sexuality and aggression.

Tragic man is defined not in terms of passionate struggles, which are but a secondary manifestation of more essential issues, but rather with respect to the human tragedy attendant upon the failure to achieve, to realize, to have expectations, hopes, justified and legitimized by potentials. Tragic man's tragedy lies in his failure to be fulfilled in his aspirations, and is tragic precisely because he suffers the pains of fragmentation and depletion that signify the unfulfilled state. Tragic man is broken and empty, and without a self in any functional sense. Tragedy, we see, is here coincident with the absence of self.

From this standpoint, clearly it is also understood as tragedy not to experience fulfillment. From the radically opposite stance adopted by Jacques Lacan, we shall see that this lack of fulfillment is precisely wherein the essence of self resides, and that perhaps the true tragedy, in this view, is the misguided pursuit of fulfillment, when absence is the nature of human being. Kohut's (1977, 1984) conceptualization of tragic man addresses issues which are typically not raised within the structural framework of psychoanalysis. Indeed, Kohut (1984) observes that "the self psychological outlook on man—that is, the expanded focus that allows us to acknowledge the significance of the problems of tragic man and to study these problems with scientific seriousness—is clearly different from the theory of cure propounded by traditional analysis" (pp. 207–208). It is different, I suggest, precisely in that with this concept of tragic man Kohut (1977, 1984) tackles issues, and proposes theoretical tenets, *beyond* a "theory of cure." By way of the self concept, and perhaps particularly in its incarnation as "tragic man," Kohut (1977, 1984) broadens the scope of analytic inquiry along the lines of, if not toward the same concluding principles of explanation, as Freud (1930) had in investigating "Civilization and Its Discontents." Rather than concluding that the nature of humankind may be understood in terms of the communal need to repress primal passions, sublimating them toward "civilized" ends, we observe a rather different conclusion. Here, the nature of the self resides in its capacity to achieve fulfillment, specifically of individually fashioned ambitions, modified by particular goals.

By way of summary, then, tragic man is, Kohut (1977, 1984) maintains, a concept which subsumes clinical data derived from the persistent application of the introspective–empathic method and which are not further reducible. Tragic man represents the psychological manifestation of the self's failure to realize its own essential nature, one which propels it toward the fulfillment of ambitions and the achievement of goals.

We observe as well, with regard to his general formulation of the self, that knowledgeable access to it is gained in consequence of the direct observation of one's own inner experiences. It is just such observation which leads to the finally irreducible psychological conclusion of a configuration of initiative and free choice (i.e., the self). Further, this self is derived in the intersubjective exchange between the infant as potential self and the adult caregiver as actual self. As well, the self in the Kohutian view is an unambiguously supraordinate structure, to which all other aspects of the psyche are subsumed.

Finally, with respect to his "theory of cure," we observe that Kohut's (1959, 1971, 1977, 1980, 1984) work offers the developing self two opportunities to constitute itself, either, as we have seen, by way of the abiding ambitions derived from archaic grandiosity, or, alternately, through the ideals and goals gained in the healthy admiration of the other. Failing this, the (tragically) depleted self may yet seek (re)constitution through a peculiarly Proustian vehicle.

> [For] the Proustian recovery of childhood memories, constitutes a psychological achievement significantly different from the filling in of infantile amnesia, which as Freud taught us, is the precondition for the solution of structural conflicts and thus for the cure of a psychoneurosis. *The Proustian recovery of the past is in the service of healing the discontinuity of the self* [Kohut, 1977, pp. 181–182, emphasis added].

Thus, again we emphasize that the self's failure to achieve its potential is about *deficiency* (i.e., about what is missing, and absent) and, significantly, we see that it is (theoretically) possible to redress this absence—to make fullness where there had been absence—by the internal recovery of what is gone (i.e., what is *past*). Such recovery is also accomplished, in this view, by providing in the present, in the analyst's function as a transferential selfobject, for example, that which will serve to "complete" the self. That is, again, make it whole and full. It is, the appellation of "tragic man" notwithstanding, an essentially optimistic view of the capacity for rejuvenation (through fulfillment) which is proposed to reside within the resilient self.

We would conclude this aspect of our discussion by remarking upon the important conceptual modifications to analytic theories of the self made by the work of Kohut (1959, 1971, 1977, 1980, 1984). We note that his efforts impact on these particular axes of theory assessment: the methodological, the metapsychological, and the developmental.

We reiterate, with respect to methodology, that Kohut's (1959) particular formulation of the introspective–empathic mode of inquiry, and his application of this mode to the analytic exploration of the mind, added considerable weight, and in many circles, theoretical authority, to subjectively derived clinical data. The method, as we have seen, is largely responsible for Kohut's (1959, 1977) ultimate conclusion that the self is the essential element of the psyche, and that its particular character is, necessarily, subjectively drawn.

Metapsychologically, Kohut (1971, 1977, 1984) challenges the structural supremacy of the ego; and his work may perhaps be expressed in terms of a theoretical coup d'etat, in which the self is "restored" to its "once and future" place of explanatory preeminence within the realm of the psyche. As a supraordinate structure, Kohut's (1977) self concept reformulates the more traditionally asserted alignment in which the ego is the structural executant of the mind. In addition to the structural component of the traditional metapsychology, Kohut (1971, 1977) also challenges a basic assumption of the dynamic point of view. Whereas the standard analytic explanation of behavior, particularly symptomatic behavior, is in terms of *conflict* among the agencies of the mind vis-à-vis the discharge of drive tensions, Kohut (1971, 1977), on the other hand, understands much of what goes by the name of *pathological* as a manifestation of *deficit* in the structure of the self. In Kohut's view, the self is depleted, not conflicted.

Among the theorists of representation and those of self psychology we note that a defining difference resides in the view each adopts with respect to the dynamics of behavior. The latter do not attribute to conflict the causal properties that the more traditional analytic metapsychology does. The primary configuration from a self psychological point of view is an evolving self whose progress toward fulfilled functioning may be impeded by the presence of obstacles in the path of development. The difference, simply put, is between an explanatory model which understands behavior in terms of conflict, and a model which understands behavior in terms of deficit.

Finally, Kohut's (1971, 1977, 1984) conceptualization of the development of the self bears little resemblance to the characteristic American penchant for correlating maturity and normality with independence. On the contrary, "self psychology asserts that normality is properly defined by positing a meaningful sequence of *changes in the nature* of self-selfobject relations throughout the course of a person's life; normality is not tantamount to the claim ... that the need for selfobjects is relinquished by the adult and replaced by autonomy" (Kohut, 1984, p. 208; emphasis added). The healthy, mature self will continue to require the support of others in order that it function adequately, but it has, at the same time, acquired the developed capacity for more complex states of need. That is to say, the active need for the support of actual others does not, as a manifestation of mature functioning, atrophy. Rather, the quality of the need is transformed from archaic, primitive need, often associated with sheer survival, to a more subtly nuanced need to rely on others with respect to such complex strivings as the pursuit of ambitions and ideals.

Concluding Remarks

The extent to which the American tradition of theorizing as a whole may be characterized as an "optimistic" endeavor is rather a different question from the extent to which it may be described as conceptual construction of "presence," and one which will not be undertaken here. However, we observe that the general thrust of theory does suggest a number of themes which perhaps can be described as "progressive," and which, in the main, speak to a self which unfolds and develops *toward* something. And that "end" toward which development tends is often a condition of mastery, and except in the notable instance of Kohut's work, independence.

The differences within the American tradition of theorizing with respect to the self concept notwithstanding, there are a number of interesting and significant positions held in common. These points of convergence, we shall see, have fashioned a formulation of the self which, despite what may be viewed as "variations in personality" from theory to theory, possesses an essentially recognizable identity. What findings with respect to the self concept may we discover at the close of our discussion of these selected American theorists?

We begin by recalling that the concept as it has been elaborated within the American tradition is largely conceived within the context, and very probably in consequence, of the particular theoretical constructions applied to selected aspects of Freudian theory by Hartmann (1939, 1950, 1952). For as we noted in some detail earlier, Freud employed the term *Ich* in a fairly fluid and interchangeable fashion, suggesting thereby that the notion that ego and self might be the *same* was at least as likely as that they would evolve along separate lines.

Subsequent theory was surely driven by Hartmann (1939, 1950) choosing to elevate the *functional* ego to theoretical prominence; the concept of a self being introduced as a representational byproduct of the ego whose sole elaborated function was to be cathected with withdrawn object (i.e., narcissistic) libido; and issues surrounding the subjective experience of one's own being left largely untouched. Hartmann (1939, 1950), in emphasizing the ego's acquisition of functions, established an atmosphere of mastery within which secondary process, the reality principle, and some degree of empirical objectivity came to characterize that aspect of psychoanalytic thought which is recognized as ego psychology. Nonetheless, we have seen that the self concept was not forsaken. On the contrary, theorists persisted in finding ways to account for that most psychological of experiences, the *sense of self*, while yet seeking to retain the theoretical preeminence of the structure ego.

Thus, we begin by noting that theorists of the American tradition have, to varying extents, had to contend with the veneer of certainty which Hartmann (1939) bestowed upon the semantically ambiguous sense of *das Ich*, effecting thereby a separation between self and ego that did not appear to be the only and necessary conceptual course suggested by the original Freudian usage. It was, in fact, this very ambiguity that allowed the self to return to analytic theory by way of the back door, so to speak. Thus we have seen both Kernberg (1976, 1982a,b) and Kohut (1959), for example, call upon aspects of Freudian theory which they contend support, in Kernberg's (1982a) case, the elimination of the "artificial" separation of the ego and the self concepts, and in Kohut's (1959), the use of a more subjectively derived methodology.

We may conclude that the self concept in American analytic theory is, in part, born of a "certain uncertainty" within the Freudian text, a fluidity of meaning which allows the reader, and the would-be theorist, to hold two conceptions at the same time. And in holding the ego and the self to simultaneous thought one may approach the interesting possibility of containing objectivity (in the ego's biologically rooted functions) and subjectivity (in the self's awareness of its own being) within one theoretical matrix of mind. Indeed, this is, I suggest, precisely what Kohut (1977) and Kernberg (1982b), by different paths, attempted to achieve.

Ambiguity, however, is only one of the conceptual parents of the self, which may also claim an inheritance from the somewhat paradoxical coupling with the definitional certainty associated with the Hartmannian ego. For regardless of the portion claimed for the self in the more introspective aspects of the Freudian text, it was Hartmann (1950) who placed the concept firmly within the cradle of the ego. It was there that it was nurtured as a "representation," and it was from there that we have seen it slowly emerge. Thus we have the *"ambiguously certain"* paradox of the self concept in its American heritage.

Second, as already mentioned, we observe the increasingly functional, and consequently influential role of the self, and concomitantly with subjectivity, within the psyche; a role which, I would suggest, came to eclipse somewhat that of the ego in the work of many of the theorists subsequent to Hartmann (1950), including both Kernberg (1982a,b) and Kohut (1977, 1984), and perhaps particularly Jacobson (1954, 1964) and Mahler (1967, Mahler and Gosliner, 1955; Mahler et al., 1975).

Thus, our review of selected theorists in the American tradition has uncovered a general trend toward an increasingly influential self; one which, from its rather modest introduction by Hartmann (1950), has moved steadily to adopt a more central structural and functional role within the psyche. We observe the self ascending in close connection with an emerging subjective sensibility; first as made manifest in the expanding proclivity for theory based in descriptively drawn elaborations of experience, as in the work of Federn (1928a,b, 1934), Jacobson (1954, 1964), and perhaps especially Mahler (1955, 1967; Mahler et al., 1975).

We recall, in this context, the work of Spiegel (1959), whose self as framework postulated a self which became a kind of *defining ground* upon which all subsequent and variant figures of experience might be assessed. We reiterate here as well the observation that Mahler's (1955, 1967; Mahler et al., 1975) work, both in method and conclusion, suggest the formative significance of the subjectively experienced sense of one's own being held for the eventual elaboration of the psyche.

Ultimately, we confront a self concept, both in Kernberg's (1976, 1982a,b) and Kohut's (1971, 1977) work, which is fully cloaked in the subjective, whether as it is seen to evolve in tandem with consciousness, or as a product of intersubjective exchanges which can only be accessed via introspective efforts. Thus we recall that both Kernberg (1976, 1982a,b) and Kohut (1971, 1977, 1984) came to view the self as a "supraordinate" structure which may be regarded as possessing an increasingly *executive* role. In Kernberg's (1976) developmental schema, as we have seen, the self became an antecedent structural event, the success of which would prepare the ground for the subsequent consolidation of ego, id and superego structures. For Kohut (1977), the self concept was now the very center of initiative from which the individual draws his or her direction. In all events, we observe a growing attention to the problem of the subject (i.e., the self as a subjective experience of being). As well, that experience is more often attired in the raiments of a (restored) centrality in psychic life that was not an aspect of its Hartmannian attire.

It is, I suggest, precisely this evolving attitude toward the subjective experience of I, that did not seem to be adequately accounted for in the more mechanical conceptualizations of the (unaltered) structural model of the mind, that impelled theoreticians from Federn (1928a,b, 1934) and Hartmann (1950) forward, to seek room within orthodoxy for the datum of the self. Thus it is that we find a self which, though it began its conceptual journey in American theorizing as an epiphenomenal byproduct of the supraordinate ego, has evolved to a position of *ascendant and formative influence*—though there is perhaps more than a slight air of ambiguity yet enveloping this ascendancy.

Despite differences among the many theorists housed within the American tradition, all share in common a particular view of the meaning of health and pathology, as well as the development of the self, in terms of some variant of the psychic process of transforming the external and objective into the internal and subjective (i.e., *making the outside inside*). All theoreticians of this bent conceive of the formation of self and/or psychic structure as a *process of internalization*, of taking in; particularly of taking the objective other in and making it an aspect of the subjective self. This process is variously described as introjection, identification, internalization, and transmuting internalization. The prevailing metaphor here is digestive, and in this connection we note, and shall here briefly review, Kernberg's (1976) metabolic analogy as well as Kohut's (1971) "transmutational" conception. Self, we shall thus see, is of a weave with other; the subject constituted in the psychic appropriation of the object.

In discussing the normal process of identity formation, Kernberg (1976), effectively employs the digestive metaphor to convey the essence of identity as consisting in a kind of transformation, or, "one might say [a] *depersonalization* of internalized object relations, [a] *reshaping* of part of them . . . " (Kernberg, 1976, p. 34), so that the object both resembles external reality and is a fully integrated part of thc self. That is, the internal object becomes indistinguishable from, identical to, the internalizing self.

This metamorphosis, as the end-product of metabolism may be characterized, is underscored in the breach by Kernberg (1976) when addressing the consequences of *failed* integration, thus: "The persistence of 'nonmetabolized' early introjections is the outcome of a pathological fixation of severely disturbed, early object relations" (p. 34). That is, a failed identity is consequent upon the more essential failure to digest that which is different from the self. Simply swallowing the other whole is an instance, perhaps a psychotic instance, of the internalization of difference. A failure to integrate the different object into the recognizably same subject results, in this formulation, in pathological experiences of being. Pathology is understood, thus, as a particular diagnostic instance of the strangeness within.

In what is, as we have seen, an otherwise distinct theoretical attitude toward the construction of individual identity, we here cite an example of a (latent) conceptual kinship in the notion of *metabolized internal objects* with what Kohut (1971, 1977, 1984) has termed *transmuting internalization.*

The latter concept, we recall, refers to the gradual assimilation of images of aspects of significant environmental objects, resulting in the creation of a permanent self-structure (e.g., Kohut, 1971, 1977, 1984; Tolpin, 1971; Wolf, 1980).

Kohut's (1971) own articulation of the concept, in the context of discussing the self as becoming increasingly capable of performing necessary functions independently, involves "a *depersonalizing* . . . of the introjected aspects of the image of the object, mainly in the form of a shift . . . from the total human context of the personality of the object to certain of its specific functions" (p. 50; emphasis added). Thus, in the face of an experience of inevitable psychic loss of the (external) object, Kohut (1971) continues, a particle of "internal structure . . . now performs the functions which the object used to perform . . . '' (p. 50).

The same transformation of what is originally nonidentical to what is identical occurs in this process as in the metabolic appropriation that Kernberg (1976) describes. Importantly, both processes require a necessary depersonalization, or stripping away of the unique (i.e., different, nonidentical) qualities of the object, as it undergoes the *trans-mutation* (or metabolizing) to selfsame and identical. Thus, the (non-identical) object is internalized, and is metamorphosed, by depriving it of personal or unique features, into an aspect of the (identical) subject.

Internalization as the controlling process whereby a psychic sense of self is elaborated, is indicative, I am suggesting, of a broader view of the self as the realization of *fulfillment*, in the sense that "taking in" via internalization is tantamount to establishing a psychological condition of "fullness" within. Thus, the explanatory constructs of the mind in general, and of the self more particularly, reflects a specific psychoanalytic instance of the rather more broadly conceived Western relationship to the idea that what is absent or incomplete is more funda-mentally either "lost," in one's "recoverable" past or "yet to be achieved," in the future toward which all development (both individual and cultural in the Hegelian sense) is progressively tending. Absence, incompleteness, and the "strangeness" (i.e., nonidentical) of the other are temporary conditions on the journey toward possession and (inter-nal) presence, and fulfillment.

We would briefly observe, in this connection, that there is perhaps an interesting argument to be made for this notion of absence become presence, or its failure to be so transformed, in the controlling meta-phors of "awaiting the messiah" and "messianic arrival and resurrec-tion" that characterize the essential core of the Judeo-Christian Western world view(s). One, of course, points toward what is not (yet), while the other proclaims its arrival and presence. In this way, it seems to me, we may cite a certain kinship with the more narrowly conceived notion of self—here, as an instance of its realization through making the inside a container for the achieved presence of the other. Our forthcoming exploration of aspects of the French formulations of the self will suggest the conceptual opposite of this notion of fulfillment. That is, we shall there see a self built upon the commitment, so to speak, to an "eternally awaited messiah," of which Beckett's Godot is so suggestive.

In addition to the idea of fulfillment achieved through internaliz-ing processes, all theorists share, as we have suggested, an accompa-nying commitment to some variant of the idea of "recovery," or "restoration." This, I suggest, finds its conceptual expression in the construction of technical processes of internalization which make the restoration possible. Thus, the experientially described phenomena of incompleteness, emptiness, or *lack* are attributed not to something to be sought after in the future, but rather to be found—more accurately refound, recalled, recovered—in the past, and reinternalized; integrated into the structure of the psyche so that fragmentation and "manyness" may yield to a united and single self. The past, in this view, is most often conceived as that realm in which the self is apt to unlock the nurturing secrets of wholeness which *once were known*. Thus the view that otherwise inexplicable experiences of nameless yearning, or a sense of one's personal incompleteness, may be understood as something having been lost, that is, as the inevitable psychic consequence of having to relinquish infantile oneness, trading it for the separation which promises mature and independent functioning. That which has been "lost," however, suggests the possibility that it is capable of being found again. Importantly, such recovery leads to the "wholeness" or completeness that I here suggest we understand as fulfillment. Thus we discover a self built upon the somewhat mythic notion of "paradise lost *and* found." We have seen this in the Freudian *fort-da* as well as in Kernberg's metabolic and Kohut's transmutational metaphors.

It is possible, we have already implied, to conceive of the commonly acknowledged sense of longing, lack, and absence not in terms of what was, but rather what is not; that is, in terms not of a paradise lost (and found), but rather of a "paradise (eternally) awaited." It will, we shall observe, be theoretically viable to speak of a desire for something, which in itself suggests its absence, as a perpetual state, *not* subject to fulfillment. In such a framework fulfillment is illusory; a misrecognition of one's actual human condition. This will be the underpinning of theorists of the French analytic tradition, discussed below.

Here we again underscore the observation that the self concept in the American tradition may be conceived as a *self of fulfillment*. And most often, fulfillment is derived from a recovery of what was.

Finally, by way of concluding our observations of the theories within the American ego psychological tradition, we observe a commonly shared view of knowing which informs this body of work, and which is perhaps most clearly underscored by the concept of the "internal representation." While, as we have suggested, the *internalization* of an image (i.e., a representation) is an exemplary instance of psychic fulfillment in the sense we discussed above, we are here placing the emphasis upon *representation* in order to highlight the particular kind of knowledge that is accessible to the mind from the standpoint of the theories discussed herein. We shall observe of this view, interestingly, that it gives us an avenue for suggesting that these theories of fulfillment have more in common with those of absence than surface alignments might readily suggest.

Generally speaking, all the theories thus far reviewed suggest, in the manner by which they construct their conceptual explanations, that the self is capable of knowing only the appearance of things, that is, the *representations*. Claiming the realization of the fulfilled self by way of internalizing a representation of the other is, I suggest, another way of saying that what we may know, and possess, of the other, of other people and otherness and strangeness in general, is but what we can make *appear before our psychic eyes* as a *re*presentation of the actual thing in itself. The actual other object is never what is actually known; rather, it is the representation of that object, as it is made to appear, to be imaged, to the mind. This "appearance" of the actual thing in itself is what Kant has termed the *noumenal*, while the *phenomenal* consists in what is made to appear, to be represented to, consciousness. We say of the self that it is a composite conceptualization, made up of those represented pictures of the world of others which have been made apparent to consciousness. We know what we are conscious of, a claim psychoanalysis has been making all along, at least from the time that Freud asserted that "where id was, there shall ego be."

It is interesting to consider that the unconscious is only knowable insofar as its nature is altered to become conscious. Further, and we shall consider this in greater detail when we discuss Lacan's view of the self, such aspects of the self as may be unconscious are not knowable but in that they be changed to conscious aspects, and thus be inevitably distorted or changed from their original (unconscious) nature. Thus we may consider the possibility, for Kohut (1959, 1971, 1977) as well as other theorists who posit a self within a representational framework, that either the self "in itself" is never obtainable, or that there is no self which is other than the appearance, the phenomenon, of a self. Thus, and we shall make this case perhaps more strongly once we have discussed Lacan, there is indeed a latent kinship among the notions of fulfillment and absence. For if an actual self, in the psychological sense, is an unknowable noumenon, then it is, in actuality, forever beyond presence, that is, it is always absent. On the other hand, if a fulfilled and realized self is recognized in the appearance, we say again that it is not known actually; it is instead an actually absent self.

We shall now shift the focus of the discussion, moving from an investigation of theories of the self in the American tradition to spotlight some views which have emerged from within the French, and then the British, perspectives. However, before doing so, we pause to address aspects of the important work of Stern (1985), whose theory of the self both challenges and affirms many of our observations in this section. For it is a theory which makes manifest the trend toward an unambiguously ascendant self, out from the shadow of the ego, which we have been tracking since Hartmann; yet it is also a theory which challenges the very principles upon which the self of fulfillment rests.

Chapter 5
THE SENSE OF SELF OF DANIEL STERN

Daniel Stern (1985), unique among theorists of the American tradition reviewed in this discussion, seeks to elaborate a theory of the infant's inner life which is explicitly organized around, first, the nonreflexive, and then reflexive, awareness of a series of patterned and invariant subjective experiences that is the sense of self. In so placing the sense of self, Stern (1985) will distinguish his work from those who have preceded him in the analytic tradition by unambiguously removing the self from the shadow of the ego, by assuming its existence from the very beginning of life, and by attributing a formative impact to subjective experience. Thus, "even though the nature of the self may forever elude the behavioral sciences, the sense of self stands as an important subjective reality [which] . . . provides a basic organizing perspective for all interpersonal events" (Stern, p. 6).

In reviewing this important contribution to the study of the self concept, we observe that, like Mahler, Pine, and Bergman (1975), Stern bases his inferential leaps upon a firm empirical, observational foundation. We shall begin by briefly addressing Stern's interesting and important methodological approach to the subject, and then proceed to a discussion of his theoretical proposals.

Methodological Observations

In keeping with an experimental and observational ethic of deriving data, American psychiatry, and academic psychology generally, has

---

References to Stern's ideas in this chapter are exclusively to his 1985 work.

141

tended to rely rather exclusively upon objective, observable events as the stuff of clinical reality. Such an approach has generated a considerable body of new information with respect to infant behavior, and many innovative methods of inquiry into the elusive realm of infant mental life. Nonetheless, a commitment to strictly observational methodologies, in accord with an American preference for descriptively drawn accounts, carries with it a concomitant disinclination to make inferential statements. Thus, while there is much empirical data available about what the infant can do, and do at earlier points in life than had previously been thought, the methodology circumscribes its generalizability; and what has been empirically garnered and is objectively known has not been employed in seeking a reply to inquiries regarding the nature of early subjective experience.

On the other hand, psychoanalysis is regularly willing to make inferential leaps, asserting claims with respect to the inner life that have enlarged clinical reality beyond the bounds of actual happenings. Such assertions are, after a fashion, also based upon "observed" events; however, the events are reconstructed from the client's own, necessarily subjective, recollections. Thus, in the obverse, the psychoanalytic methodology is largely subjective and has not responded well to calls for objective corroboration.

It is at this juncture, between objectively derived data which abjure subjective inferences, and subjectively generated data which elude objective confirmation, that Stern, astride both approaches, will attempt a combinative methodology in seeking to say something more about the infant's subjective experience. Thus, Stern aims to employ the new data on infant behavior in order to construct a working hypothesis which makes some descriptive inferences about the origins and nature of the inner life; and, Stern unambiguously asserts, "I plan to start by placing the sense of self at the very center of the inquiry" (p. 5).

We note that Stern speaks of the *sense* of self, and that by this he means to address the self at the level of direct, nonreflexive, experiential awareness rather than at the level of conceptual formulation. In turn, this notion of "sense" as denoting awareness bears directly upon his understanding of self as a series of particular kinds of awareness, occurring under specifically circumscribed conditions. To wit, the self is here an "*invariant pattern* of awarenesses that arise only on the occasion of the *infant's actions or mental processes*" (p. 7; emphases added), and such invariant patterns are ways of organizing experience.

Thus, the "self," Stern continues, "is the organizing subjective experience of whatever it is that will later be verbally referenced as the 'self' " (p. 7). That is to say, the self is a subjective organization of experience which is derived from the infant's actions and thoughts and, importantly, exists prior to any verbal capacity to name, or reflect upon, the experience. Stern employs considerable infant research data, which will not be reviewed here, to buttress his assertions, particularly that the self exists from the outset of life, but for our purposes we highlight that this assertion is at odds with the predominant American psychoanalytic tradition of an ego which develops over time; a tradition which stems from Freud's (1914) own assertions that the ego is *not* present from the outset.

Indeed, it is one of Stern's basic assumptions "that some senses of the self do exist long prior to self-awareness and language" (p. 6), and his work represents an effort to elaborate a set of organizing principles which may explain the epigenetic patterning of subjective experience in its preverbal as well as verbal states. In this he belongs to a "developmentalist" tradition whose beginnings may be traced to Freud's oral–anal–genital progression and which includes, although from a quite different standpoint, the work of Mahler and Melanie Klein.

For Freud and Mahler have also sought to account for observed behaviors in terms of the infant's experience of self and other. However, whereas Freud's is a theoretical statement about the progressive reorganization of the drives, and Mahler's developmental schema is largely a theoretical exposition of the restructuring of the ego, and the id (this despite its recounting in terms of the infant's experience of self and other), Stern's unambiguous focus on the self is, as he notes, "not encumbered with or confused with issues of the development of the ego or id" (p. 19). That is to say, while Mahler and others, such as Erikson, Spitz, Jacobson, Kernberg, and even Kohut, all adhered, more or less, to psychoanalytic principles in constructing a genetic explanation, Stern is quite able to place them to one side if the data do not call for them. Thus, for example, Stern cites recent findings from infant research which question the developmental sequencing of the pleasure principle prior to the reality principle, and concludes that "this position leaves the infant unapproachable by psychodynamic considerations for an initial period, resulting in a *non-psychodynamic beginning of life''* (p. 255). How, we may now ask, does Stern elaborate the subjective life of the infant which he draws from the developmental data at hand?

Domains of the Self

Stern opens his theoretical inquiry by posing the question, ''is there a self to begin with . . . ?'' and in so doing implicitly challenges the long-standing American ego psychological, largely Mahlerian developmental paradigm which, in positing a merged state of ''dual-unity,'' replies in the negative. For traditional theoretical explanations claim a self which develops over time as specific tasks are realized. That is, the major developmental advances in the self occur in consequence of the successful assimilation of social experiences, as in the processes of separation, establishing basic trust, orality, and independence, for example. As well, traditional theoretical explanations posit, as is again most clearly illustrated in but not exclusive to Mahler, an initial phase of dedifferentiation in which there is no self to speak of, that is, no awareness of self, even a nonreflexive awareness. Rather, developmental theory has envisioned a time of boundaryless merger from which a self ''hatches'' into being.

Stern, by contrast, proposes a sense of self from the very beginning of life, and in so doing he not only has done away with an initial state of merged unity, but has, as well, disassociated the development of the self from a set of specific clinical issues, such as separation, individuation, or basic trust. In fact, what Stern has done is reverse the direction of traditional developmental causality. Thus, whereas the increasingly complex and aware self had been attributed to (was dependent upon) internalizing social experiences with others, Stern redefines self so that it becomes the causal agent which makes increasingly complex social interactional experiences possible. In this model, the self is the independent variable upon which the achievement of social experience is dependent. Thus, ''the sense of self serves as the primary subjective perspective that organizes social experience and therefore now moves to center stage as the phenomenon that dominates early social development'' (p. 11).

There are, in Stern's view, four different senses of the self, each denoting a realm, or domain, of self experience generated by the extent of matured capacities and abilities available to the infant. These senses include an *emergent self*, covering a period from birth to 2 months; a *core self*, which is elaborated in the span from 2 to 6 months; a *subjective self*, formed between 7 and 15 months; and a *verbal self*, which begins to develop subsequently. Importantly, Stern does not envision these as successive senses of self, but as concomitant, for "once formed, each sense of self remains fully functioning and active throughout life [and] all continue to grow and coexist" (p. 11). The self, we begin to sense, is not an entity so much as a felt experience, or *areas* of experience, more or less accessible to reflexive awareness, and always available as a background of nonreflexive awareness. How does Stern describe these senses of self?

The Emergent Self

This domain of self experience seeks to descriptively capture that period of time from birth until 2 months, a developmental phase most familiarly conceived of as presocial, precognitive, and lacking in organization. It is the stage of "normal autism," during which little or no awareness of self or other is traditionally thought to exist. Stern reformulates this typically obscure and often vaguely described period of life, asking how, in fact, the infant might experience the social world that had been previously theorized to be beyond his or her ken at this early juncture.

Stern rejects the notion that newborns exist in a formless, boundless state of "bloomin', buzzin' confusion." He relies upon a wealth of observational research on the first two months of life, including studies which found that 3-day-old infants can recognize the smell of their own mother's milk; that they tend to be particularly responsive to the human voice as measured by an increase in "nonnutritive" sucking in order to induce it; and that infants can discriminate patterns and prefer to look at the human face. On the contrary, he asserts that "infants are not lost at sea in a wash of abstractable qualities of experience. They are gradually and systematically ordering these elements of experience to identify self-invariant and other-invariant constellations" (p. 67).

Thus we observe that Stern reconceptualizes this early period, envisioning the infant as a proactive agent who engages with his or her environment, and who possesses capacities and abilities which allow for the creation of patterns and groupings of experience. Now Stern does not stop at the claim that the newborn is busily involved in organizing the world at an earlier age than had been previously thought: that is, observing no more than the uninterpreted data display. Rather, employing a combinative methodology alluded to above, Stern employs this empirical data to aid him in replying to his own inquiry about the *subjective* life of the infant in these first months.

What, he is essentially asking, can it feel like to be a newborn infant? To answer is, of course, to make an inferential leap into the basically unverifiable, but Stern takes with him as a kind of "candle in the dark" the accumulating evidence of research. Employing the objective as a springboard, Stern makes just such a leap into the subjective, concluding that "during the first two months the infant is actively forming a sense of an emergent self. It is a sense of organization in the process of formation, and it is a sense of self that will remain active for the rest of life" (p. 38). Stern is thus asserting that even in this early period, even and especially from the start of neonatal physical life, there is also a neonatal subjective life.

Now Stern is by no means arguing for a reflexive, contemplative self at this point. On the contrary, this is a self which is here preparing the ground for the much later acquisition of reflexive subjectivity. The emergent self is, nonetheless, an awareness, but a direct experience of events rather than a self reflexively mediated awareness. One is here reminded of the earliest stages of subjectivity drawn by Kernberg (1982b). The sense of self here described as emergent is the simultaneous experience of the organized patterns it creates *and* the process of creating itself. Further, this is a self which gets its start, contrary to predominant ego and object relations theories, without the benefits of external experience. Indeed, Stern asserts, "infants do not need repeated experience to begin to form some of the pieces of an emergent self and other. *They are predesigned to forge certain integrations*" (p. 52; emphasis added).

The emergent self consists of two interrelated aspects. First, it is, as we have suggested, the creation of invariant, and hence recognizable, patterns of experience in relation to one's own being and in relation to others. These patterns are the result of the infant's innate organizational capacities; they are the product of his or her efforts. Thus, one significant aspect of the "sense" of this self is precisely as the set of organized and invariant patterns established. The emergent self is, in part, the nonreflexive awareness of these organizational products. But Stern does not define this early sense of self in terms of the results of its patterning activity alone. The emergent self is also that which is "on the way to being."

Thus, a second aspect of the emergent self is the sense of self which *is* as it engages in its own becoming. The "sense" here is the felt experience of emerging; the self feels or experiences itself *in the process* of forming, as there is not yet a formed sense of self with a fixed reference point; the first such anchor will be the body and it will serve to organize the core self. Here, the self is "known" only as a fluid state of "coming into being." A point of reference is first emerging here, and the sense of self is the experience of that emergence as it occurs. The emergent self is truly a "happening."

In conceiving of an *active, patterned, and organized* subjective experience in these first moments of life, Stern abjures any notion of a dedifferentiated period of life as an adultomorphic reification. For what appears to be an undifferentiated state when compared to the relative complexity of the older child, is simply attributed to the infant from the point of view of the adult observer who is able to conceive of a state in which nothing is discernible or subject to awareness. The infant, if she or he has a subjective life, and that of course is the inference Stern makes, cannot have an undifferentiated one simply because there can be no awareness of what is not known; and, conversely, as soon as it is discerned, it is differentiated. It is only later, with the acquisition of more complex capacities, that one can conceive of knowing what she or he has not discerned.

The emergent self is the "domain of emergent relatedness" (p. 67), and is essentially an organizing process. It is the act and the experience of creation, and this act and this experience *is* the emergent self. All subsequent senses of self will be products of this process. Thus, the emergent sense of self is present and plays a causal role in establishing each of the domains of self experience which follow. Let us see how each of them is constituted.

The Core Self

The core self introduces Stern's first genuinely overarching perspective regarding the self. For as we have observed, the emergent self is not an encompassing, fixed point of reference, but a *process*. Now, for the first time, and in consequence of that process, an initial invariant self referential sense is established. It is a sense of self composed of a set of principle experiences which, when taken together, yield a sense of a central core of being.

These experiences include *self-agency*, or the sense of causing one's own actions, and importantly, of not causing the actions of others. It is, in this way, a discriminatory activity in which initial psychic dividing lines are drawn. A second experience contributing to the core self is that of *self-coherence*, which is the experience of being whole, and in possession of palpable, and "locatable" physical boundaries. *Self-affectivity* is a third constituent element, and refers to the patterned and invariant experience of certain feelings in association with other experiences of self. That is, one feels regularly "happy" when feeding; or "irritable" when wet. Finally, Stern includes a sense of continuity or sameness over time that he refers to as *self-history*, and which enables one to endure change and yet feel that one's being has not changed.

Each of these four experiential constellations is understood as a *self-invariant*, or a thing that remains constant even as all other things may change. It is the integration of these core experiences which allows for the successful realization of the primary task of this period, the establishing of an interpersonal world, which in its turn is accomplished by distinguishing a core self from core others. These experiences, we see, constitute one's first fixed, nonreflexive sense of self and other. For in the aggregate, these experiences reflect an awareness of a regularly volitional, coherent source of affect which endures over time. These elements constitute the very essence, or core, of "selfhood" and accompany, in an experiential as distinct from a cognitive, sense all other self experience.

Now, Stern posits that this core self is elaborated during the span from 2 to 7 months, a period which fairly closely coincides with Mahler's period of "normal symbiosis." And it is during this period, as Mahler et al. (1975) have maintained, that "the infant behaves and functions as though he and his mother were an omnipotent system—a dual unity within one common boundary" (p. 44). In contrast, Stern is suggesting a core self and core other differentiation just at the time when most prevailing views would have the infant enmeshed in an unbounded self–other orbit. Thus, just as we observed that Stern had, in proposing an emergent self from the outset, reversed the order of causality in establishing the infant's social interactional life, we note that here, as well, he engages in some reversals.

For rather than adhering to the developmental schedule in which the infant is first merged with mother and only secondarily evolves from within that fused state to an increasingly complex self and other differentiation, Stern makes that merger experience contingent upon the prior emergence of a fixed core self. Thus, new research evidence suggests that "the capacity to have merger- or fusion-like experiences as described in psychoanalysis is *secondary to and dependent upon an already existing sense of self and other* . . . first comes the formation of self and other, and only then is the sense of merger-like experiences possible" (p. 70; emphasis added).

The core self is a bipartite experience in which the first sense, as just described, addresses the emergence and certain establishment of a self as distinct from, or over and against, the other. The first part of the core self experience is a kind of sorting out process, in which self is discriminated from other on the basis of direct, nonreflexive sensations and behaviors which mark off self and other boundaries. The second half of this sense of self involves the experience of being *with* the other and requires, as we have noted, the successful realization of the core self in the first sense.

Involved in the sense of core self *with* the other is the objective fact of what Stern refers to as the self-regulating other. That is, the ministrations of the mother, which have an observable, empirical impact upon the infant. Stern's more fundamental question, however, much as it has been all along, is what might the infant's subjective experience of this objective, regulatory relationship be?

These experiences with the self-regulating other, it turns out, "are the same ones that have been called mergings, fusings, [and] security gratifications" (Stern, p. 104) but, as we shall see, they are not the traditionally defined psychic mergers of analytic theory. For the experience which Stern is addressing is neither the primary fusion of infancy in which self and other are felt to share a single encompassing boundary; nor is it the remergings, or feelings of engulfment, which are theorized to occur subsequent to the acquisition of individuated subjective boundaries. In these descriptions we recognize, in the latter instance, the pathological states of symbiotic psychosis, and in the former the notion of an initial, or primary, fusion of self and other which was posited as entirely normative in the early days and months of life. However, rather than imputing to the infant's subjective state what is observed in the behavior of the psychotic child, Stern suggests that the experience the child has with the self-regulating other is a different order of experience.

To begin, positing the *experience* itself—of the self *with* the other as a subjective event—requires the antecedent presence of a self, and this, we have seen, Stern has done by theorizing that the first aspect of a core self is that which develops its own sense of agency and cohesion. This, in Stern's view, must occur prior to any mergerlike experiences with an other. Thus, the first distinguishing characteristic of the subjective state of the self when it interacts with the self regulating other is that, unlike normal autism or symbiosis, a core self is already in existence.

Second, and predicated upon this first condition, is the nature of the experience itself. Because a self already exists, one whose emergent sense allows for the creation of invariant patterns, it is able to experience changed feeling states as particularized, inner-directed events, and is capable of discriminating those things which emanate from self and those which emanate from other. It is "skill" which had begun to evolve in the emergent self and had become established, according to Stern, in the consolidation of the core self as differentiated from the core other. That is, being with the other is not an indistinguishable mass of unattributable, merged feelings. Rather it is a *self-altering* experience in which the particular feelings the infant has could only be mutually created, but which are recognized as belonging to the core self.

Thus, the self, because it is already a subjective entity, can and does experience specific feelings which are generated by, indeed which can *only* be generated by, being in interaction with the other. Furthermore, the feelings which this self correctly identifies as his own are, consequently, *not distorted*. The self's experience of being with another is, again, because there is a subjective sense of a separate, bounded self, *not* felt to be a fused, boundless condition, but "simply the actual experience of being with someone (a self-regulatory other) such that self feelings are importantly changed" (p. 105). So, what Stern refers to as merger experiences bear little resemblance to traditional psychoanalytic formulations, for there is *no fusion* of boundaries between self and other; *no distortion* of the interaction; while there *is* *affective self-ownership* of altered feeling states.

This second aspect of the core self is a transformative one, in which, as the infant is engaged in being with the other, she or he becomes other than what she or he had been. For in the course of being cared for by the self-regulating other (i.e., fed, diapered) the infant, as we have seen, experiences alterations in affect, many of which occur as "silent" byproducts of the primary caregiving role. Nonetheless the infant self in its very core is forever changed by these ministrations, and one is reminded, in Stern's formulation, of Kohut's (1977) selfobject, of Winnicott's (1958) notion of the infant's "going on being" in the silent presence of the mother; and perhaps most significantly, of Bollas' (1987) concepts of the "transformational object" and the "unthought known." These latter ideas will receive considerable attention below and so it will suffice for now to note that Bollas conceives of the infant as being affectively transformed by the other in ways which are prearticulate and "silent," and as "knowing"—nonreflexively—what he has not and cannot yet think or say. In similar fashion does Stern's infant nonreflexively "know" the feelings generated in mutual interaction with the transforming mother.

Stern introduces two very interesting concepts in the course of elaborating the role of the subjective experience of being with the other that merit attention. These concepts are representations of interactions that have been generalized (RIGS) and the closely related notion of evoked companions.

RIGS and Evoked Companions

Stern ties all the elements of the subjective experience of being with the other into one unit, the "lived episode," in which the elements were first manifested. These elements include the other person as they are felt, seen, and heard at the moment of the altering interaction; the sense of a core self and other which serve as a background for the specific interactional event; and the important alterations in the infant's feelings. Thus, the subjective experience, interestingly, is neither the self altering experiences of the infant self nor the regulatory role of the other. Instead, both are "embraced by a larger common unit of subjective experience, the episode" (p. 110) in which each retains its distinct identity as a component of the unit.

Now, while each lived episode may become a specific memory, as they are repeated (i.e., as there are many feedings or many diaperings) they become "generalized episodes of interactive experience that are mentally represented—that is, representations of interactions that have been generalized, or RIGs" (p. 110). These RIGs, Stern suggests, are constellations of interactive experiences with others which form generalized representations of these interactions, and whenever the infant experiences a particular affect, that affect stimulates, or activates, those generalized interactions, or RIGs, of which the affect is an attribute. Recalling such attributes serves to reawaken the RIG as a palpable, present experience, such that the infant, or the adult, reexperiences the moment in a visceral and mnemonic fashion. Thus, the sound of the ocean or the aroma of cut grass, no less than the press of hunger or the taste of milk, can stir a feeling which is itself an attribute of a more generalized experience "and whenever a RIG is activated, it packs some of the wallop of the originally lived experience in the form of an active memory" (p. 110).

The RIGs, we note, serve as a kind of depersonalized (i.e., generalized) pattern against which the self is able to assess new lived episodes, for "it is important to remember that RIGs are flexible structures that average several actual instances and form a prototype to represent them all" (p. 110). In this we recall the conceptualizations of Spiegel (1959) who posited a self which was, in fact, an invariant framework composed of like elements from a number of experiences, and which served as a steady and coherent background against which to assess and assimilate new events.

Now Stern raises the question, which is quite central to the organizational lines of this inquiry, of how to distinguish between being with self-regulating others who are present and being with those who are absent. That is, what is the qualitative difference in experience, as it is felt subjectively, between actually interacting with a self-regulating other and the subjective feelings associated with the RIG of a self-regulating other who, as a RIG, is actually absent. Is there a subjectively felt difference between relating to the present other and to the absent other? Stern's reply is an interesting one, which places his concept of the sense of self, no less than those of his colleagues in the American school, within the "self as fulfillment" tradition, albeit with some nuances of difference.

Thus, Stern will maintain that there is essentially no difference between the subjective experiences of being with an actual other or a "RIGged other," because "in both cases infants must deal with their *history* with others . . . [which] involves the *subjective experience of being with an historical self-regulating other*" (Stern, p. 111; emphases added). That is, whether the self-regulating other is actually present or not, the infant must still call upon his generalized representations (RIGs) in order to grasp what he is experiencing subjectively. In both instances it is his own subjective historical constellation of lived, generalized episodes, to which the infant turns for a "reading" on his current state. Thus, presence and absence, in this view, are not as definitive as the RIG itself in subjective experience.

But this is the juncture at which we observe that Stern tends toward a "fulfillment solution" to the presence–absence dichotomy. For here he suggests that when a RIG of being with a self-regulating other is retrieved, so too is the experienced presence of the (self-regulating) other. The RIG not only reawakens the memory of an event, or episode; it also conjures the felt experience of being with the other, or in his or her presence. This other, not unlike the psychic endproduct of Kohut's (1977) transmuting internalization, is not the veridical depiction of the other, but is rather a more depersonalized "exemplar" of an aggregate of self-regulating others. This other, called an *evoked companion* by Stern, serves to assess a current interactive episode, helping the infant self to evaluate how the new interactive event may compare with the "simultaneously occurring experience with the evoked companion" (Stern, p. 113). The companion is evoked in order that it aid the infant in establishing the subjective meaning of the new interaction.

This mnemonic companion, which may also be evoked when the infant is alone in situations that had historically had another present, is, we observe, a concept which sits on the border between the present and the absent serving to reestablish what is absent. This is much the same as object constancy, the transmuted object, and the internalized self and other representations. The evoked companion, a constituent element of the RIG, becomes the internalized "content" of the subjective life; it fulfills the psychic inside, making the subjective experience of self a composite of absent companions reevoked. The evoked companion's character is essentially a collection of "all that was," for the evoked companion recalls, that is, makes present again, that which *once was* present and is no longer.

As we move to consider the third of Stern's senses of the self, we conclude our discussion of the core self by observing that the key accomplishment of this realm of subjectivity, particularly in the experience of self with the self-regulating other, is the foundation of the interpersonal world. For we see that the infant's subjective experience is inexorably bound to social experience with the other, the affective memory of which becomes the very fabric of internal life and which is evoked to assess ongoing interactions. How will subsequent self experiences build upon and enlarge this interpersonal self?

The Subjective Self

The core self and core other, we recall, is essentially about establishing *sensory and physical differences*, which allow for the elaboration of invariant patterns of discrimination. The core self provides the physical assurance that the self is separate from the other, and such assurances are an absolute precondition for the realization of that realm of exchange which is uniquely human (i.e., intersubjective relatedness). Psychological "knowledge," of one's own discrete being, in the form of nonreflexive sensory experience, must precede any psychically "intimate" knowledge of the other; indeed, such core certainty "is the existential bedrock of interpersonal relations" (p. 125).

Having so established this core self and core other knowledge, the infant, Stern asserts, takes a "quantum leap" in the nature of the sense of self such that some time between 7 and 9 months there is the "momentous realization that inner and subjective experiences . . . are potentially shareable with someone else" (Stern, p. 124). Minds can now begin to touch minds, whereas earlier only bodies could make contact. Phylogenetic paths here diverge as the distinctly human capacity for reflexive awareness of one's own thoughts and feelings arises (i.e., reflexive subjective knowledge), along with the concomitant awareness of like thoughts and feelings in the core other. Of course the ontogenic manifestations of the newly discovered capacity for sharing will depend largely upon the idiosyncratic inclinations of particular core selves with core others, but the principal accomplishment stands: the infant has, in Stern's words, achieved the "acquisition of a 'theory' of separate minds" (p. 124).

Thus, the infant is able to conceive of the possibility that what she or he is thinking or feeling may bear sufficient similarity to what mother is thinking or feeling that they "can somehow communicate this (without words) and thereby experience intersubjectivity" (Stern, pp. 124–125). This ability to experience intersubjective communication expands the range of the sense of self, for relatedness itself, as well as the "content" of that relatedness, has been forever altered. The self is now primarily organized in terms of intersubjective contact although, as we noted, core-relatedness must have been securely established if this new domain is to take root. Now this order of contact is still prior to the advent of language, and consequently the intersubjectively shared experiences need necessarily to be of a kind that do not call for words. Let us see what Stern has in mind here.

Preverbal Mental States

Stern suggests that we may identify three specific preverbal states which empirical data suggest are indicative of the infant's capacity for intersubjectively shared experience. These include a sharing of joint attention, intentions, and affective states.

That the focus of attention can be shared is suggested, Stern believes, by research evidence which indicates that 9-month-old infants can point, follow the visual direction of another's pointing behavior, and check back with the "pointer" to confirm that they have found the intended target. The data thus allow Stern to make the inference that the infant can have an attentional focus and that, even if different from the mother's, it can be made similar. What he calls *interattentionality* becomes a reality (p. 130).

In similar fashion is the inference made that intentions and affects can be shared. Thus, Stern's formulation of the concepts of *interintentionality* and *interaffectivity* have been derived from data suggesting that infants of this age range engage in "protolinguistic forms of requesting" such as placing the hand palm up and accompanying such behavior with verbal intonations when the mother is holding, for example, a cookie; or that infants can appreciate the similarity between their own affective state and the expression seen on the face of another.

Interestingly, Stern's own observations suggest that the sharing of affective experiences "may be the first, more pervasive, and most

immediately important form of sharing subjective experiences'' (p.
132). This is a finding which accords well with long-standing psychoanalytic assertions regarding the early formative impact of affect, both
as medium and message. The defining influence of affects has been
psychoanalytically pursued by Kernberg (1976) among many others.

Autonomous Function or Motivational System?

In seeking to understand how it is that the infant comes to adopt "an
organizing perspective about the self and the other that opens the door
to intersubjectivity'' (p. 133), Stern reviews some of the relevant research data offering cognitive, social, and genetic explanations for the
intersubjective capacity. Concluding that all of these views must play
a role in any adequate explanation, noting perhaps especially that the
"special awareness" that is intersubjectivity unfolds maturationally,
Stern moves to a question of particular relevance to the long-standing
ego–self dichotomy we have observed throughout our discussion of
the American tradition. Thus he asks whether, once "tasted," can
intersubjectivity become one more in an armamentarium of capacities,
to be employed or not as one chooses; or rather, "does it become a
new psychological need, the need to share subjective experience?"
(p. 135).

This is indeed an important query. For the response will illuminate
the position of the self concept in Stern's, or any other, theoretical
framework. If intersubjective relatedness is but another autonomous
ego function, one among many, then the self can hardly be thought of
as more than a representational capacity within that ego. It is surely an
overarching essential of the very idea of self, irrespective of theoretical
origin, indeed a characteristic of the human condition itself, that one
is able to engage in some form of intimate exchange with others (i.e.,
make intersubjective contact).

In fact, as the ego psychological theoretical approach attests, attributing autonomous status to a capacity has suggested its *relative*
independence vis-à-vis other needs and demands. However, as we emphasize, the status is only relative, for in the ego psychological view
these capacities are always subject to a "deneutralizing" process; they
are, that is, ever "at the service of the 'basic' psychoanalytic needs,
[i.e., the drives], whose higher status is protected" (p. 135). Is this the
fate of intersubjectivity as well?

While not saying so directly, it seems reasonable to assert that Stern understands intersubjective capacity to merit the status of a fully developed, idiosyncratically human motivational system. He observes that research offers no conclusive evidence regarding the supraordinate status of this form of relatedness, but notes that evidence does suggest that the ability to share with others is a uniquely functional survival mechanism for humans, providing, as it appears to, both security, and inclusion in the group. And, "the more one conceives of intersubjective relatedness as a basic psychological need, the closer one refashions clinical theory toward the configurations suggested by Self psychologists and some existential psychologists" (p. 136); that is, toward placing the self at the unambiguous center of explanation.

Developmental Modifications

We conclude our discussion of the subjective sense of self by observing how Stern's characterization of this domain of experience imposes some modifications upon traditional developmental theory. Thus, the 7- to 9-month age period in which Stern places the emergence of the subjective sense of self, characterized as it is by an active psychological *sharing* with the mother, is just the instance which established explanations understand as "the time when toddlers invest so much libido in their own *autonomous* functions" (Mahler et al., 1975, p. 69; emphasis added). In this chronological span, the Mahlerian youngster, for example, enters the *practicing subphase*, and is actively engaged in what Greenacre (1957) has felicitously anointed a "love affair with the world." And it is precisely at this moment that Stern introduces a significant modification.

The subjective sense of self, we have seen, is often about sharing one's focus of attention with the mother; about the joining of intentions; and about the union of minds in the likenesses among their affective states. But we note, as we did in discussing the emergent and the core senses of self, that Stern has undertaken to amend the traditional sequence of developmental evolution. Basing his inferences here, as throughout the development of his paradigm for the evolution of the sense(s) of self, upon research evidence, Stern thus asserts that conjoint subjective experiences are occurring "just at the developmental moment when traditional theory had the tide beginning to flow the other way" (p. 127).

Stern is arguing, as he notes, not so much that the order of developmental events ought to be thought of as reversed (i.e., placing subjective union prior to autonomous "hatching"), but rather that they appear to occur within the same time frame. Thus, "in the present view, both separation/individuation and new forms of experiencing union (or being-with) emerge equally out of the same experience of intersubjectivity" (Stern, p. 127). Intersubjectivity itself creates an "atmosphere" within which the child may simultaneously experience *psychological mutuality* and an omnipotent love affair with the world and an increasingly individuated self. For knowing what is shared, one also experiences what is not; knowing what belongs to "us" allows knowledge of what belongs only to "me." One condition does not cancel, but rather enriches, the other.

We have seen that the subjective capacity radically reorganizes the sense of self, enlarging its reach beyond the sensate knowledge of the body; indeed, as far and as profoundly as the mind of the mother, and forever after setting the human child on a reflexive course. This sense of the self as a subjective, and then intersubjective, experience is organized, as we have seen, prior to the advent of verbal capacity. We turn now to a review of how Stern envisions the sense of self as it is impacted by the acquisition of language.

The Verbal Self

The sense imparted by the verbal self is significantly different from that in any of the foregoing domains of experience. For here, unlike antecedent self experiences, the child is able to link the internally represented, inexorably silent, subjective world to the external world of events. Prior to reaching this juncture, the infant could do little more than record the impact of reality; from the moment the child becomes a self in the verbal sense she or he is increasingly able to alter that reality. How has Stern elaborated this pivotal realm of experience?

A World in Words

Perhaps the single most profound change in the sense of self may be attributed to the advent of language, the acquisition of which permits hitherto quite literally unimaginable ways of engaging with the other.

While prior to the ability to employ language the infant, as we have observed, surely was able to "be with" the mother, the quality of that relatedness was circumscribed in particular ways by the absence of words.

Thus, "being with" the self-regulating other was a hallmark achievement in the sense of the core self, and played a major role as well in the subjective sense of self, in which sharing of subjective states is the primary organizing principle. The nature of the relatedness, changes significantly as we move from the core sense to the subjective sense in that for the first time, in the latter instance, infant and mother *share a state of mind*, such as intention or affect, in contrast to a bodily state. But it is not until language is available that *meaning* can be made, because words permit idiosyncratic experiences to be shared with, and thereby possibly confirmed by, the "speaking other." A verbal self is the sense that one can, by representing one's particular experience in the commonly shared medium of language, which is the thread of communion running through an otherwise unspeakably diverse human experience, be understood.

Language makes it possible to *share in the world* of many others, for linguistic representation is a child's cultural membership card. With it she or he can gain access to the larger world of distinctly human being. Language also makes it possible for the child to *share with the world* his or her personal life. For it allows the child to tell his own tale, or to create what Spence (1982) has called "narrative truth"; and it permits the child to actively engage with another in creating a meaning which had never existed before, a mutually created and mutually shared meaning. For meaning is the dynamic relationship of thought and experience to word and "results from interpersonal negotiations involving what can be agreed upon as shared."

Thus language, as human kind's portable version of the public square, becomes a new meeting ground upon which the child may encounter the mother in a fundamentally altered manner. For in being able to link personally conceived mental representations to events and actions of the external world, the child begins, quite literally, to have a say about those events, and his or her role in them. Thus, the self which emerges in consequence of language is now not only able to renegotiate the ongoing issues of his or her life, such as separation, intimacy, attachment, and autonomy, but possesses as well the capacity to *reinvent* him- or herself. For now the child, and the adult to come, is increasingly able to create and alter personal meaning, for "the advent of language ultimately brings about the ability to narrate one's own life story with all the potential that holds for changing how one views oneself" (p. 174).

Nonetheless, for all that language enables the child to share his inner life with another, thereby creating meaning in that life, it is, Stern suggests, a "double-edged sword [as] it also makes some parts of our experience *less shareable* with ourselves and with others" (p. 162; emphasis added). How is it that language, which so greatly enlarges the realm of relatedness, can also foreclose it in other respects?

A Self Divided

Language, Stern argues, makes experience less shareable the more one is able to speak of it, precisely because it enables the child to arrive at an *agreed upon* meaning. A meaning which the child and the mother have negotiated together and which thus bears the assent of each is no longer the same experience. For that which is verbally represented is not the actual experience. The word is a wedge placed between the palpable and the shareable. It must be thus, for meaning is a public reconstruction of private events.

One must "say" an experience, represent it with words, even if only to echo it back to the self, if meaning is to accrue to that experience. To speak the experience is to publicize it, to make it objective, and thus, no longer what it was (i.e., subjective). Thus, while there is no meaning that cannot be put into words, there are no words which do not separate the speaker from that of which she or he speaks. "Language," Stern asserts, "causes a split in the experience of the self [and] . . . moves relatedness onto the impersonal, abstract level . . . and away from the personal, immediate level intrinsic to the other domains . . . " (p. 163).

Language appropriates aspects of the more global, preverbal, subjective experience and transforms it such that it is an experience entirely different from the original. But, as Stern emphasizes, the other levels of relatedness (i.e., the core and intersubjective senses of self) are not obscured by the acquisition of language. Rather, these domains now exist in two distinct, and simultaneously present forms, "so that they lead two lives—their original life as nonverbal experience and a life as the verbalized version of that experience" (p. 174).

The cooccurrence of these two qualitatively very different realms of being, the preverbal and the verbal, or the private and public, can often explain the kind of relationship one has with one's self. Thus, for example, it may happen that, under ideal circumstances, language proves capable of capturing just that aspect of the larger preverbal experience that expresses the full experience in what is felt to be a truly coincident manner. Here we may imagine that the sense of feeling "at one" with one's self is most intimate.

More usually, however, language does not represent the global subjective experience very well and, being inadequately articulated, "it wanders off to lead a misnamed and poorly understood existence" (p. 175). This, of course, is an instance of the bifurcating impact of language upon the self, for words are most characteristically unable to accurately represent what is felt. Finally, Stern notes that there are portions of preverbal experience that simply do not allow access to language—there are literally "no words to describe what happened." In such cases, the experiences lead an *un*named, rather than a *mis*-named, "underground existence."

Thus, while poetry, and some fiction can come quite close to the first of the conditions Stern outlines, in which there is a nearly perfect congruence of the spoken with the unspoken; more typically, language tends to misrepresent preverbal subjective life, or cannot represent it at all. What language always does, however, is bind experience to words, specifying a particular way in which the experience is expressed, and importantly, comes to be understood and subsequently experienced. Thus, prior to language, an infant may, in Stern's example, experience the many properties of a patch of sunlight. Language will circumscribe that experience by claiming it as a primary *visual* experience—henceforth the child is more likely to say "see the sun" —and is increasingly apt to leave behind the many other aspects associated with the patch of sunlight to which she or he had preverbal access precisely because it could not be spoken. Language does not possess the range to cover all that was, and is, known inarticulately, and so it necessarily fractures preverbal experience, separating the self from parts of itself.

In this way we observe that Stern attributes to language the power to most profoundly transform the sense of the self, expanding and contracting it, making it more completely whole while yet dividing it from itself. For language, we have seen, enlarges the sense of the world by affording access to a public, communal culture, but exacts as its entry fee, the splitting of the preverbal senses of the self from the domain of verbal experience. Language thus empowers the self, allowing it to transcend, even to alter, and possibly distort, via the symbolic, the parameters of given reality. This permits the child, and then the adult to envision a future which is not bound and determined by the events of the past. But language also contracts the domain of self experience by delimiting and diverting "attention" or awareness from the also present but now ever elusive domains of silence. With language comes the sense that all things are possible and knowable except, perhaps, one's self which seems just out of speaking range.

Concluding Remarks

For the first time since Federn (1928a,b), whom we shall encounter somewhat later in this volume, we see in Stern's position, the unambiguous elevation of the subjective self; and he is able to do so precisely because he does not feel compelled to tie observed behavior to prior and specific analytic concepts, as ego. Rather, Stern's assertions, inferential though they necessarily remain, are data driven. He seeks to draw conclusions from the objective evidence at hand, rather than reinterpret that evidence in the light of already established concepts.

Here, we observe, Stern stands as the culmination of a theoretical trend which we have seen moving in the direction of the elevation of the subjective self as the central explanatory concept, but was always, in some more or less pervasive form, burdened precisely by "issues of the development of the ego." Thus, previous theoretical efforts in the American tradition have, as we have seen, grappled with the shadow of the ego, and even Kohut, whose self was, after all, a "center of initiative," yet remained, to a certain extent, tied to a dual track explanation of behavior in order to retain a role for the ego.

In focusing upon the sense of self, Stern takes as his theoretical starting point the inference of a subjective life in the infant. The principal "working parts" of his theory are "subjective experiences themselves . . . in contrast to the main working parts of psychoanalytic theories, which are the ego and id from which subjective experiences are derived" (p. 26). His position argues for the existence of some sensation (i.e., some sense) of self which antedates the ability to speak that self; indeed it is "a basic assumption of [Stern's] that some senses of the self do exist long prior to self-awareness and language" (p. 6).

Singly, no less than in the aggregate, Stern's senses of self suggest the thoroughly interpersonal nature of the infant, asserting that relatedness in some form is coincident with human being from birth onward. Stern understands the self initially as awareness of subjective experiences, at first nonreflexive, and later reflexive. The self need not, in this view, await the cognitive capacity for mental representation; nor is it dependent upon the social world to be roused from a postulated autistic sleep. On the contrary, the Sternian self becomes the determining variable, itself fashioning its interpersonal world.

In its highly sensate, preverbal nature Stern's concept of the self bears some interesting similarities to the French theorist Anzieu's (1985) work, in which considerable impact is attributed to the previsual sensations of sound, temperature, and smell as they contribute to the early formation of the self. We shall review Anzieu's (1985) contribution below, with particular attention to what he has called the *sound envelope* and the *skin ego* in discussing his view that sensory qualities play a significant role in organizing an inner space, or self. Here we pause to observe that arising from a very differently inclined tradition of theory making, relying rather heavily upon the data of empirical observation, Stern arrives at a similar conclusion. To wit, that the self starts out as a series of nonreflexive sensate experiences of relatedness to the mother. The self is neither a dependent function nor solely a creature of the other; but rather an a priori entity whose subjective nature has a formative impact upon the objective.

Developmental Turnabouts

We have noted as well that Stern's theory of the self undertakes to modify aspects of traditional theory, and in some instances actually reverses the direction of causality. Among the many innovative implications of his work, we select four which highlight the unambiguous ascendancy of the self concept.

First, we recall that Stern inverts the traditional causal relationship among the self and the social environment. Thus, whereas the emergence and evolution of the self have more typically been characterized as being dependent upon the initiating action of the mother, in Stern's formulation the sense of self becomes the independent variable, whose actions account for the infant's emerging interpersonal world.

Second, we have seen that Stern reconceptualizes the nature of early infancy, envisioning it as a *proactive* rather than a reactive period. This is accomplished largely by dispensing with an initial dedifferentiated, autistic phase. Instead, we see an *emergent self* which is actively engaged in organizing its world. The self is present and active from the start.

Third, just at the chronological moment when traditional developmental theory proposes a psychic state of symbiotic merger with the mother from which a self will subsequently emerge, Stern is asserting, on the contrary, that a core self is separating and differentiating itself from a core other. Rather than merging, the core self is actually distinguishing its own boundaries from that of the mother. In fact, Stern has maintained, no psychic merging can occur at all prior to the establishment of such boundaries. Here is a startling reversal of the traditional view: Instead of the self arising from a formless mass of unattributable sensations, we observe that an antecedently differentiated self yields the possibility of merger. Again, causality is reversed; and again the self is clearly the independent, determinative agent.

Finally, we note that Stern modifies yet another tenet of established developmental theory when he asserts that the period between 7 and 9 months is not characterized simply by the infant's moving away from the mother. It is a period when, we recall, the capacity for intersubjective relatedness now makes it possible for the infant to share more intimately, more closely, with the mother. The subjective sense of self gives rise for the first time to a period when "the *joining* of subjective psychic experience can actually occur" (p. 127; emphasis added). Thus does Stern modify the developmental expectation for individuated exploration of the world (i.e., "practicing") by asserting that there is a simultaneous "moving toward" the mother in consequence of the acquisition of an intersubjective capacity.

Thus, these modifications, and frank reversals, of established developmental timetables, coupled with Stern's focus, which is, as he asserts "not encumbered with or confused with issues of the development of the ego" (p. 19), yield a self concept freed of the constraints which we have observed in some form in all preceding theories. It is a concept which is not fettered by the anterior claims of a structural ego, nor bound to adhere to a schedule of development which observed data do not support. It is a concept which unambiguously serves as the organizing principle of the psyche, and claims a central role for the subjective, both elements of which we began to sense in Jacobson (1964) and Mahler et al. (1975), and which became more candidly apparent in both Kernberg (1982a,b) and Kohut (1977), though all these works still struggled to accommodate the ego. It is, finally, a concept which celebrates, in traditionally American fashion, the marriage of the empirical and the intuitive; the objectively obtained data inferring a subjectively derived self. Stern's hypotheses, it seems fair to say, are a chorus of assertions that the self is indeed the "center of initiative and . . . recipient of impressions" that Kohut (1977) envisioned.

In subsequent chapters, we initiate a discussion of a very different approach to the self concept, in which issues of adaptation, mastery, and external reality do not begin to approximate the central role afforded them in the American tradition. The French tradition, we shall see, is more aptly characterized by a kind of Freudeo-Hegelian union, in which it is largely a pre-1923 Freudian language which is spoken, and Freud's theory is modified by a Hegelian language which is spoken through the medium of Kojeve (1947).

However, before undertaking to view the self from a French psychoanalytic perspective, we will pause to assess yet another American formulation of the self, this time from a cognitive conceptual foundation.

Chapter 6

THE TOTALITARIAN SELF OF
ANTHONY GREENWALD

It is a principal thesis of Anthony Greenwald's (1980) classic paper, "The Totalitarian Ego," that the *self*, or the *ego*, for he uses the terms in a frankly interchangeable manner, "is an organization of knowledge" (p. 603). Put somewhat differently, we may say that the self is conceived not so much in terms of the content of what is known, as it is the method by which that content is ordered. And that ordering, or arrangement, Greenwald proposes, is not only the emblematic methodology of the self, yielding what may be considered its defining characteristics, but also "correspond[s] disturbingly to thought control and propaganda devices that are considered to be defining characteristics of a totalitarian political system" (p. 603) as well. Not only is the self the way in which the mind structures knowledge, it turns out, in this schema, to structure knowledge in the way in which the total state structures lives. The self is a tyranny. Let us see what Greenwald has in mind.

Biases, Fabrications, and Personal History

Differing from dynamic conceptions of the self, Greenwald comes at the discussion from a distinctly cognitive perspective. Here, we shall see, the self is less the distillate of emotional events, and more the outcome of processes of thought. This is noted at the outset in the particular way in which he operationalizes the self. As we have noted,

---

References to Greenwald's ideas in this chapter are exclusively to his 1980 paper.

it is an organization of *knowledge*, with the particular functions of observing and recording personal experiences. That is, the self organizes knowledge, or becomes its own self, by *perceiving* and *remembering*—quintessential cognitive functions—what has happened to it. The self is not, in this view, a summary of emotional reactions, or conflicts, but is instead, the mental understanding of those events. Thus, *how* the self perceives, and *how* it remembers, is everything. In this way, Greenwald suggests, the self is a "personal historian," recording events, and indeed fashioning a kind of "curriculum vitae."

But what is of especial interest here is that this historian undertakes the task from a frankly partial, or "biased," perspective. Already committed beforehand to writing this personal history so that it reads as a coherent, balanced narrative, the self is not so much recording events as constructing them; not so much engaging in mnemonic preservation as retrospective invention. Greenwald's self is a "fabricator," and a revisionist, and these "not ordinarily admired" characteristics are what he refers to as cognitive biases. We shall have occasion to return to this important notion of the self as fabricator, for it is an interesting, and perhaps ironic, harbinger of what I might refer to as a postmodern "anarchy of self."

These "biases," which are the distinctive methodology of the self, include *egocentricity, beneffectance*, and *conservatism*. Together they function to produce not a veridical but a fictive self, constructed in the interests of maximum survivability. What are these biases?

Egocentricity, not surprisingly, refers to the tendency to both recall events in terms of one's own self, and to overestimate the causal impact. The concept here speaks, first, to the bias of memory to preserve events as if they were data in an autobiography; remembering the past "as if it were a drama in which self was the leading player" (p. 604). Memory is thus episodic in character, capturing those moments for later recall that feature the recorder himself. Second, *egocentricity* tends to perceive the self as the fulcrum of both cause and effect. There are two sides to this aspect of *egocentricity*. The self is either understood as the reason that others act; that is, the cause of the other's behavior, or the effect of such behavior. In the latter instance one understands oneself as the target of another's action and is reminiscent of the general worldview of some paranoid personalities. The overall impact of *egocentricity*, as a behavioral or mnemonic bias, is to conceive of events as they happen and as they are recalled, with the self at the center.

The second bias, *beneffectance*, bears some considerable similarity to *egocentricity* in that it also places the self at the causal nucleus of events, but with a twist. Here the self eagerly accepts credit for successful outcomes, and only rather unwillingly for those which have not done so well. Thus, *beneffectance*, a coinage introduced by Greenwald, literally refers to people's inclination to see themselves "as the origin of good effects and reluctantly as the origin of ill effects" (p. 605). An interesting extension of this bias is what Greenwald refers to as *vicarious beneffectance*. Here, the same tendency to take credit is reflected in the readiness of the self to share in the good results, or "victories," of others while distancing the self from "defeats." The example cited notes how when one's university wins a game it is "we" who won, while should the team lose, it was "they" who were defeated. One is reminded here of the similar function served by what Anna Freud (1936) has referred to as "identification with the aggressor." Though different in other respects, both serve to place the self on the "winning" side; to allow it to bathe in the reflected light of "glory" and strength.

Finally, Greenwald observes that the self is predisposed toward a *cognitive conservatism*. That is, in concert with conservative tendencies generally, this bias describes a "disposition to preserve existing knowledge structures" (p. 606). In other words, the self seeks to confirm and reconfirm what it already knows, or believes. Decisions or judgments, once reached, tend to be justified and promoted as "right" by selectively attending to information which supports them.

The principle of conservation plays a significant intrapsychic role, both cognitively and dynamically, in the elaboration of theories of representation generally, and it is worth taking a moment to review the ideas as they have been most frequently employed. Object permanence or perceptual constancy, as Greenwald points out, "is the fundamental achievement of a conservative nature" (p. 606), and both object permanence in the sense of Piaget (1952) and other cognitive psychologists, and object constancy as a psychodynamic principle, describe the important function of conservatism, or conversely, the inherent reluctance to let go, which plays so prominent a role in self formation.

Indeed, first establishing and then conserving a permanent percept or constant and essentially invariant image of the other, it seems to me, affirms the enduring (intrapsychic) *presence* of the other as a feature of self. Object constancy in the psychoanalytic sense makes the same assertion, but here the constancy refers to, and must include, conserving the image, even and especially when it is the target of conflicting and often hostile emotions. Object constancy is viewed in many psychoanalytic developmental circles as the intrapsychic *sine qua non* of separate and individuated functioning. Thus, we may say that a kind of psychic prerequisite to being a "self" is mastering the cognitive–dynamic capacity to "keep the other in mind" and "ever present."

Here we observe Greenwald's implicit argument that object permanence, for example, is not only a feature of an inherently conservative nature, but that the process of conserving *is* self. That is to say, self is that which conserves and is also the product of its conservations. It is what it retains of the other. It is what it can recall, represent, and make available to itself as it will. We may say that as the self is a bias to conserve, so also is it the process of *presencing* which conservatism triggers.

Thus, the bias toward conservatism is, in my view, a significant affirmation of another bias of the self, namely to sustain the image as a visceral experience of *presence*. And as we have already noted, many theorists of representation have conceived of a concept of self which relies upon the steady accretion of increasingly complex, and intrapsychically maintained images. The self becomes the integration of its many (re)presentations. Here, it seems to me, Greenwald at least infers this presencing principle as an inherent bias. But let us return to the elaboration of the "totalitarian self."

By way of the biases then, the organization of knowledge (i.e., the self) is being structured under the influence of a self-focused (*egocentric*), self-aggrandizing (*beneffectant*), and self-justifying (*conservative*) process. These traits are the hallmarks of a self which, in the interests of its own coherence, will regularly conceive of itself as the center of action and memory, will rarely acknowledge, or even record error, and will strive to maintain what has already been established. These are the very traits, Greenwald asserts, that also characterize both totalitarian states and scientific theory. This is an interesting and significant proposition, and we pause here to explore and comment upon it.

Extrahuman Analogies

To have biases is not the same as having bona fide organization or structure. The elements must be linked and interdependent. Greenwald argues for this interdependence, which in effect is the self (i.e., as an organization of knowledge) by analogy to extrahuman organizations of knowledge which possess the (self) same biases.

He reasons thus: The biases we observe in individuals are also present in totalitarian societies and the models of science. Both of these are recognized organizations of knowledge. Therefore, individuals possessing the same characteristics are also organizations of knowledge. Greenwald than proceeds to demonstrate that these biases do indeed describe totalitarian societies and scientific paradigms.

In assessing the organization of knowledge in totalitarian societies, Greenwald draws upon Orwell's famous depiction, *Nineteen Eighty-Four*, to demonstrate the similarities among thought-control and self-control. He quotes, for example, Orwell's description of the totalitarian society which requires that the past be "readjusted," in order to "safeguard the infallibility of the Party" (Orwell, 1949, as cited in Greenwald, p. 609). Further, that controlling the past in this manner demands the necessity "to remember that events happened in the desired manner." Such techniques, called "doublethink" by Orwell, bear a clear relationship to *benefectance*, for example.

But of equal interest in this respect is Greenwald's references to Hannah Arendt, whose thought-provoking comments on totalitarianism reflect the view that the state undermines individual initiative by making itself the absolute organizational center of thought. Aspects of her commentary indeed impress as an interesting analog to the intrapsychic development of identity, or self. The following quote from Arendt (1966), I believe, demonstrates this point quite nicely: "Total domination, which strives to organize the infinite plurality and differentiation of human beings as if all of humanity were just one individual is possible only if each and every person can be reduced to a never-changing identity . . . " (as cited in Greenwald, p. 609).

Thus we see that for Arendt, and clearly for Greenwald, "total domination," whether of the state or the self, requires a rewriting of history such that it is read in one consistent voice, without dissent. In order to achieve a sense of unified (i.e., total) self, of singular voice, it is necessary to suppress the "infinite plurality" of impressions which impinge upon (psychological) being. The self is an idea created by way of (self-imposed) thought control, or at least restriction, in the interests of order. Meaning and consistency are won at the expense of randomness and multiplicity.

In this connection one is reminded of some of the psychotherapeutic approaches to multiple personality disorder in which, after an initial "mapping" of the plurality of "persons," the dominant self is sought and cure is in large part thought to be a matter of setting up one executive self with sole (psychic) authority to speak, in one voice, for all. Here, perhaps we may say, with Arendt (1966), that what is wanted is a psychological "band of iron . . . [which] holds them so tightly together that it is as though their plurality had disappeared into One . . . " (as cited in Greenwald, p. 609). Arendt was describing "total terror," but we see that it serves as well to describe a kind of "total identity."

Thus we observe that dynamic theories of representation, indeed psychoanalytic tenets generally, are themselves descriptive of total systems, for they also depict a self, or ego, which comes into being by effecting a "domination" over (i.e., an "intrapsychic organization" of) the vast plurality, or multiplicity, of early sensory input, or the chaotic press of id impulses; "reducing," or distilling or sublimating such experience into a more or less consistent, "adapted," or "never-changing identity." Manyness must be subdued in the interests of oneness, which is the equivalent of achieved identity; and to live the variety of experiences which impact the psyche is to threaten the disorder, the anarchy, of "identity diffusion."

Indeed, anarchy is the very nemesis of all total organizations. For if many voices speak many views, then there may be many "true" selves; and many inconsistent, even contradictory, directions which may be followed in episodic and inconclusive fashion. This is not a conception of humankind at all compatible with, or palatable to, predominant cultural ideals of personhood.

The *anarchic self*, a term I have coined to describe an intrapsychic multiplicity, presents a direct assault upon the idea of self as having personal depth, moral character, loyalty, all of which have long described a nineteenth century romantic view of the self. As well, the principle of multiplicity threatens the very different characteristics associated with the "modern" self. Here anarchy is hazardous to the view of self as using reason and intentionality as a means toward achieving carefully considered ends. Normal persons are, in this view, above all predictable. Contemporary psychological theorists working from a cognitive, as well as a "humanist" perspective, have tackled this issue of the viability of the singular, or individual, self in the light of such considerations as "alternative narratives," and "multiple identities." We think here of Rosenwald (1988a,b), of Sampson (1985, 1988, 1989), and perhaps most notably of Gergen (1985 1990, 1991), who had much to say about both "romantic" and "modern" selves in the light of a postmodern technological "saturation" of the psyche. Thus does Gergen (1991), for example, suggest that romantic and modern views of self are rapidly giving way in the face of newly emerging cultural imperatives which are changing the very manner in which we understand our (many or multiple) selves.

Greenwald's concept of self, we have seen, is, in a sense (cognitively) programmed to evolve, that is, it is biased in the direction of total entity, editing experience to fashion a coherent narrative of the self as a consistent and rational being. Viewed in this way, we may say that Greenwald's total self is a cognitive explanation which lends confirmation to a cultural ideal. (This, of course, is not to say that any explicit cultural ideal admires totalitarianism as politically desirable, but rather that the features that fail in the body politic appear to succeed admirably in the "body human" in producing "capable," culturally admirable selves.) Greenwald himself, however, does not appear to be arguing in quite this way. Conversely, he concludes his essay by proposing a kind of "Darwinian" explanation of the cognitive biases, suggesting that they serve in "facilitating [the self's] own existence" (p. 612).

It is possible to read Greenwald, in a kind of retrospective manner, as a theoretical explanation which lends additional mortar to the edifice of self as a particular kind of structure, that is, a theory in support of a cultural ideal. Greenwald, however, is rather proposing an explanation along the lines of an "intrapsychic genetics." This view suggests that the self is the kind of self it is because the particular (total) structure has considerable "survival value" for the self itself, and does not arise because the culture shaped it. The process is biased, as all evolutionary processes are biased, in favor of survival (of the fittest self). Thus, whereas I am suggesting that it is possible to understand Greenwald's self as a *reflection* of cultural imperatives, something which postmodern theorists argue, Greenwald himself appears to be asserting a concept of self as an original entity arising from "intrapsychic imperatives."

Greenwald's self concept, in asserting a definite bias to become a particular kind of organization (i.e., of knowledge), also describes a self which is psychocognitively *destined* to become. It is present from the beginning, in embryo; that is, it will become a (total) presence, structured in a determined way. It is a self which, not unlike Orwell's protagonist, Winston Smith, will win a "victory over [its]self," as it yields to recognizable oneness and eschews the random chaos of many-ness. A self which is "victorious" is one which is filled with the total, structured presence of a unified explanatory narrative (e.g., a "Big Brother"), and has overcome the multiple voices (and persons) which speak in the absence of surety.

Nonetheless, Greenwald's "personal historian" also suggests a different kind of self. One which, as it suppresses the multiple personalities, points toward their very being. For, albeit in the interests of (self) survival, this historian, as we have seen, "fabricates," and "revises," that is, it changes and interprets events to suit its needs. Presumably, such activities may happen more than once or twice. Presumably, there are endless revisions (and decisions) which a personal moment may reverse. Fabrications are constructions designed to suggest one thing when another was what occurred. Presumably, a fabrication indicates by *its* presence, the absence of some *other* thing. Perhaps the self, even a biased one, hints at another and absent one.

Scientific paradigms as well, Greenwald maintains, rely upon similarly biased operations in the development and elaboration of theory. In common with total societies, and human beings, scientific thinking is also organized so that a prevailing paradigm (read "self") can contain a broad array of data under its conceptual umbrella (read "consistent identity"). In this, and other "biased" ways, does the paradigmatic scientific theory also conserve its dominance and identity. "Thus," Greenwald asserts, "a successful paradigm accounts for an increasing range of phenomena ('paradigm-centricity'), credits itself with confirmed, rather than with disconfirmed, hypotheses, and preserves the integrity of its theoretical constructs" (p. 610).

Greenwald attributes this thesis of analogy between cognitive processes and scientific theory to Kelley's (1955) foundational cognitive theory, which conceives of the individual as a kind of scientist who, in the course of his daily living, constructs and tests numerous hypotheses which may contribute more effectively to anticipating and handling life events. This interesting notion notwithstanding, Kelley does not devote much time to the concept of self per se which, along with the emotions, plays a relatively minor role in his work. Epstein (1973), however, does expand upon Kelley's theory of *personal constructs*, or "hypotheses of daily living," applying them directly to the idea of self, submitting, indeed, that "the difficulty has been that the self-concept is not really a self-concept at all . . . " (Epstein, 1973, p. 405). If not a concept, then what is the self? Let us pause to investigate this particular slant for what it may contribute to our present pursuit of many selves.

The Riddle of Self

In seeking to reconcile the views of those who argue that the self cannot be adequately defined as a construct and ought, therefore, to be abandoned, with those who nevertheless insist that there is unquestionably a phenomenological feeling state of "self," Epstein (1973) proposes a solution which dispenses with the concept of self itself, though surely not the idea.

Epstein (1973) concludes his summary review of a number of prominent theorists of self, including Cooley (1902), James (1890), Mcad (1934), Sullivan (1953), and Allport (1955), among others, by observing that all have attributed similar characteristics to the self. By teasing out these similarities it becomes possible, Epstein reasons, to see the "overall picture" in a new way. Putting the elements together in the form of a riddle, Epstein asks the reader to consider "what is it that . . . ," among other things, has a set of ideas arranged progressively and which are consistent with one another; is both unified and differentiated; is necessary for solving problems in the real world; and if it fails will leave chaos in its wake?

These descriptors are, of course, the features of a well-constructed theory, but are also those of a similarly constructed "self." Indeed, "the answer" to the riddle posed, Epstein (1973) proposes, is that *"the self-concept is a self-theory*. It is a theory that the individual has unwittingly constructed about himself as an experiencing, functioning individual . . . " (p. 407). It was Epstein's stated aim to attempt to accommodate the divergent views of behavioral and phenomenological theorists with respect to the notion of self. By redefining the self-*concept* as self-*theory*, that is, "by recognizing that individuals have implicit theories about themselves" (Epstein, 1973, p. 415), which are constructed like all other theories, the objection that the self is not scientific is, in Epstein's view, dispensed with, unless one is willing to dismiss theory in general.

It is in this way that Epstein's proposal serves to underscore Greenwald's contention that the self operates like, and possesses the characteristics of, scientific theory. But Epstein's (1973) paper, in conjunction with Greenwald's, also serves, I believe, to bolster another contention.

The idea of self is in a transitional state; indeed, it is undergoing what might well be described as a "paradigm shift." For we note that the old model of self, as a "never-changing identity," is beginning to give ground to the paradoxical notion of "everchanging identity." To be sure, neither Epstein nor Greenwald make this assertion, but in my view the evidence for just such a shift is contained within some of the central theses of their proposals.

Thus, if self is a theory, then surely it may be overturned, abandoned, indeed, rewritten. Self as a theory, is no longer essentially fixed, but open-ended; no longer achieved, but becoming; instead of a "never-changing" actuality, self as a theory is more accurately an "ever-changing" potentiality.

If self is a "personal historian," engaged in revising events, elevating some, and discarding others, in order to reconfirm the total structure, then other equally actual events may be reclaimed from this personal "scrap heap of history" to write another (subversive) version.

In this way, it seems to me, both Epstein's and Greenwald's statements contain the seeds of a self considerably less stable than what has preceded them, and do so within discussions which yet draw the self, in its particulars, as familiarly coherent, reasonably predictable, substantially unified, and, indeed, fundamentally stable.

But many postmodern theorists of the self argue quite explicitly that the paradigmatic self of unity fails to satisfactorily account for the increasingly frequent assaults of multiplicity, both as a cultural and a phenomenological experience. The model of the self as a competent master of new events, some arguments run, fails to absorb the rush of diverse events which can be attended to, and the self, as Gergen (1991), for example, has suggested, becomes *saturated*. The theory of self as an achieved state, in this view, is not able to reliably account for the datum of its experiential world; its explanatory power vis-à-vis perceived reality has been compromised. The postmodern position on the idea of the self might well assert, in common with all conceptual revolutions, that the self as "an existing paradigm . . . [may have] ceased to function adequately in the exploration of an aspect of nature to which that paradigm had previously led the way" (Kuhn, 1962, p. 92). Nonetheless, despite the implications of both Epstein and Greenwald, they are, after all, still theorists of a relatively stable self. Let us see what we may conclude from our reading of both, noting that Greenwald remains, in the main, an important part of the traditional paradigm of self.

Concluding Remarks

In common with other theorists of representation, Greenwald also envisions a self which imparts a sense of centralized, continuous, and internally balanced mastery. His too is a concept of the self which emerges from and is indistinguishable from the process which gives rise to it and, importantly, is also a self which not only emerges, but also "arrives." At the end of all the processing and structuring, there is a recognizable entity which henceforth remains more or less consistently stable and goes by the name of (my) self.

Here we recall Spiegel's (1959) proposal that the self seeks to overcome chaos and discontinuity as it constructs an internal paradigm, or framework of archetypical mental representations against which all subsequent representations are assessed. In this way, the framework, which "is the self," according to Spiegel's lights, becomes, essentially, a fund of information, an organization of knowledge.

Stern (1985) as well, we recollect, defined the self as an "invariant pattern of awarenesses" (p. 7) that are occasioned by the infant's own actions or mental processes. Similarly, it is these patterns which organize experience, and that organization, again, is the self.

Finally, we see as well, that Greenwald's concepts are not unlike those of Mahler et al. (1975) and other theorists whose essential commitment is to an individuated, distinct self, however arrived at. In this way, we are able to understand Greenwald's self, whose origins are largely cognitive at the end, rather than dynamic, as nonetheless an achieved state, and one that conforms to the belief that health is commensurate with organized actuality and that, conversely, not to be able to sustain an equilibrium or, as the saying goes, to "lose one's grip," threatens psychological disarray.

This psychic infrastructure has traditionally had, in contradistinction to its political counterpart, considerable survival value for the self in that it serves to reduce chaos, favor predictability, and insure continuity. These are features that are perhaps more attractive to intrapsychic than to social and political comfort. However, as we alluded to earlier in this discussion of Greenwald's paper, the survivability of the infrastructure is now in considerable doubt. Indeed, a body of sociocognitive theorists, including Gergen (1985, 1990, 1991), Sampson (1985, 1988, 1989), and Rosenwald (1988a,b), among others, have made some very interesting arguments for the postmodernist self.

Part II

THE SELF OF ANTICIPATION

[H]uman history is the history of desired Desires
[Kojeve, 1947, p. 6].

Just as we have noted that the theorists of the American school of psychoanalytic concept formation had lent a particular cultural cast to the evolving view of the self, and in this way may be said to have reformulated psychoanalysis for its particular audience, so too have the French, most notably in the work of Jacques Lacan, "reinvented" Freudian thought as it passed through a Gallic sensibility.

The psychoanalytic opus as initially conceived and formulated by Freud contains, as we have regularly noted, many ambiguous, and often frankly contradictory, propositions, assertions, and models. The lack of definitional certainty which accompanies, and inclines, the psychoanalytic text to lend support to a multiplicity of interpretations, coupled with the certainly formative influence of a particular cultural worldview, inevitably plays a leading role in determining which portions of that text are selected for emphasis over others. Simply put, and as we have in part already observed, some segments of Freud's thought are more compatible with some cultures than with others.

Thus, the conflict-free, or at least in part energically neutral, adaptational ego, empirically derived and normatively predictive by development, seeking to achieve a mastery over its environment and a maximum degree of independence consonant with survival, fit uniquely well with a characteristic American sensibility. It is a sensibility which understands maturity and adult functioning as the ability to "get along," overcome obstacles, and redirect unruly passions in the interests of self-control and a "higher" good. In this context one is particularly moved to observe that many of the early theorists of ego psychology were themselves immigrants to the United States in consequence of the Second World War, thus perhaps lending a dimension of overdetermination to the importance of the adaptational axis of the American ego.

By the same token did the French psychoanalytic movement, notably in the Lacanian voice, find a far more compatible Freud residing
in the unconscious. Indeed, it is possible to characterize the French
psychoanalytic effort in a metatheoretical sense as a movement to
"recapture" and "restore" the id-dominated unconscious to what was
understood to be its rightful centrality. In order to do so, as we shall
see, Lacan had to reconstruct theory in such a manner that the ego
was decentered.

In fact, Lacan's outright rejection of the "American ego" as a
"ridiculous attempt to reduce [psychological concepts] to the suppos-
edly supreme law of adaptation" (Lacan, 1949, p. 3) is frankly hostile,
and clearly indicates that he will characterize things quite differently.
Indeed, Lacan (1949) asserts that experience:

> [T]eaches us not to regard the ego as centered on the *perception-
> consciousness system*, or as organized by the "reality princi-
> ple,"—a principle that is the expression of a scientific prejudice
> most hostile to the dialectic of knowledge. Our experience shows
> that we should start instead from the *function of meconnaissance*
> that characterizes the ego in all its structures [p. 6].

We shall have occasion to investigate Lacan's (1949) particular meaning as we enter into a discussion of his "mirror stage" below. Here
his comments will suffice to highlight the vastly different vantage
points from which the Hartmannian ego and the Lacanian subject approach the self.

The French preference for the less predictable, more mysterious
unconscious, or conversely, the Lacanian aversion to adaptational re-
ductions, may perhaps be understood as a consequence of the initial
psychiatric resistance to psychoanalysis in that country. Failing entry
into the medical world, as it decidedly did not in America, psychoanalysis was rather more warmly embraced by the literary, artistic, and
political worlds where it was given a distinctive reading by literary
critics such as Julia Kristeva (1982a,b,c) and her mentor and teacher
Roland Barthes (1972), and philosophically reconceptualized by Mi-
chel Foucault (1965, 1977) and Jacques Derrida (1967a,b), for example.

Thus, psychoanalysis in France was not initially saddled with the
mandate to *solve problems* that is the natural domain of the medical
profession, and which, indeed, did color the psychoanalytic proclivities

of its American adherents. Instead, French psychoanalysis was nurtured on poetic articulations and derives from artistic images, themselves primary process, and weaned, quite literally, in the lecture halls of (Kojevian) philosophy. Surely we must expect this child to have a different nature.

To attempt to unravel the labyrinthine history of psychoanalysis in France, however, would take this discussion far afield, and is, in any event, extensively documented elsewhere (Roudinesco, 1986; Oliner, 1988; Turkle, 1992). We shall here mention in schematic fashion those defining elements of thought which bear directly upon our subsequent exploration of the psychoanalytic formulation of the self in selected aspects of the work of Lacan (1949, 1953, 1960).

The particular coloration given to Germanic thought in France came by way of a native Russian philosopher and naturalized French citizen, Alexandre Kojeve, whose idiosyncratic interpretation of Hegel would play a significant role not only in the formulation of Lacan's thought, but that of a generation of French cultural commentators and philosophers. Those who regularly attended Kojeve's seminars on the many chapters of *The Phenomenology of Mind* (1807) during the period 1933 to 1939, and thereby became acquainted with his slant on the Hegelian notions of desire, recognition, and self-consciousness, for example, included Raymond Aron, Georges Bataille, J-P. Sartre, Maurice Merleau-Ponty, and Raymond Queneau, who would later collect his notes on Kojeve's lectures, and publish them as *An Introduction to the Reading of Hegel* (1947).

But it would remain for Lacan to marry these notions, of desire and recognition, to his own inventive reading of Freud. The consequences of this reading, as they are elaborated in his early and defining paper, "The Mirror Stage as Formative of the Function of the I" (1949), and as they continued to be a force in all subsequent work impacting upon the idea of the self (regularly referred to as the subject), will be seen to yield a radically reconfigured concept from that of the ego'psychological tradition. Indeed, Lacan's (1949, 1953, 1960) work may be understood, at least in part, as a crusade to dethrone the ego, decenter the subject, and stand the human psyche upon a newly structured unconscious. Thus, before it is possible to understand Lacan's contribution to the self concept, it is necessary to grasp Kojeve's contribution to Lacan.

Chapter 7
ALEXANDRE KOJEVE'S DIALECTICS OF DESIRE

Kojeve (1947) sets out to elucidate the manner in which being (i.e., human existence) reveals itself to itself; asking, essentially, what it is that propels the individual toward the realization of his or her particular nature as a "knowing subject." How, in other words, does the self come to know itself and, thus, to be?

He will fashion his ontological response upon the outcome of the exchange between *desire* (conceived as the absence of something) and *satisfaction* (or the presence of that thing). This exchange is a dialectical one in which desire, in order to realize its positive satisfaction, must pass through negative action. We shall see that Kojeve discerns two distinct levels of relationship characteristic of humankind: those in which there is a relationship to and transformation of *things*; and those in which there is a relationship to and transformation of other *human beings*. The dialectic of negative transformative action governs both.

It is in the relationship to things that humankind first develops a sense of its own being; a level of awareness Kojeve refers to as "Sentiment of self," and which evolves in consequence of the experience of a desire for something that is absent. Such a desire may, for example, be a hunger for food which stimulates an awareness of one's self as that which is hungry and desirous of satisfaction through food. This "sentimental awareness" stirs the self to action which will satisfy the desire, and it is, in dialectical fashion, an action which is both the opposite of, is dialectically opposed to, and necessary to, the condition it seeks.

References to Kojeve's ideas in this chapter are based exclusively on his 1947 work.

Thus, desire prompts negative action, in the form of the destruction, alteration, or transformation in some fashion, of the object of one's desire. The hungry self must necessarily destroy the reality of the object which will serve as its food. By way of such negative action it transcends the reality of the other in order to positively satisfy its own desire. Thus it is that in relation to a desire for the "things" of the natural world, a simple awareness of self is first aroused.

Interestingly, it is not, we note, in the quietude of thinking or contemplation that the consciously aware self is aroused. On the contrary, "contemplation reveals the object, not the subject" (p. 3). Thus, it is neither reason nor contemplation which stirs the movement toward awareness. It is *not*, that is to say, because the I thinks that it therefore is.

Rather, what impels human beings toward some feeling of self is, as Kojeve here maintains, *desire*, which is itself a "disquieting" experience. It is wanting something which is not there, as food. (Indeed, we observe that desires of all kinds are often described as a "hunger for.") And it is this gnawing sense of incompleteness, or emptiness, which, in turn, transforms the human being, stimulating awareness of I as an I which desires. It is this desire for some other thing which is absent that causes one to notice oneself. Desire, which is the experiential affirmation of absence, gives birth to the I, and one may imagine, in this way, that the first utterance of I is more closely characterized as "I desire."

Now, Kojeve continues, the relationship to things is but one of the ways in which the human being becomes aware of self and, as it turns out, it is *not* the way in which she or he becomes *distinctly* human. For in this relationship to things one is merely living a "natural" existence; a life in nature as a "natural I," but not in possession of an *awareness* of self as a sentient being. Instead, this "natural I" is an I which is of the same essence as that which it desires; it is, as Kojeve says, a "thingish" I, which is desirous of other natural, "thingish" objects.

On the other hand, an indispensable characteristic of *human* being, Kojeve asserts, resides in the pursuit of that which is *not* of the natural, "thingish" world. It is a desire which does not desire things. It is, on the contrary, a desire for that which is *not a thing*, literally the desire for *no thing*.

It is in this sense that we may speak of that characteristically human trait, the desire toward "nothingness." This need not at all be a nihilistic understanding of the nature of the human self, but rather an assertion regarding what marks the essence of human being. For it is this very capacity to project itself out from its "thingish" confines toward what is not a thing, that indicates the presence of the human self. That the essence of the self rests in its "nothingness," in its being *not a thing*, is underscored in the breach by our attributing pathology to those who *do* conceive of themselves as things.

Now we see that the Kojevian formula for the uniquely human awareness of self requires that desire forego the pursuit of things. But what, then, can desire seek, if not things? It turns out that, to be *human* desire, it must desire itself. For it is only pure, objectless, "thingless," desire, that is not a thing. It *is* no thing; instead, such desire is "the revelation of an emptiness, the presence of the absence of a reality" (p. 5).

The human self is that being which desires not a thing, but another desire. This can only be made manifest in the company of other desires, that is, in the presence of other beings who also desire another desire. Desire becomes, in Kojeve's analysis, the desire for the *recognition* of the other. The "satisfaction" of pure desire is made manifest in winning the desirous gaze of the other. Thus, it is in the relationship between and among human beings, in a necessarily *social* setting, that the human subject is born. More particularly, in the specifically dialectical relationship of desires, each seeking to appropriate, via recognition, the desire of the other, the truly self-conscious I emerges.

Now Kojeve has characterized the nature of this distinctly human relationship in terms of Hegel's paradigmatic master–slave configuration, which is to say a relation of ascendancy–dependency. For "the human reality can come into being only . . . on the basis of its implying an element of Mastery and an element of Slavery, of 'autonomous' existences and 'dependent' existences" (pp. 8–9). One is here readily reminded of the analytic model of human being in which the dependent infant and the autonomous mother each desire and require the recognition of the other. Lacan (1949) as well as Winnicott (1958, 1963, 1967), for example, will, we shall see, make much of this desire for recognition.

Thus, simply put, the "master–slave" relationship is a narrative about the pursuit of recognition; a story about the distinctly human desirc to be desired; to be seen, affirmed, and wanted for one's own sake, as a value in and of itself. It is a tale of becoming, won in the passage through the crucible of desire for recognition; for one becomes distinctly human in managing to be seen, recognized. In this Kojevian model we see that what is being pursued, and what marks the pursuit as human, is the willingness to risk all else, even one's vital survival, for the sake of the literally unreal.

For recognition is not of the "thingish" world of reality at all; rather, it is the child of a radically human, nonnatural, *imagining*. And to be human, in this Kojevian setting, is to take that leap across the divide from the real(ity) of the body to the image(ry) of the mind. Thus, says Kojeve, "Desire is human only if one desires, not the body, but the Desire of the other . . . that is to say, if he wants to be 'desired' or 'loved' or, rather, 'recognized' in his human value" (p. 6).

In this way Kojeve develops a concept of the fully human (i.e., self-conscious) self as one which alone is able to partake of *both* versions of desire. In the first instance, human kind shares the same desires as all animals, a desire for "things" which serve to insure survival and which stimulate only the dim sentiment of self. It is in the second instance, however, in which desire becomes a desire which is not directed toward things, but toward recognition from other human desires that the truly *human* self is realized.

This form of desire is what distinguishes human being from other forms of being, and what makes the self-conscious I a solely human formulation. The "origin," so to speak, of the self may, in this framework, be said to be conceived and maintained only as a "*recognized* self*." For "it is only by being 'recognized' by another . . . that a human being is really human, for himself as well as for others" (p. 9).

In what follows we shall have ample occasion to recognize the influence of these Kojevian ideas as they are adapted to more specific analytic purposes in selected relevant aspects of the work of Jacques Lacan.

Chapter 8
JACQUES LACAN'S SELF LACKS FOR NOTHING

The work of Lacan is a far-reaching and complex reconfiguration of central psychoanalytic concepts which Lacan (1949) himself avowed is both a "return" to an earlier and "truer" Freud, and a bold use of nonanalytic formulations to break theoretical ground for psychoanalysis. The very scope of the Lacanian corpus forecloses an exhaustive review, and in any event, such is not the aim of this book. Rather, we are endeavoring, in the work of all the theorists represented herein, to highlight those features of their theoretical efforts which cast light upon the concept of the self. Thus, in keeping within the bounds of this discussion, we will cull from Lacan's multifaceted theoretical compendium a selected number of conceptual contributions which most distinctly clarify what is intended when one speaks of the "Lacanian self." Following a brief review, for contextual purposes, of these distinctly Lacanian viewpoints, we shall enter into a discussion of what is arguably one of the most innovative and fertile contributions to theoretical speculations on the formation of the self, Lacan's (1949) "mirror stage."

We begin, however, by noting that Lacan (1953, 1960) understood the self (i.e., the subject) in terms of its elaboration within the defining structure of language; and regarded the ego as a misconstrued and distorted image which is mistakenly linked to the actual self of the unconscious. The unconscious itself is understood to be structured along the lines of a language, and is conceptualized as the core from which "true" self-realization derives. The *unconscious*, in this view, is the formative center, not the (misapprehended) ego. Thus does Lacan (1953, 1960) conceptualize a *spoken self*, fashioned by the language

187

of the unconscious; and a *decentered self*, which is the conscious
"ego." Thus did Lacan (1953, 1960) come to suggest a true self which
is spoken from the "offstage" of the unconscious. Perhaps above all,
however, Lacan (1949) is addressing a self which is constituted by a
particular understanding of *desire*, and this is most clearly observed
in his genetic formulation of I. Lacan (1949) seeks the origins or
beginnings of the self—the I—in a specific developmental stage which
he called the *stade du miroir* or mirror stage, and it is in this phase of
his work that the Kojevian influence is most clearly discernible. For
it is in the "mirror stage" that Lacan (1949) fashions Kojeve's (1947)
concepts of desire and recognition to fit his theoretical view of the
formation of the self, and it is this period of theory building that, we
shall see, influenced Winnicott's (1963) own "mirroring" formulations. Thus, we shall focus the balance of our discussion of Lacan's
(1949) formulation of the self upon this analytically reflective work.

An Imaginary Self

Lacan's mirror stage, first elucidated in 1936, was reintroduced by
Lacan at the International Congress of Psychoanalysis in 1949 "for
the light it sheds on the formation of the *I*" (Lacan, 1949, p. 1), and
is, in this way, precisely suited to the purposes of this investigation.

Lacan (1949) establishes the foundation for his concept of the
mirror stage when he reminds his audience of the rather well-known
fact that the child, not unlike the monkey, can, from rather early in
life, recognize its image in the mirror. However, unlike the monkey,
who soon abandons the image as "empty," the child is prompted by
his image toward a series of playful movements which allow him to
experience a relationship between his own gesticulations and those
reflected in the mirror.

Now what is occurring, Lacan (1949) asserts, is revelatory of a
particular "ontological structure of the human world" (p. 2) in which
the human child is "predestined" toward "the transformation that
takes place in the subject when he assumes an image" (p. 2). The
child, we may say, is hardwired to respond to the specular image as
if it were coincident with his own being, thus triggering, via the mechanism of identification, a series of alterations, or "transformations,"
culminating in the arrival of the symbolic subject.

Now, Lacan maintains, the assumption, at this early stage in the child's life, of the image in the mirror is deceptive. It is an image that suggests by its appearance a unified totality which hardly accords with the actual child's "motor incapacity and nursling dependence" (p. 2). For the actual child's fragmentary psychological state is not accurately reflected in the mirror. What the child sees, and identifies with, is an idealized image, a symbol of what is not. Thus, the child's assumption of the mirror, or "specular," image illustrates the "symbolic matrix in which the *I* is precipitated in a primordial form . . . [and] this form would have to be called the Ideal-I" (1949, p. 2).

Thus we observe that in saying that the child "assumes," or "takes on" (*identifies* with) the image in the mirror, Lacan (1949) is distinctly *not* saying that the image is an accurate reflection of the child's nascent self. On the contrary, "the important point is that this form [the Ideal-I] situates the agency of the ego, *before* its social determination, *in a fictional direction*, which will always remain irreducible for the individual" (Lacan, 1949, p. 2; emphases added). We underscore that Lacan is here making a Januslike assertion with regard to the essential character of the self; to wit, that the I comes into being prior to any social identifications; that one's first "other" is his own inverted image; and, in consequence of that very origin, the specular genesis, faces toward the fictive.

Thus, the self in its primordial configuration antedates any identification with others; establishing the I as a prearticulate, presocial, identification with one's own image. An idealized alter ego, the image in the mirror is an inherently alienating one. Through the medium of the mirror the ego becomes the self's other. The ego, then, is not coincident with the self, it is merely a reflection, and a deceptive one at that, of the (other) self.

The first other which the child experiences is the self's own (mirror image) other. In this way we note that the Lacanian I is truly mythic, born as it is of the self's own preoccupied gaze in a latter-day reflecting pool. Like all myths, it is not a veridical depiction of reality, but rather an idealized account of the way in which one imagines the world or the self is, or will become.

The self from the outset is directed by the fictional need to be understood in terms of the particular meaning Lacan (1949) attaches to the "imaginary." For in seeking to understand his intent in claiming that the I, even prior to its assumption of the social, is fictive, we must

understand something of the manner in which he employs the term
imaginary. At the time that Lacan was working out the formation of
the self as a function of the reflection in the mirror, he clearly viewed
the "image" as a formative, explanatory analytic concept. As we have
already noted in discussing this paper, Lacan turned to the mechanism
of identification as a fundamental explanatory tool. The term *identification* means to assume or take as one's own, via internalizing processes, the features of a visual image. Identification was the underlying
dynamic in the formation of Lacan's (1949) self, much as we have
seen that it was for those of the American tradition of theorizing, and
indeed, for the British as well. Lacan, however, is already attributing
some variant meanings and outcomes to this rather orthodox mechanism as it is coupled with the image.

Now, the imaginary is employed within the context of the mirror
stage, and the term bears at least two sensibilities. Thus, the imaginary,
which here is the realm in which the self is determined after all, connotes both a resemblance and a fiction.

In the sense of a resemblance, the concept is seen to belong to
reality, for the image is understood to "be like," to "resemble" the
actual. The imaginary refers to the fictional in the sense that the first
image the child identifies with is his own deceptively autonomous and
unified image. The child's counterpart in the mirror does not approach
a veridical resemblance to his actual self; it is, in this sense, a deceiv-
ing, fictive, or imaginary identification.

So, we may say that Lacan employs the term *imaginary* in two
distinct senses: the first refers, by way of resemblance, to the true, the
actual; the second refers, insofar as the genesis of the I is concerned,
to what is inherently deceptive, and thus not true or actual. The image
reflects what is and what is not.

We may now understand Lacan's (1949) important assertion that
the I is, in its inception, a fictive construct, in the light of his use of
imaginary in the second sense. In direct consequence of its derivation
in an *image*, not in reality, the I is necessarily unreal; a fictive construct
which shall forever remain the irreducible core of the self.

At its heart the self is a fiction, constructed upon what, for Lacan
(1949), is a *meconnaissance*, or literally, a "failure to recognize" the
actual state of affairs. It is a deception, resting upon a foundation of
erroneous perceptions of the image in the mirror as actually "fairer,"
stronger, and far more autonomous than it is in reality. In this sense

of the word, the image bears little or no resemblance to the child's psychological reality.

Now it is this *meconnaissance*, this originary failure to accurately recognize, which implants the deception of autonomy (from the unconscious) to which the conception of the ego has been, in Lacan's (1949) view, falsely wed. For the image that the child sees is one which is both psychologically and physically outside of and beyond the viewer.

The image is, in size and wholeness, in marked contrast to that of the small, powerless, and psychologically fragmented infant; and second, the image with which the child identifies is reversed, that is, inverted. It is, thus, a distortion which establishes both the subject's illusion of endurance (where there is discontinuity), and the later conditions for its own separation from itself. Thus, "this *Gestalt*," Lacan (1949) asserts, "symbolizes the mental *permanence* of the *I*, at the same time as it prefigures its *alienating* destination" (p. 2; emphases added). The subject begins its existence by tying itself to, identifying with, and even projecting itself into, the "statue," the nonvital reflection, according a deceptive reality to what was seen in the image residing in the mirror. In this connection we may observe a kinship with Bion's "bizarre object," which has been pathologically invested with an animism it does not in fact possess. Thus, the self begins its psychological journey as a misperception, particularly with respect to its permanency and autonomous functioning. Later, by dint of the transition in the nature of the I which will bring the mirror stage to a close, we shall see that this self is destined to be alienated from itself.

In reflecting upon the very formative impact of this reflected gestalt, Lacan (1949) is led to what might well be considered the core of this paper and may stand as a defining mark of his subsequent work. We note, as we proceed, that Lacan's (1949) discussion of ethological data with respect to the developmentally stimulating effects of the visual image highlights the dual meaning he imputes to the term *imaginary*. For we shall see that he calls upon the early visual gestalt both to demonstrate the *real* impact of the image, and the *deceptive* effect of the image, at one and the same time.

For other living creatures, Lacan observes, as for the human infant, the visual image, the gestalt, provides the stimulus for behavior. Thus he notes that for the maturation of the pigeon to proceed apace it is a recognized ethological fact that it needs to "see," in fact or in mirror image, another of its kind. So it is with the human infant, that she or he too will respond to the visual reflection, in fact by a "jubilant assumption of [the] specular image" (p. 2).

However, whereas for other living creatures there appears to be a seamless coincidence of itself with its supporting context (i.e., a pigeon *is* insofar as it is in its surround) there is, for the human, Lacan (1949) conjectures, "an organic insufficiency in his natural reality" (p. 4). From the outset, the natural environment, though surely necessary, is not, in and of itself, sufficient to sustain the distinctly human project.

The Kojevian influence becomes clear as Lacan (1949) goes on to suggest that the I of human being requires something other than what is supplied in the world of nature; that the natural world cannot, by itself, produce the human subject. (In other terms, and via other solutions, we recall, with Mahler, Pine, and Bergmann [1975], the *psychological* birth of the human infant.) In the Lacanian formulation, this insufficiency, or lack, is addressed by the imago in its specific incarnation as the mirror stage. Thus, it is the particular function of the imago, in consequence of this original insufficiency, "to *establish a relation* between the organism and its reality" (Lacan, 1949, p. 4; emphasis added).

Thus Lacan (1949) advises his audience that the mirror stage serves to establish a (reflected and imagined) tie between the actor and his context that presumably exists without intercession in other living creatures. Indeed, common parlance may be quite revealing in this connection. For it is only the human being about whom it may be said, "she or he is *reflecting* upon that"; or "she or he is a particularly *reflective* person." Only humankind, presumably, reflects on its experience, whereas other living creatures, it would seem, simply are. The human being's connection to the natural world from which she or he is derived is not, so to speak, a perfect fit. Indeed, and importantly, Lacan asserts that "this relation to nature is altered by *a certain dehiscence at the heart of the organism*, a primordial Discord" (p. 4; emphasis added).

The human organism is, in its peculiar species-specific nature, oddly ill-suited to the natural surround in which it is inevitably embedded. Its essential capacity to reflect upon, and thus detach, or stand at a psychological remove from, the natural (i.e., the actual, and nonmediated) world to which it owes its origin requires some additional mechanism by which the human organism can reestablish psychic coincidence. As we have noted, Lacan (1949) here asserts that it is the

I as a reflection in the mirror which serves that function. But it is, as we have also noted, a deception, for the visual image in its initial configuration as one's other in the mirror is an inverted, reversed, and idealized picture, bearing no psychological resemblance to the actual psychological self. Later, as the I adopts its social identity, Lacan (1949) will say that an even deeper alienation sets in, for at least this imaginary or specular I is still tied, even if in distorted fashion, to the child's inner world. In the postoedipal world, the I will be a captive of the social. Nonetheless, in both situations we note that what runs through the nature of the I from its very inception is this notion of insufficiency, of lack.

But the mirror stage is a two-part development, in which the assumption of the deceptive, specular image is but the first step. A second step will involve the turn from the specular I of the child's inner life, to the social I of the outer world. The transition from the one to the other psychological world in fact marks the close of the mirror stage.

We recall that the initial formation of the human subject began at the point at which the infant assumed an identification with his own, presocial image, giving rise to the specular I. And it is here, we noted, in the beginning of the mirror stage, that the I's deception of permanency is established. An identification of a different order heralds the close of this stage, and protects Lacan's (1949) formulation of the self from charges of its being an "absolute" and purely subjective concept; that is, only a product of the imaginary.

The close of the mirror stage is initiated in that moment "which dates from the deflection of the specular *I* into the social *I*" (Lacan, 1949, p. 5), an event which transpires when the child enters into identification with its "parental counterpart." In other words, as the oedipal conflict evolves toward its successful resolution, as the child assumes aspects of the actual other, "the dialectic that will henceforth link the *I* to socially elaborated situations" (p. 5) is initiated.

A critical and inevitable consequence of this process is the certain separation of the self from its initial self of the mirror image; for as this specular I of the child's inner world, his *Innenwelt*, is "deflected" into the "social," or *Umwelt*, the I assumes the "armour of an alienating identity, which will mark with its rigid structure the subject's entire mental development. Thus, to break out of the circle of the *Innenwelt* into the *Umwelt* generates the inexhaustible quadrature of the ego's verifications" (Lacan, 1949, p. 4). That is to say, the ego is necessarily and inevitably self-alienating and its "inexhaustible quadrature" locks away the self of the *Innenwelt*. To become a social being, as the self inevitably must, is to become, as it inevitably will, a self alienated from itself.

"It is this moment," Lacan (1949) asserts, in which the self moves to make its social identifications, "that decisively tips the whole of human knowledge into mediatization through the desire of the other" (p. 5). For now the self, in having assumed the identity of the other, requires the other for its continued being. All desires are now subject to mediation by culture, the collective other.

In this paper, the alienated self is the outcome of the necessary transition from the inner world of identification with one's own image, to the outer world of identification with the images of one's increasing number of "counterparts." As the self moves toward the *Umwelt*, it is, in Lacan's (1949) view, "captured" by the social.

We conclude this aspect of our discussion by observing that, in its entirety, "the *mirror stage* is a drama whose internal thrust is precipitated from insufficiency" (Lacan, 1949, p. 4). The I is propelled into existence in consequence of an originary and defining *lack* which is the very mark of human being. We recall in this context that there is a similar lack, or absence, which distinguishes Kojeve's (1947) formulations, and we see in Lacan's (1949) assertion regarding the formation of the I the commitment to a self which is stimulated into being and is henceforth characterized by this fundamental lack, or "dehiscence" which we recognize as desire.

For we cannot fail to note that Lacan (1949) is here proposing a self whose very "precipitation" results from an absence toward which desire points. Nor can we ignore that Lacan (1949) here attributes the "sealing over" of this absence to the interposition of the imaginary, that which is a deception, and not real; that which is no (actual) thing.

Now it should be noted at this point that the self of which we speak here is not coincident with subjectivity. On the contrary, the function of perception, of the image in the mirror, is to yield an *alienated* image (of the self), rather than a subjective experience of I. Nonetheless, it is only through the acquisition of subjectivity that the child may be freed of the alienating image, although whether such freedom comes to pass is surely an open question, the resolution of which, as we noted earlier, rests in the achievement of the "full speech" of the unconscious. Subjectivity is encountered in the assumption of language from the actual other. It is cloaked in language that the child passes into the symbolic order of the subjective. Lacan (1953) dates the particular psychoanalytic moment of entry into the world of language, the realm of the subject, to that instance when the child encounters the reality of the *fort-da*.

Thus does Lacan (1953) turn to this quintessentially psychoanalytic narrative, applying a far more spacious connotational intent to its operative terms; and in so doing, radically recasts the Freudian scenario that it may accommodate the Lacanian intent. So fundamental to an understanding of Lacan's conceptual substrate is this recasting that we shall here take a moment to review his meaning.

We recall that Freud (1920) turned, in the course of elucidating the many ways in which the mind "works," to an illustrative description of a game invented by his grandson who was, Freud (1920) observes, "greatly attached to his mother" (p. 14). This game involved tossing a reel, attached by a string, over the edge of his covered cot so that he could not see it, accompanying this action by what Freud (1920) believed to be the utterance *fort*, or gone. Immediately following, he pulled the reel out from behind the covered cot and "hailed its reappearance with a joyful *'da'* ['there']" (p.15).

Now, Freud (1920) admitted of multiple possibilities in attempting to grasp the psychoanalytic meaning of this game, some related to instinctual renunciation, others to the achievement of some small yield of pleasure, but all, it seemed, tied to the larger project of explicating the nature of the pleasure and the newly introduced death instinct which stood beyond it. Lacan (1953), we shall see, applies a rather more expansive interpretation to the fundamental meaning of the *fort-da*.

For Lacan (1953) the child's game, characterized as it is by the repetition of the words *fort-da*, is both "the moment in which desire becomes human [and] is also that in which the child is born into language" (p. 103). For in this moment the child, Lacan (1953) asserts, is not only mastering his deprivation, the absence of mother, but recasting the nature of this desire (for mother), transferring it, as it were, to a different order of expression. The child now spoke his desire, *fort-gone, da-there*, and its fulfillment. He symbolized his desire in the word; and the specific nature of that desire, Lacan continues, is the desire for the other. That is, the child desires that the mother desire, and thereby *recognize*, him, for "the first object of desire is to be recognized by the other" (Lacan, 1953, p. 58). This is, we recall from Kojeve (1947), the distinctly human desire. Language, says Lacan (1953), here outfitted in psychoanalytic garb, is wherein the subjective self is born.

Fort-da comes to mean, as "gone" and "there," the psychoanalytic reconfiguration of the Kojevian notions of "absence" and "presence." The self, Lacan (1953) asserts, is fashioned upon the horns of this idiosyncratically human dilemma. Thus we conclude that the Lacanian self, conceived in deception, and nurtured by desire, is "irreducibly" and forever driven by absence, and composed of what is not present. The self is here understood as the psychological manifestation of pure desire in the Kojevian sense; the immanent representation of the absent.

Now, as we have suggested throughout, it is the central thesis of Lacan's (1949) paper that the earliest formation of the I is itself indicative of what makes the self an imaginary construction. For the very mechanism which serves the function of establishing the I via the child's first relationship (i.e., the image) is also the initial signpost pointing toward a world which is not actually present, but *is* actually imagined. The self in its imaginary origin, then, is constituted by and stands for what is actually absent, while the self in its symbolic transition indicates a (linguistically symbolic) *presence*. Now in referring to this presence, we are not saying the self has achieved "real" presence. On the contrary, Lacan (1960) avows that "the real is the impossible," the never attainable. The closest we get to reducing this inevitable alienation from reality is the successful acquisition of the symbolic. And the closest the self gets to reducing its own self-alienation is the "full speech" of the unconscious, a speech which promotes the subject's own linguistic construction. For it is "the psychoanalytic experience," Lacan (1953) asserts, which "has rediscovered in man the imperative of the Word as the law that has formed him in its image" (p. 106).

Thus the self concept stands at the very crossroads of two levels of being, the present and the absent orders of being. For the self, composed as it is of the Lacanian image, both *resembles the actual* and *reflects the fictive*. It is the human self, as a product of the *image* (and the imagination), which serves to bridge these two worlds.

By way of summary in the *stade du miroir* Lacan (1949) has formulated a self which has an imaginary origin, a beginning in the child's mistaking the specular and idealized image for a true resemblance to his own self when it is actually a fictional, even mythic, depiction of who she or he is or may anticipate becoming.

Later, as the mirror stage draws to its close, this specular I is transformed, Lacan (1949) would say "captured," by the postoedipal situation, in which identification with the imaginary world of the mirror is relinquished in favor of the "lure" of identifications with actual other counterparts.

Finally, in making this transition, the self is inevitably alienated from itself because all that it henceforth can ever know of itself, all human knowledge, will be mediated through the subject's desire of the other. Whereas the initial relationship to the self was imaginary, it was yet a relationship to one's own "innerness." In the evolved relationship to itself, after the resolution of the oedipal and the entry into the social, the self is only related to itself through the filter of desire. A person's self now may be realized only insofar as she or he succeeds in winning the desire of the other; that is, in becoming desirable to the other.

The "stade du miroir," as we suggested at the outset, is largely a psychoanalytic hypothesis regarding the genetic origins of the self. It proposes, as we have seen, a self derived from the imaginary, and predestined to its own alienation in consequence of its necessary "capture" by the social and inevitable domination by desire. However, even as it is a specific stage in development, the mirror stage also reflects a particularly Lacanian epistemology, which makes some quite different assertions about the self and self-knowledge than the theorists of the American tradition, for example, might easily recognize as analytic.

What characterizes this ego is not the successful mastery of skills, nor its adaptation to environmental and social requirements. Rather, as we have underscored, this is an ego which, at its very core, is made up of failures in recognition, indeed is a function of those failures (i.e., *meconnaissance*) which accompany the child's first identification and which continue to characterize all future self-knowledge. It is, as well, a self which can only possess knowledge of itself as such knowing is mediated by desire, and we recall that desire is the pursuit of the absent. It is, thus, in the pursuit, rather than in the forever elusive possession, that knowledge resides.

We recognize in these observations reflected in the Lacanian mirror, a theory of knowledge that asserts two particular tenets. First, that all knowledge is indirectly acquired, filtered through the effort to satisfy desire, that is, to fill the absence that desire is. Second, that knowledge is built upon the inevitable failure to recognize the real nature of what we perceive; that all knowledge is inevitably qualified, and compromised, by its derivation in a reflected reality rather than a real actuality. As Lacan (1953, 1960) has suggested, such perceptions of the "real," it turns out, are never humanly attainable.

We conclude this aspect of our discussion by briefly restating a number of central organizing principles of the Lacanian self, including:

1. The Lacanian self is an *imaginary* self, derived as it is from the image in the mirror. This self is thus real in the sense that it bears a resemblance to the actual, and unreal or fictional, in the sense that it depicts a reflected, that is, reversed, picture.

2. The child's first identification is with this image, thus making the earliest aspect of his internal life his own reflected other. The Lacanian self is a *presocial* entity, owing its origin to the misperceived projections of the child's inner world. The self emerges prior to the psychological influence of the actual other.

3. The self's mirror other, his or her ego, is a case of mistaken identity, what Lacan (1949) has called a *meconnaissance*. For the *gestalt* in the mirror is an idealized reflection, bearing little kinship to the dependent and largely incoherent psychological bundle that is the actual child. The Lacanian ego, as the child's mirror-derived and idealized other, is a forever unobtainable product of the imagination.

4. The imaginary self inevitably moves, as it resolves the oedipal crisis, into the social world of actual others. In identifying with actual others, the self turns from the inner world to the outer world and adopts the ways of culture. In so doing the self is separated from itself, largely by repression and the introduction of the mediation of the desire of the other. As the child moves into the social, a lasting residue of the oedipal is the persistent desire not for the actual other's body, but for the desire of the other, that is, to be what the other desires. This is the transition to the uniquely human; a transition which perforce separates one from the preoedipal, presocial inner world. Thus, the Lacanian self is an *alienated self*.

5. In consequence of the postoedipal repression and the desire for the other, the Lacanian self is also a *divided* subject, which largely labors under the misapprehension that his "true" self is the one he is conscious of while in fact this is only his mistaken image of the true.

6. The "truth," which is not coincident with the real, resides in the *language* of the unconscious, and it is only insofar as one succeeds in being spoken by one's unconscious that one is fully one's self. The Lacanian self is an (unconsciously) *spoken self.*

7. Thus, the self is "located," and desire realized, in the capacity of the self to *recognize itself;* to achieve the recognition of his own unconscious. Of course it is in the nature of such desire, as unconscious, that it can never actually be recognized, for such would imply consciousness and hence the loss of the unconscious, the source of desired recognition. Thus, desire remains forever unfulfilled, and the self forever absent.

8. Resolution, if there be any, rests in consciously recognizing that the unconscious be permitted to recognize and speak the self, although the (conscious) self cannot recognize this. Thus, the Lacanian self is *recognition of the self as absence.*

We see that in these numerous ways the Lacanian self appears to bear little resemblance to the self we encountered in the American tradition. There we observed a self, whether as a function of the ego or as an increasingly influential conceptual entity in its own right, whose first psychic images derived from actual others. The American concept is of an *interactionally derived self,* whereas, as we have just noted, the Lacanian conception attributes no initial formative influence to the *Umwelt.*

Perhaps the single most distinctive difference rests in observing the ubiquitous role of the internal representation, itself an image, in the construction of the self in the American school. The representation of the self, in Jacobson's (1964) work, or Mahler et al.'s (1975); in Kernberg's (1976) or Kohut's (1977); even, and perhaps especially, in Spiegel's (1959) or Sandler and Rosenblatt's (1964), serves to establish the *presence* of the self to the self, a coincidence, as we have just observed, which cannot occur for the Lacanian self.

The internal image serves, the more so as it becomes a secure and *constant* image, to attest to the "psychic fact" that there *is* a self. In the American conception, the self which originally was not there (i.e., was absent) comes to be constituted as *there*, as *da*, as images of the actual other are internalized, and "taken in." In the American conceptualization, the image indicates the *fulfilled and present self*, while for Lacan (1949, 1953, 1960) it reflects a *false presence*, obscuring an actual absence.

It is interesting to observe, in this connection, the latent similarity among these seemingly disparate formulations. Thus for example, we are reminded of the ego psychological view that the achievement by the ego of "frustration tolerance," and "delayed gratification," are signs of maturity and psychological health. At first glance it would seem that Lacan's (1953) assertion that the ego itself is the essence of frustration would hold little in common with the American notion. However, let us briefly consider what is involved in *delaying gratification*, or tolerating *frustration*, after all.

In both these instances, I suggest, we encounter the face of desire. For in delaying gratification, are we not putting off the moment of satisfaction, and thus perpetuating a condition of desire? In bearing frustration, are we not enduring the absence of what is desired? Indeed, the argument that the mature ego, or the healthy self employing the functional capacity of a sound ego, is that ego which can tolerate frustration and delay its gratification, is surely related to the argument which proposes that the self is propelled by desire and comes to tolerate the (perpetual) absence of fulfillment. In this way I suggest that the manifestly distinct formulations of the American ego psychologists and Lacan bear an interesting latent comity.

In yet another respect, we observe that Lacan shares a common emphasis with his frequently disavowed colleagues of the American school. Both place considerable conceptual confidence in the formative impact of the visual. That is to say, the image, whether as actually seen in the mirror, or as it is (re)constituted mentally, as a representation, in consequence of the ministrations of the mother, establishes the self in the first instance as a pictorial manifestation. We shall have occasion below to note that this is a predominant feature of many of the theorists of the British school as well, perhaps most notably Winnicott (1960a, 1963). An interesting departure from the constituting impact of the visual are the hypotheses of the French psychoanalytic theorist Anzieu (1985), whose innovative approach we shall also undertake to discuss in the following section.

Part III:
ANOMALOUS SELVES

> Symbolism conveys both absence and presence. To see three
> truths with the same mind: things are real, unreal, and neither real
> nor unreal
>
> [Brown, 1966, p. 261].

We have observed, with respect to the "self of realization" and the
"self of anticipation," that the formulations which shaped these concepts emerged in the light of their respective theoretical progenitors.
Thus, so much of what characterizes the American tradition, for example, particularly with respect to the self concept, is based upon the
manner in which subsequent theorists responded to Hartmann's innovations; and, similarly, the essence of the French psychoanalytic movement, in all its political as well as theoretical turmoil, was a debate
derived from Lacanian principles. As is often the case, and surely
has been with psychoanalysis vis-à-vis Freud, bursts of innovative
contributions are frequently, and even necessarily, followed by long
periods of refining and elaborating upon that initial contribution. New
paradigms, novel ways of seeing and of interpreting, occur rarely and
are followed by extended stretches of consolidation, or what Kuhn
(1962) refers to as "normal science," during which research derives
from "achievements that some particular scientific community acknowledges for a time as supplying the foundation for its further prac-
tice" (p. 10).

Much of what we have discussed in the preceding sections were
the elaborations and variations upon how to allocate defining psychic
influence to the paradigmatic Freudian themes of conscious unconscious, of surface interior, of rational (ego) and irrational (id). Here
we will consider those theorists whose work, in some significant respects, does not so much represent "normal science" as it suggests
anomalous thematics, those running counter to prevailing (paradigmatic) expectations. Because it is in the nature of "normal science" to

201

enunciate and reinforce what the paradigm has already provided, it is distinctly an "enterprise [which] seems an attempt to force nature into the preformed and relatively inflexible box that the paradigm supplies . . . indeed those that will not fit the box are often not seen at all" (Kuhn, 1962, p. 24). Here, we plan to take another look in the box.

Other Ways

The work of Federn and Anzieu, aspects of whose theoretical contributions serve as metaphorical as well as theoretical bookends to this aspect of our investigation, can stand, it seems, as illustrations in the breach of this general axiom of normative research. For both represent work which, though noteworthy, and even formidable in content, in significant ways pursue lines of investigation outside the bounds of the prevailing paradigm. For one of the fundamental functions of a working paradigm is that it serves as a guide in the selection of problems for study. Indeed, paradigms only "permit," that is, recognize as legitimate, the investigation of those problems which meet the criterion supplied by the paradigm itself, while "other problems, including many that had previously been standard, are rejected . . . " (Kuhn, 1962, p. 37). Works which raise extraparadigmatic questions win little or no recognition during the life of that paradigm.

Thus, we shall see that Anzieu, for example, unlike those within the Lacanian tradition, does not disavow the ego as a distortion. Rather, he will emphasize the antecedent influence of the tactile as the fundamental source of the psychological self. Indeed, he will assert that *sensory*, rather than visual–cognitive experience serves as a primary source of self awareness, providing both internal and external perceptual experience.

Anzieu eschews the supplanting of the topographical theory by the structural theory, and instead reconceives the ego and the id in terms of what he refers to as a "second topographical theory." In so doing he will assert the tactile and the topographical origins of the ego, but will not make the emergence of the self coincident with this ego. Significantly, the self Anzieu will propose is distinct from and *prior* to the topological evolution of the ego. The self he proposes will correspond to the "auditory and olfactory envelope" which antedates any tactile distinctions between inner and outer. Anzieu's is a self immersed in smell and sound, and whose (albeit primitive) existence predates the ego. This is a self without a visual or tactile referent and surely does not accord with predominant views on the elaboration of the psyche, and the self, in terms of the ego.

The maxims of normal science are perhaps especially apt with respect to the theoretical contributions of Federn. For Federn's ego psychology represents, I believe, a substantial and coherent alternative statement concerning the nature and functions of the ego-self and its relationship to the vicissitudes of narcissistic cathexis which have been accorded a kind of footnote status vis-à-vis the Hartmannian paradigm. We shall not address the many possible explanations for this, beyond observing in passing that Hartmann's model had the advantage of providing a number of satisfactory solutions while at the same time adapting to the contemporary sociocultural investment in mastery and a devotion to empirical confirmation that Federn's methodology did not provide. (We recall, after all, that one of Hartmann's primary goals was to make of psychoanalysis a "general psychology." To do so, analytic models of investigation needed, of necessity, to conform to a more encompassing cultural paradigm.)

Indeed, Federn's methodology, phenomenological in character, sought "evidence" for its theoretical assertions in the subjective reports of private experience, "evidence" not, of course, warmly received within the confines of an investigative paradigm which prized objective confirmation. In framing the problem to be studied in terms of subjective experience, and in employing subjective criteria as a source of confirmation, Federn violated the methodological expectations of the prevailing model. Thus, in attributing the origins of the psychological self to *felt* experience, to sensory phenomena which, interestingly, also precede visual and cognitive apprehensions of being, Federn was indeed a kind of anomaly within the prevailing ego psychological tradition.

Federn's concept of self was itself paradigmatically invisible. He underscored the formative influence of the vague, the idiosyncratic, and the nonvisible (i.e., the invisible). That is to say, of course, he emphasized the distinctly nonempirical and nonobjective elements in the psychological elaboration of the self just at a time when psychoanalytic investigation sought to establish its principles upon the pedestal of objectivity. In pursuing the impersonal and largely latent sources

of self confirmation, Federn was not employing the criterion of a Hartmannian model of ego psychological investigation any more than was
Anzieu, in not spurning the reality-oriented ego, pursuing solutions
within a Lacanian framework.

And Middle Ways

Appropriately enough, between the work of Federn and Anzieu we
shall address the contributions of a selected number of theorists who
emerged from within the ranks of the British Psycho-Analytical Society, and are broadly referred to as the "middle group." This loosely
organized assembly of clinically immersed and inductive theorists,
themselves the anomalous effect of unanticipated causal events, took
a path distinctly other than that which had been hewn by either of the
heir apparents to the Freudian legacy, Anna Freud and Melanie Klein.
The middle group constructed a set of analytic hypotheses which addressed the paradoxical nature of the self and which, paradoxically,
came to characterize much of British psychoanalytic thinking. Interestingly, this group initially emerged not so much in response to theoretical as to political demands, and the fertile innovations in theory which
were eventually attributed to the middle group may be understood as
a fortunate byproduct of pragmatic efforts to reconcile orthodoxies.

For the British psychoanalytic community, not unlike its French
and American counterparts, has been the site of many and often divergent trends of thought and theory development. Thus, much of what
characterizes the American tradition, particularly with respect to the
self concept, is based upon the manner in which subsequent theorists
responded to Hartmann's innovations. The essence of the French psychoanalytic movement, in all its political as well as theoretical turmoil,
was a debate derived from Lacanian principles. Much of British psychoanalysis was shaped largely by the responses, and rivalries, stimulated by the work of Melanie Klein.

Much has already been said concerning the passionate schism
within the British Psycho-Analytical Society among the followers of
Melanie Klein and Anna Freud (see, for example, Kohon, 1986;
Rayner, 1991) and we shall not attempt to discuss those events in any
detail in this context. However, in order to set the stage for the appearance of the theorists whose work we wish to look at, we shall undertake

a schematic overview of those tumultuous events, observing as we do so that the consequences of this rift gave rise to a particularly British, and especially fertile, if paradoxical, resolution, one that altered the direction of thinking about the self.

The rift itself, as is well known, was occasioned by the theoretical positions proposed by Melanie Klein and the opposition to them by Anna Freud. It was not only Klein's particular ideas, however, but a set of circumstances, historical and otherwise, to which we may attribute both their success and the fact that they occasioned the level of tension that they did.

Among the many provocative departures from prevailing analytic attitudes which Klein proposed we note the following: her assertion that the infant's psyche was far more elaborate, far earlier, than had been thought, and included a complex unconscious phantasy system; and an emphasis upon the guilt engendered by the child's destructive, aggressive tendencies, deriving from the forces of the death instinct. These "Kleinian" foci, we observe, reveal her theoretical commitment to seeking explanatory principles of behavior within the psychobiology of the instincts and the inner life generally; but her unique contribution rests in having transformed the impact of significant other objects into *intrapsychic*, as distinct from actual and interpersonal, events. This becomes especially apparent when considering her very important work on the influence of the *internal* object, aspects of which we shall have occasion to discuss below in connection with the elaboration of the self concept.

But at the same time that Klein was proposing these views, the psychoanalytic atmosphere in mid-1920s Vienna was turning distinctly toward possible environmental explanations of behavior. It was at this time, for example, that Anna Freud (1926) published her book on the analytic treatment of children; a work which bore no resemblance to the far more instinctual arguments of Melanie Klein. The atmosphere in London, however, bore no resemblance to that of Vienna, and consequently Klein's work was receiving a rather enthusiastic reception in the British Society, where there was considerable sympathy for and interest in the determining influence of hate and aggression. By 1927 Klein had taken up residence in London and continued to receive a generally positive hearing.

While the psychoanalytic relationship between Vienna and London remained tense over the next decade or so, events might well have taken a very different turn for the British Society generally, and theory in particular, had politics not taken the turn they had. As it was, history forced a great number of analysts from Austria in the late 1930s, and while many only passed through England on their way to America (e.g., Hartmann, Loewenstein, Rapaport, Federn), Freud and Anna Freud settled in London. In so doing, the tensions which had existed across the expanse of the European continent now lit sparks within the same meeting hall.

The British Society eventually worked out a solution among the Kleinians and the Anna Freudians which allowed for the continued training of analysts under one roof, a solution revealing a penchant for compromise radically at odds with, for example, the French preference for more dramatic and absolute breaks which characterized the disputes over Lacanian principles and techniques. Thus, the A and B groups of Kleinian and Freudian adherents were formed, and because the solution required that a second training analyst come from neither group, the "middle group," or "independents" as they were also called, came into being. It is from this group of analysts, neither Freudian nor Kleinian in commitment, that some particularly innovative theoretical positions were advanced, particularly with respect to the self. It is to this group that we shall shortly turn, noting as we do that they can be understood to represent, both individually and as a collective, a distinctly paradoxical response to the instinctual and environmental poles from which they sprang.

Before engaging these theorists directly, however, it may prove useful to comment briefly upon the nature of theoretical formulations within the British tradition, noting that it reflects a rather distinctive turn of mind which informs the character of the middle group as surely as it does British thought in general.

Thus we recognize that the accommodations made by the British Psycho-Analytical Society, which allowed both groups, and a newly created third, to coexist fruitfully, represent the essence of compromise; and such compromise was, after all, based not upon favoring one or another theoretical position, but rather upon the pragmatic concern to preserve the effective training of analysts. The nature of this solution is as much a reflection of a distinctly Anglican sensibility and intellectual tradition as those we have seen in the American and French schools of thought. What, then, is this sensibility?

Unlike their continental counterparts, the British were not as influenced by that tradition of philosophical romanticism that holds with the metaphysical principle that reality, which is to say, all that is knowable, derives from some antecedent, innate, and transcendent idea, an Absolute Spirit or *Geist*. One thinks here of Hegel, although Kant's work also reflects this philosophical attitude quite well. In this view human kind is one aspect of Spirit, the natural world (i.e., Nature) another, and fundamental knowledge of either or both is reliant upon intuitive rather than rational processes. Thus, the idealists, such as Fichte and Schopenhauer, underscored the determining import of, for example, "mind," and "soul."

On the other hand, the empirical emphasis upon corporeal, factual, and sensory-derived experiences has a long and influential history in Britain, and the views of the English philosophers such as Locke, Berkeley, Hume, and J. S. Mill, contributed much to a distinctive British propensity for evaluating phenomena and drawing conclusions based upon data derived from direct, sensual observation. For it is from this philosophical and methodological commitment to observation and reliance upon the data of the senses, that the commitment to knowledge which is born of experience may be seen to arise. Where the senses conflict they are subject to reevaluation and compromise within the mind of the observer such that an overall picture of reality may be rendered.

We recognize in these principles of observation, accommodation, and reliance upon direct experience for knowledge, the essence of the compromise reached by the British Psycho-Analytical Society referred to above. Rather than draw upon one or another of the positions as unalterably "correct," a solution was crafted which allowed both to proceed, and eventually, for a third position to gain a certain ascendancy. In addition, in the inclination toward compromise and pragmatic solutions based in experience which an empirical tradition fosters, we observe many of the hallmarks of theory development in the British tradition.

There is a reliance among British theorists generally, and notably in the work of Klein, Fairbairn, and Winnicott, upon the observed evidence of clinical data. In large part, what they perceive to have transpired in the consulting room serves as the basis of their hypotheses and the source of their theoretical conclusions. This is, for example, in marked contrast to the French theorist Andre Green (1972) who has observed in connection with the use of clinical material that it does not serve to decide any theoretical debate. Thus, Green (1972) continues, "I do not think that presenting clinical observations constitutes proof of what an analyst advances from a theoretical point of view" (p. 4).

In large part due to the British preference for basing conclusions upon direct observation, theory has tended to be built by a kind of empirical accretion rather than by abstract assertion. As a consequence of the variety of clinical experience and clinical observers, British psychoanalytic theory tends not to be easily categorized in terms of its adherence to one or another aspect of the Freudian paradigm, as the Americans had been with the poststructural Freud and the French with the prestructural Freud, for example. The British, and the middle group or, perhaps more fittingly the "independents," however, may be understood, in terms of the Freudian paradigm, as a particularly innovative instance of anomaly.

A final observation is perhaps in order before we proceed to the heart of our discussion, and it is this: the British have tended, perhaps with the notable exception of Fairbairn, to make their most significant theoretical contributions as they addressed the developmental rather than the structural axis of psychoanalytic thought, particularly with regard to the origin and evolution of the self. Thus we shall observe, in addressing selected aspects of the work of Winnicott (1958, 1960a,b, 1963), Balint (1968), and Guntrip (1971) that the thrust of investigation, the balance of hypotheses, and the weight of conclusion, is couched within early mother–infant relationships. Observation of experience is the source of (British theoretical) conclusions; and those conclusions largely refer to the course of development, much of it attributable to experiences in the real world.

The overall focus upon developmental themes, however, changed the character of the theoretical debate in Britain, as well as the direction of theory, especially with regard to the self concept. For by not dwelling upon the mechanics of structure, many theorists bypassed the frequently casuistic discussions, designed to tease out the precise shades of meaning among the ego and the self, for example, that we have noted in the "self of realization" fostered by the American tradition. As well, an emphasis upon the developmental also allowed the British theorists to more readily discuss self and ego in an interchangeable fashion reminiscent of the pre-1923 Freud.

Our investigation of the self concept in this section will focus upon selected theorists of the middle group of British psychoanalysts, whose work illustrates an interesting blend of ideas bearing, as we shall see, a conceptual kinship with presence *and* absence, yielding a formulation of self which, in paradoxical fashion, suggests fulfillment and loss together. We shall open, however, with a Viennese Freudian loyalist whose later years were spent in the United States in the shadow of Heinz Hartmann, and close with a contemporary French psychoanalyst; for in the work of Federn and Anzieu, respectively, we discern some of the same elements of paradox which characterize their British counterparts.

Chapter 9
THE PHENOMENAL SELF OF PAUL FEDERN

When Paul Federn (1932) asserted that "the cardinal feature of 'ego experience' is not thought or knowledge but sensation" (p. 62), he clearly distinguished himself, both methodologically and conceptually, from many of his psychoanalytic contemporaries, perhaps most notably Hartmann (1939, 1950). For we have seen that Hartmann's (1950) approach to the study of the ego was decidedly objective in spirit; seeking to underscore, and even to define, the ego by those features which may more readily lend themselves to empirical verification.

Thus, whereas Hartmann (1939, 1950) sought to explain his notion of the ego in purposive, functional, and above all, nonsubjective terms, we encounter in Federn, (1926, 1928a,b, 1932, 1934) the antithetical claim that the ego is characterized by the most subjective of phenomena, one's own *feelings* or sensations. Methodologically, this claim would commit Federn (1926, 1928a,b, 1932, 1934) to a series of phenomenological investigations, describing the subjective experience of assorted transitory psychic states, such as the moments just prior to falling asleep, or just upon awakening, as well as his rather better known depictions of estrangement, depersonalization, and aspects of psychotic experience.

Conceptually, as we shall see, Federn's ego is also quite a different entity from Hartmann's. For whereas the latter conceived of the ego as a functional structure of the psyche, responsible for the "whole person's" adaptation to and mastery of reality; for the former, the ego *is* the self; that is, the enduring, and more or less continuous, *subjective feeling* of one's own unique being. This subjective experience Federn (1926, 1928a,b, 1932) would call *ego feeling*, and define it as "the

211

totality of feeling which one has of *one's own living person*" (Federn, 1932, p. 62; emphasis added). Lest there be any doubt as to the coequivalence of ego and self, we pause to note that in an earlier discussion of estrangement, Federn (1928b) observes the patient's reaction to a diminution of affects when in such a condition by commenting that the patient "misses them and states that he him*self* (that is, *his ego*) has changed . . . " (p. 287; emphases added).

Federn's ego psychology represented a distinct conceptual and methodological alternative to the functional and adaptational elaborations of Hartmann, accentuating instead the far more qualitative aspects of being, and indeed, seeking to explain selected healthy and pathological phenomena in terms of subjective experience rather than observable behavior. As a discrete ego psychological position, Federn amplified the role of the subjective, and the accompanying elevation of the self from a circumscribed mental representation contained within the structured (Hartmannian) ego, to terminological and conceptual coincidence with the ego itself. But these ideas would never gain the theoretical prominence achieved by Hartmann's body of work, though the influence of his many tenets would be subtly dispersed among major theorists of the American tradition.

Thus, in the course of this project, we have detected the steadily growing influence of the subjective upon the formulations of the self, notably in the work of Kernberg (1976, 1982a,b), Kohut (1959, 1971, 1977), and perhaps especially Stern (1985), whose concept of the self owes its origin and nature to the formative influence of the unambiguously subjective. Somewhat earlier, Jacobson (1964) began to take account of the role of the subjective generally, and, more specifically and in limited fashion, of Federn's work itself, in her own formulation of the self. Thus, for example, does she observe, as did Federn (e.g., 1932), that conscious knowing, or observation, of the self, more specifically for Jacobson (1964), the self representation, is a circumscribed avenue of approach at best, and that the self is also shaped by less quantifiable influences. "The self representations will never," Jacobson (1964) asserts, "be strictly 'conceptual' . . . [for] they remain under the influence of our *subjective emotional experiences* . . . " (p. 20; emphasis added). In a footnote to this comment Jacobson (1964) acknowledges that "Federn's concepts of ego feeling and ego experience emphasize this point" (p. 20, n 11). Let us take a closer look at some of the central concepts of this "other" ego psychology.

"Inner Reaches" and "Outer Limits"

Federn's psychology rests upon the rather detailed investigation of a selected number of states of being, most often characterized by their transitory nature. He studied waking and falling asleep, as well as the assorted variations associated with the feeling of one's own "realness," pursuing both the inner reaches of one's own being, the source of the self-evident experience of being, and the outer limits of that experience, in the vaguely felt and indeterminant psychic region where the self ends and the other begins. The former would come to be designated as *ego feeling*, and the latter as *ego boundaries*, while both would be explained in terms of a revised formulation of narcissism.

For just as narcissism occupied Freud (1914) as he began to think about revising the libido theory; and just as it called Hartmann's (1950) attention to a set of incommensurate conceptual equivalences which led him to formulate an ego psychological concept of the self; so too did narcissism play a major explanatory role in Federn's (1928a,b) own psychology.

What is the origin of the experience of self, and what is the evidence for it? What accounts for the transition from self to nonself experience? Federn (1928a,b, 1932, 1934) sought, in his reconceptualization of narcissism, and his particular use of the libido theory, to fashion a distinctly psychoanalytic reply to what is essentially an inquiry into the ontological status of the self. He gave expression to his formulations in the interrelated notions of *ego feeling* and *ego boundaries* as they are both sustained by narcissistic cathexis.

Feeling One's Self

Federn (1932) took exception to the emerging functional–structural view of the ego which would soon become known more generally as Hartmann's (1939) ego psychology. He believed instead that the ego is more than an abstraction designed to suggest a collection of actions, and this view is immediately confirmed in his assertion that, among other things:

> I do not regard [the ego] merely as the sum of the ego functions . . . nor yet simply as the "psychic representation" of that which refers to one's own person . . . these are all aspects of the ego . . . the ego, however, is more inclusive . . . *it includes the subjective psychic experience of these functions* [and] this *self-experience* is a permanent . . . entity, which is not an abstraction but a reality [pp. 60–61; emphases added].

Federn's ego, we see, is the palpable feeling of the functioning body and psyche both; and, importantly, that feeling *is* the experience of the self. Further, we underscore that this experience is decidedly more than the *idea* of one's self. Indeed, the consciousness of self devoid of affective investiture, constitutes, in Federn's (1926, 1928a, 1932, 1934) view, a form of pathology. But from whence does this feeling of ego, the feeling of self, derive? And how is it recognized?

On Feeling Strange

Federn (1928a) initiated his studies of the subjective experience of the ego with a series of investigations into the nature of some selected ego states, paying special attention to estrangement and depersonalization. Thus, Federn (1926, 1928a, 1932, 1934) essentially encountered the phenomenon of "ego feeling" in the breach. For it was only in its absence, as described in these symptomatic manifestations, that he retroactively assumed its normative presence.

Estrangement, then, is described as that condition in which the outer world remains recognizable, and fundamentally unchanged, yet at the same time is lacking in the feeling of warmth or familiarity that imparts a sense of the individual's own "realness." Thus, while the patient can correctly identify the items of the world, "his feeling, wishing, thinking, and memory processes have become different . . . [and] in still more severe cases even the unity of the ego has become doubtful; in its continuity the ego is *only perceived, not felt*" (Federn, 1928a, p. 40; emphasis added).

That is, the person knows that all is the same as before, but his own bodily sensations do not accord with this knowledge. The self feels detached from the outer world, and indeed, a "stranger in a strange land." Federn (1928a) believes that this may be accounted for by a disturbance in bodily feelings. Normally in accord with one's psychic image of the body, in cases of estrangement "we find that . . . the bodily ego feeling, this psychical representation of the bodily ego boundary, is always disturbed" (p. 42).

Depersonalization, on the other hand, is an interference with "inner reality." Whereas in estrangement the external perceptions are in jeopardy, in a depersonalization experience it is rather the "estrangement of some psychical functions" (1928a, p. 51), such as affect or memory, which are subject to feelings of unreality. The depersonalized individual has feelings, but complains that he does not feel them. Cognitively, there is no loss of knowledge of these affects, but there is a profoundly diminished capacity for subjectively experiencing them as belonging to one's own self. Thus, "these feelings of the patient do not seem to him genuine or evident; he feels them to be different" (Federn, 1928a, p. 52).

In both instances, we note, there is no loss of recognition, of consciousness, of either the objects of the outer world or of the content of the inner world. What *is* lost are the *sensory* elements which normally accompany encounters with the world and with the self, and for which we employ such nominals as "feeling" or "emotion." It is clearly Federn's (1928a,b, 1932, 1934) contention that it is the palpable or sensory component of being which imparts a conviction of one's "realness"; feelings, he argues, constitute the evidence of one's living self. Conscious awareness, devoid of affect, provokes the experience of the "thing-in-itself," shorn of the affective modifiers which impart life, and is why, Federn (1928a) claims, "at heart the patient feels as if he were dead . . . he feels like this because he does not feel" (p. 40).

Federn (1928a) is thus clearly asserting that while consciousness is surely a necessary aspect of being, it is not sufficient. In order that the self be truly present to itself, it is not enough to *know* that "I am"; the *cogito* is not, alone, affirmation enough of a certain self. Indeed, as the instances of estrangement and depersonalization illustrate, consciousness shorn of affect constitutes psychological pathology. Ego consciousness, in Federn's (1928a) conception, would be sufficient only if estrangement were the normative existential condition. Thus, "to repeat our formulation: combined with the consciousness of the self, there is also an *affective sense of the self*, which we designate briefly as 'ego feeling' " (Federn, 1932, p. 63; emphasis added). But what is the origin of those feelings which impart palpable reality to the self, and what explains their absence?

Borderlines

We have seen that "ego feeling" is the experience of one's own person; a persistently felt sensation of our own processes within us which imparts a sense of actuality. The I is not an idea, but "me," and "the ego must be conceived of as a *continuous experience of the psyche* and not as a conceptual abstraction" (Federn, 1928b, p. 283; emphasis added). Nonetheless, there are always variations in the extent to which some psychic processes or bodily functions are invested with ego feeling; that is, ego feeling fluctuates. Indeed, we have seen that it can be lost altogether in such instances as estrangement. Now, Federn (1928b, 1932) maintains, ego feeling changes as the cathectic investment of the ego *boundary* changes.

In fact, it is the change in ego feeling which alerts one to the very existence of ego boundaries, which normally are not sensed. It is only when an impression, either internally generated or garnered from the outside, is experienced as foreign that we become aware of the limits of the ego; of where self ends and other begins. For if that which passes an ego boundary from the external world is experienced as familiar, then, Federn (1928a, 1932) argues, it has been "egoized," or made of the self. The same may be said of affects, memories, and desires generated from within. If they pass across the internal ego boundary as recognizably "mine," then they too have become part of the self and are experienced as familiar.

Thus, the "term 'ego boundary,' " Federn (1928b) says, "shall not designate more than the existence of a perception of the extension of our ego feeling" (p. 285). It marks the scope and limits of what is experienced as self and what is not. The boundary itself is characteristically invested with ego feeling, and it is, as we have noted, only when such feeling is absent that there is any awareness of the boundary.

Now, it is at this juncture that we pause to inquire as to the source of this "feeling" which invests the ego and its boundaries and allows all that passes across to enjoy the benefits of psychic familiarity. The answer Federn (1928a,b, 1932) supplies involves an interesting modification of the libidinal explanation of narcissism and deserves a closer look, for in his reformulation Federn (1928a,b, 1932) makes some thought-provoking assertions about the self.

An Energic Assertion

In "Narcissism in the Structure of the Ego" (1928a), Federn concludes that estrangement is the result of a loss of libidinal cathexis at the ego boundary, while object cathexes remain intact. Thus, there is no loss of interest in objects, but there is an estrangement from them caused by a depletion of ego or narcissistic cathexis. Here, Federn draws the conceptual distinction between narcissistic libido and object libido, underscoring that, with respect to estrangement, "my explanation emphasizes the reduction of narcissistic cathexis" (p. 43). The evidentiary feeling of one's existence relies, in this view, upon a continuous narcissistic investment in the many functions of the body and the psyche which comprise the "whole person," and its absence is Federn's (1928a) theoretical explanation for the feelings of "unreality" of the self associated with estrangement and depersonalization. Indeed, it is not only feelings of "unreality," but the very metapsychological foundation of the ego itself which, in Federn's (1934) view, relies upon "a state of psychical cathexis of certain interdependent bodily and mental functions and contents" (p. 94). The self is sustained by, and feels real in consequence of, the continuous, simultaneous, and ongoing cathexis of all its bodily and psychic functions. Thus, the self not only requires a perpetual libidinal cathexis, the self actually is "located" within the cathexis itself. As narcissistic libido is present, so too is the self. Conversely, as narcissistic libido is diminished, so also is the self diminished. The self is present in the psychic energy which pervades the body and mind and which permits consciousness to affectively recognize (i.e., *feel*) itself.

Now narcissism had been, at least since Freud's (1914) formulative assertion, generally conceived as a libidinal cathexis of the ego, and recognized behaviorally as an excessive preoccupation with the ego. At the same time, estrangement and depersonalization both fit the behavioral description of a preoccupation with the ego, or self. How is it, then, that Federn (1928a,b) asserts that these conditions are due to a *lessening*, rather than an increase, in narcissistic libido? "How then," he asks of himself, "could Federn speak of a 'decrease in narcissism'?" (Federn, 1928b, p. 285). His reply is a curious one, and relies upon an interesting distinction which he makes between "object-loss" and "estrangement."

According to the libido theory, "object-loss" is the occasion for a withdrawal of libido back into the ego where it increases the stores of narcissistic libido and triggers a behavioral preoccupation with the self. Where there is object loss there is an increase in narcissistic libido. However, estrangement, Federn (1928b) maintains, is *not* object-loss; it is, rather, "a specific occurrence, a particular mental sensation" (p. 285), and as such it does not provoke a withdrawal of object cathexis. Indeed, we have seen that object interest remains intact despite the decrease in sensations associated with estrangement.

Now, the particular mental sensation which constitutes estrangement turns out to be a reaction of "diminished affectivity," and at the point where such diminishment occurs, that "ego boundary is less cathected with libido" (Federn, 1928b, p. 285). Thus, Federn (1928a,b) is arguing that narcissistic libido, that quality of libido which is associated with the ego itself, is what is withdrawn in instances of estrangement and, conversely, that such (narcissistic) libido is the necessary prerequisite of a sensate experience of being. In fact, Federn (1928b) continues, it is not only the ego boundary which is cathected with narcissistic libido; but rather, all of consciousness is so imbued—hence the ego feeling.

To this point we have see Federn (1928a,b, 1932) argue that estrangement illustrates the general psychological principle that the normal evidentiary sense of self is attributable to a cathectic investment of the ego boundaries with narcissistic libido. The boundaries themselves are changeable, and thus cause a concomitant change in ego feeling, which is itself an investment of consciousness with narcissistic libido. In the course of elaborating this position, Federn (1928a,b, 1932) modified the analytic understanding of narcissism by asserting that the absence of a sensory affirmation of the self is the outcome of a depletion of narcissistic libido, while the presence of such libido sustains the feeling of self. We shall now observe that he carries his argument even further, maintaining that there is a unitary feeling of ego from the start, and that the feeling is fueled by a particular manifestation of libido here introduced by Federn (1928b).

A Metapsychology of Ego

When assessed broadly, we see that Federn's (1928a,b, 1932, 1934) was an effort, not unlike Hartmann's, to elaborate a set of principles which, when taken together, would serve as the foundation for a fully developed psychology of the ego within the paradigmatic outlines of psychoanalytic theory. In following the line of his reasoning we discover that Federn (1934) has, in fact, provided a topological, economic, and overall metapsychological, formulation of the ego which serves to explain the very *phenomenology* of the ego. That is to say, the traditional axes of psychoanalytic assessment are brought together, in Federn's (1928b, 1934) formulations, to account for the subjectively felt experience of self.

From a phenomenological standpoint, then, Federn (1928a,b, 1934) conceived of the ego as the felt continuity of body and mind across time and in space, experienced as a unity. His theoretical efforts amount, in some respects, to establishing the psychoanalytic "truth" of this phenomenon and he sought to do so both by topographical and economic means.

Federn (1928b, 1934) thus endeavored to explain the uniquely human experience of *being* and at the same time *being aware* of being (i.e., "knowing that I know"), by emphasizing the ego's singular topographic relationship to consciousness, a relationship which impacts directly upon one's own understanding of and relationship to self. Thus, "the ego is both the vehicle and the object of consciousness. We speak of the ego, in its capacity as the vehicle of consciousness, as 'I myself' " (Federn, 1934, p. 95), while the ego as the object of consciousness is known as the self. In this way we see that Federn's ego, as the signification of the *feeling* experience, the I, and the *knowledge* of that feeling, the self, is the descriptive and conceptual container of a distinctly human psychology; both the source of experience, and the knowledge of that experience, it is a vessel of duality. But upon what foundation does this ego stand?

Because the ego may be experienced more or less vividly at different times, because ego feeling is a dynamic phenomenon not a static one, Federn (1928b) reasoned that the explanation for this fluctuation, as in estrangement and depersonalization, is a changing distribution of cathetic investment in the ego itself. Thus, the extent to which libido is available to the ego will determine its capacity to function and to experience itself as functioning, that is, as being. The metapsychological "basis of the ego is a state of psychical cathexis of certain independent bodily and mental functions and contents" (Federn, 1934, p. 94).

For this investment with ego feeling, Federn (1928a) has employed
the term *narcissism*.

Now, Freud (1914) himself said as much when he formed "the
idea of there being an original libidinal cathexis of the ego" (p. 75).
What distinguishes Federn's (1928b) formulation is his hypothesis that
this ego feeling, this primary narcissism, is both *present from the outset*
and is *empty of content* (i.e., is without a thought of the other object)
and *still* qualifies as fundamentally narcissistic in character (Federn,
1928b, p. 290). It is, as yet (an ego) feeling too rudimentary for mentation or emotion; it is an objectless feeling, narcissistic in the sense of
sustaining, rather than desiring, the self.

Thus, unlike Freud (1914), who asserted that "we are bound to
suppose that a unity comparable to the ego cannot exist in the individual from the start; [but that] the *ego has to be developed*" (pp. 76–77;
emphasis added), "I hold," Federn (1928b) says, "that an ego feeling
is present from the very beginning, earlier than any other content of
consciousness" (p. 290; emphasis added). It is true that at first the
feeling is vague, and the content is negligible, but there is, nonetheless,
a *sense of self* present at the inception. (We think here of Stern [1985]
who has also, as we have seen, spoken to a subjective sense of self
from the very start.)

This early "content of consciousness" is referred to by Federn
(1928b) as a "rudimentary ego feeling," and it serves as the first sense
of one's bodily ego and "also, distinctly, [as] a psychic ego feeling.
The latter is empty of mental and emotional functions" (Federn, 1928b,
p. 291). Thus does Federn stake a claim for the originary presence of
some form of discrete psychic entity, a realm of being in its own right,
and not a bodily derivative. This subjective sense of being is assigned
coequal footing with the material, and interestingly, is an objectless,
or empty sense of being, absent the other. Indeed, this "rudimentary"
self feeling is the phenomenological counterpart of Federn's (1928b)
particular metapsychological sense of primary narcissism.

An Objectless Self

In referring to the ego feeling "I might just as well," Federn (1928b)
says, "speak of . . . 'objectless narcissism' " (p. 290), for this feeling,
though it concerns self feeling and is thus broadly narcissistic, contains

no representational capacity, and is thus without an idea of the objective. The ego feeling is only the experience of the subjective. So, "as long as the child does not yet have a representation of his own ego, the ego exists only as subject . . . primary narcissism may therefore be designated as the *subject* level of the ego" (Federn, 1928b, p. 295; emphasis added). The "object" level of the ego, on the other hand, develops over time and is established and reestablished for each relationship that is encountered. This is another way of saying that while the self, the "object" level of the ego, must await representational capacity before it can successfully emerge, the I, the "subject" level, is present, and continuous and objectless from the start. Federn's (1928b) ego, then, is a descriptive term for the dual nature of the self as subject and object.

As subject, Federn's (1928b) I is formulated as a curiously "unsatisfied" state, a kind of "evenly hovering tension," in which the subjective ego feeling is constituted by the libidinal cathexes which fuel narcissism, "without, however, being autoerotically satisfied" (p. 289). Satisfaction is forestalled because the "self," the ego at the object level, is absent, for it cannot be represented. While what is absent is not subject to satisfaction, it *is* subject to desire. However, Federn (1928b) informs us that, "such a state of *lack of satisfaction* does not need to bear the character of displeasure" (p. 289; emphasis added). Indeed, the absence of satisfaction, in this objectless state of being, is more closely akin to a posture of literal suspense, in which (libidinal) desire is a state of being in itself, a kind of *"agreeable forepleasure"* (p. 289) in which, at this fundamental level, the I perpetually awaits the (self)object of desire. This condition of agreeable forepleasure, a kind of relentless anticipation, "does full justice," Federn (1928b) avows, "to the quality of the experience of healthy ego feeling" (p. 289). A "healthy" self is a self of perpetual anticipation; a self in a state of ongoing desire, absent fulfillment. Federn's I is, in this fundamental sense, defined by a lack of satisfaction. We shall have occasion to return to this view in our concluding remarks, as it bears an interesting relationship to some of the formulations of Lacan (1949) with respect to the self of desire.

An Intransitive I

We have seen that the ego feeling is invested with and sustained by an objectless primary narcissism which provides a kind of "agreeably" libidinal character to the subjective I. It is a condition in which there is, indeed, a "sensation of craving for pleasure and its satisfaction in one's own person, [but] not yet a *directing* of the libido toward oneself" (Federn, 1928b, p. 312). Federn seeks to express this psychological state by calling upon classical Greek grammar to speak his meaning. Thus does he attribute to primary narcissism the character of the "middle voice." Neither active, as in the ego's planning and thinking, nor passive, as in awaiting stimulation, the middle voice strikes a grammatical pose which is distinguished from the reflexive stance as well. For in the latter the self is able to contemplate itself as object, as in the self-love which describes actual narcissism. The middle voice is rather an intransitive or constant state reminiscent of Winnicott's (1958) "going on being," which may be expressed as "I breathe," "I grow," and "I am."

Interestingly, the British analytic theorist Balint (1958a) takes a nearly identical approach to the selfsame material, when in his paper entitled "The Concepts of Subject and Object in Psychoanalysis," he begins by observing that "the Greek originals" for the terms *subject* and *object* "were created by the philosopher grammarians of the Stoic school," and goes on to note that the meaning of subject in this school was "something essentially constant" (p. 83).

Now, as development proceeds, representational capacity emerges, and more complex, dynamic feelings and thoughts come to overlay the relative simplicity of the intransitive I. But the original ego feeling is not lost. Rather, it remains "most deeply hidden, even from one's own consciousness, [and] the entire world of primary narcissism remains extant . . . for the primary narcissistic ego (which comprised external world and individual) is repressed and becomes unconscious in its totality" (Federn, 1928b, p. 302).

Thus we see that Federn's (1928b) formulation implies what Winnicott (1960b) and later, Bollas (1987, 1992), openly propose. That there is an aspect of one's being which is unavailable to (i.e., "most deeply hidden" from) the self but which yet wields psychological influence. In Federn's (1928b, 1934) case, in health, this ego feeling is responsible for the largely unnoticed sense of continuity which is commonly felt as I, and, in pathological instances, for the feelings of estrangement, depersonalization, and psychotic detachment that he so thoroughly investigated.

The Limits of Infinity

Until Federn, psychoanalysis had not given much attention to such seemingly peripheral states as falling asleep, awakening, and, broadly speaking, to objectively unverifiable and ungeneralizable phenomena such as "feeling real," and experiencing, to varying extents, one's own sense of I. But in seeking to apply psychoanalytic principles to these intensely subjective, and distinctly psychological, sensations of being, Federn contributed to a subtle but certainly growing dimension in analytic investigations of the self which, as we have seen, would make itself increasingly manifest in the concerns of subsequent American theorists who would feel the theoretical need to account for the subjective.

Specifically, we may say of Federn that he sought to graph the vicissitudes of the subjective feeling of I along metapsychoanalytic lines, providing, for example, a distinctly libidinal explanation of the waxing and waning of self experience observed in estrangement and depersonalization; as well as attempting to provide a topographic and economic explanation for the source and original presence of a subjective sense of self. In constructing his account Federn (1926, 1928a,b, 1934) became a theorist of both the psychological limits of self and, somewhat more subtly, of its originally boundless, indeed "cosmic" reach.

As a theorist of limits, we have seen Federn (1928a,b) pursue the question of how the I is able to know, or more accurately, to sense, what is me, and what is not; what is intrinsically familiar, and what is essentially alien. We have noted his reply in the conceptualization of a differentiating ego boundary which, so long as it is libidinally charged, retains the sensate capacity to discriminate self from nonself. To a certain extent, as we shall observe at a later point in this discussion, the French theorist Anzieu (1985) will employ a related formulation of limits in elaborating his idea of the skin ego and the initial development of the self through the senses.

Now the presence of such libidinized boundaries are a necessary and desirable feature of psychological life, enabling the self to be "localized," as it were, within the confines of one's own corporeal being. One comes to believe, more or less, that one is, and can only be, where the body is. This, of course, is a psychological necessity, and we need only recall the delusional conviction of the psychotic woman cited by Norman Brown (1966) who asserts that "that's the rain. I could be the rain" (p. 160), to underscore the impracticality of adhering to psychic boundlessness. Nonetheless, in an aspect of his work whose implications have not been systematically explored, Federn (1926) asserts both that originally the I was coextensive with the universe of encountered experience, and that it precedes any perception of the body as a distinct source of sensation.

Thus, in declaring an originally limitless and commingled experience of self, or what Federn (1928b) has characterized as the "*stage of predominant primary narcissism*," in which "*the ego boundary coincides with the child's entire conceptual world*" (p. 294), he suggests a formulation of the self which began as, and to a certain extent remains, an existentially infinite psychic experience, unfettered by bodily boundaries. Thus, quite unlike Freud (1923) who, we recall, unambiguously asserted that the ego "is first and foremost a body-ego" (p. 27), Federn (1926, 1928b) rather avows the initially "mental" and "cosmic" nature of the I.

Now, as we suggested, the exclusive retention of this boundless sense of felt identity with all else leads, in Federn's (1926, 1928b, 1934) formulation, to a psychotic experience of the world. Thus, he postulates that, normatively, primary narcissism (i.e., the cosmic sense of self) is renounced, but not entirely abandoned. In fact, Federn (1928b) suggests that while "on the surface the ego feeling separates the external world from the ego" (p. 302), the initial sense of cosmic unity and universal identity continues to lead a "covert" psychological life. Thus, "clandestinely, as it were, the narcissistic cathexes . . . of the external world persist . . . [and] most deeply hidden, even from one's own consciousness, the entire world of primary narcissism remains extant" (Federn, 1928b, p. 302).

In this way, Federn is proposing that an original, and fundamentally descriptive, aspect of the self, as a cosmic commingling, is repressed as the child becomes acquainted with, and then comes to associate his being, with being in the body. Such a formulation asserts that a primary (cosmic) self is sealed over by what may be conceived of as a secondary or corporeal self, intimately allied with the body. These infantile ego feelings of absolute identity with the world "become completely unconscious in the adult, but [we] evidence their existence by the fact that they may return in psychoses. I believe," Federn (1928b) continues, that "this is a new conception since usually only repression of the object representations and their elaborations are discussed" (p. 302). Indeed, Federn does offer the innovative notion, not unlike Winnicott (1960b) would, that the self we recognize is a psychological "latecomer," one of whose essential functions is to obscure, or protect, a chronologically antecedent, and perhaps more "true" experience of being.

We conclude our discussion of Federn's (1926, 1928a,b, 1934) work by observing that his I is originally a mental experience of the infinite which is but incrementally shaped and confined by the secondarily evolved awareness of the body. Thus does Federn (1926) assert that *"mental ego feeling*, corresponding to inner perceptions, *is the first to be experienced* by the child; ego feelings related to the body and to perceptions conveyed through the body come only gradually" (p. 35; emphases added). This is, as we have suggested, a rather innovative theory of mind, particularly from a psychoanalytic standpoint, in which Federn (1926, 1928b) has declared the priority of mental experience. For we have seen that in his conceptualization, it is the psyche, not the soma, that serves as the first, and the foremost, conduit of being.

We have seen as well that Federn's is a body of work elaborated through the use of an unmistakably subjective methodology which, in turn, yielded a concept of the self decisively subjective in character. Although Federn's assertions, as a coherent theory of the phenomenal self, did not themselves secure widespread recognition, his explicit elevation of the subjective life of the self foreshadowed an unequivocal commitment to the role of the introspective in the work of Kohut (1959, 1971, 1977), and perhaps, especially, Stern (1985).

Chapter 10

THE GOOD-ENOUGH SELF OF DONALD WINNICOTT

Perhaps foremost among Klein's lasting contributions to psychoanalytic theory in general, and theories of the self in particular, remains the assertion of the determinative import of the internal psychic world of the infant. There is no more eloquent advocate of the theoretical coincidence of the self with that world than D.W. Winnicott.

The cumulative thrust of Winnicott's theoretical contribution may be read as what he himself characterized as a "search for the self" (Winnicott, 1971). Many of his most significant papers (e.g., 1958, 1959, 1960a,b, 1963, 1967) represent explorations of facets of this search, investigating as they do the circumstances under which the self's emergence is most likely to be facilitated, and the quality of experience which is apt to foster true or false self systems.

Above all, the Winnicottian self is a paradoxical phenomenon, the emergence of which relies upon the good-enough facilitation of the mother, but whose fundamental authenticity, recognized in the capacity to generate one's own sense of "realness," rests in a developed "capacity to be alone" (Winnicott, 1958). The essential and true self, we shall see, is a noncommunicative, isolated sense of realization which can only be discovered in the gaze of the other. It is the interpersonal which gives rise to the ultimately inaccessible personal, and it is the mother which occasions the birth of that which, if genuinely established, no other can truly know.

Winnicott's work is not a unified theoretical statement, but is more accurately characterized as a series of fertile reflections upon the nature of selfhood drawn from clinical experience. The ensuing

227

discussion will select from among the many Winnicottian contributions a few particularly salient, and in some instances less frequently assessed, papers which when taken in the aggregate offer a view of the self as an interpersonally facilitated private creation.

Perhaps we may best proceed by imposing a somewhat artificial division upon Winnicott's theory of the self such that we tease from the flow of his work two distinct tributaries. The first of these we shall understand as the external, or environmentally triggered, source of the self; the second the internal, or privately created, source. Without the former, the potential for the latter will wither; without the latter, the former is but a stage upon which the self is "merely a player." Thus, we shall proceed in this discussion by exploring the outside, the inside, and finally, the paradox that true being is an isolation capable of creation only in the presence of the mother. We begin, then, by asking, from whence the self?

Being and Not Being

Winnicott (1960a) has addressed many aspects of the human infant's journey from absolute dependence toward the achievement of independence, but for our purposes in seeking the origins of the Winnicottian self, perhaps none is so central as the role of maternal care in triggering human being, and then protecting it from the vortex of nonbeing or annihilation. It is certainly so, of course, that maternal responsiveness must include attention to the somatic demands of the helpless infant, and indeed, it is precisely in the course of such ministrations that the ego is transformed from an unintegrated to an integrated state, and the infant attains what Winnicott (1960a) has called "unit status."

That is to say, by dint of the good-enough presence of the mother the infant undergoes a linking of previously discrete functional events, such as motor and sensory experiences, which yield a continuous sense of being. Thus, the "holding phase" enables the infant to become a biologically organized entity in which the sensory, motoric, and to a certain extent cognitive functions of the ego are synthesized. But of particular significance to our search is the recognition that adequate environmental holding is the singular condition under which such integration may occur. Indeed, so critical to the Winnicottian theory of the origin of the self is the environmental function, made operational by each particular mother, that "there is no value whatever in describing babies in the earliest stages except in relation to the mother's functioning" (Winnicott, 1962a, p. 57).

Thus, we see that the infant achieves a sense of his own integrated, continuous being, his "selfness," as she or he is held by the mother. Holding provides the essential condition for transforming the infant from an unintegrated biological potential to a psychological reality cognizant of its own being. Indeed, as we shall have occasion to note below, aspects of the work of the British object relations theorist Bollas (1987) will underscore and build upon the transformational impact of the prearticulate mother in the formation of the self.

Now the experiential knowledge of continuity, that is, of being, carries with it the inevitable anxiety associated with *dis*continuity or nonbeing. Prior to the stage of ego integration, disintegration could hold no meaning, but once this stage has been attained, "the infant retains the capacity for reexperiencing unintegrated states" (Winnicott, 1960a, p. 44), and the possibility of such an event coming to pass is the occasion for profound infantile distress.

The maternal environment is thus not only the condition under which the infant's inherited potential for a particular personal being (i.e., the self) is actualized, it is also the matrix within which such being is sustained or jeopardized. This self is a fragile continuity, readily subject to the psychological experience of what Winnicott (1960a, 1962) has called annihilation. Thus, both being and nonbeing are in the hands of the mother.

Nonbeing is not, at this first dawn of infantile selfhood, a fear of death, for as Winnicott (1960a) observes, it is only when "a whole human person can be hated [that] death has meaning" (p. 47). At this early juncture there is not yet any conception of a whole other. Nonbeing is, rather, the simple interruption of being. When the thread of continuity is broken, "going on being" is annihilated. Being is a steady state and is to be understood as the experiential opposite of reacting, which necessarily disrupts the balance of being. Thus does Winnicott (1960a) assert that "being and annihilation are the two alternatives" (p. 47). Any invasion of the infant's steady experience of being, such as hunger, wetness, noise, is an immediate threat to that being, an anxiety associated with the possibility of nonbeing. Such invasions or impingements demanding the infant's reaction, jeopardize the fragile integrity of the germinating self. For this "central self could be said to be the inherited potential *which is experiencing a continuity of being''* (Winnicott, 1960a, p. 46; emphasis added), and when such continuity is not protected, that is, when the infant must react rather than be, she or he is subject to not being. Thus, "the holding environment . . . has as its main function the reduction to a minimum of the impingements to which the infant must react with resultant annihilation of personal being'' (Winnicott, 1960a, p. 47).

But we have here only partially responded to our inquiry, whence the Winnicottian self? We have seen that, not unlike Hartmann (1939), Winnicott (1960a, 1962) also asserts that the inherited potential to become a personal self emerges within an *environment*. Unlike Hartmann (1939), however, and perhaps more in kinship with Mahler (1967; Mahler et al., 1975) in this respect, Winnicott (1960a, 1962) has personalized that environment (i.e., distinctly placing other persons in determinative roles), specifically attributing to each child's particular mother the weight of an individualized environment, charged with the task of bringing forth, of birthing in the psychological sense, an infantile self and protecting it from fragmentation. So the self, we may conclude, emerges and is sustained within the holding environment of the mother, who is, of course, the child's first and original other (i.e., not-me). But what is it, in particular, about that environmental mother that sparks the self into being?

In the Eye of the Holder

When the infant looks at the mother's face what, Winnicott (1967) asks, does she or he see? The baby, we learn, sees no less than his or her own self residing there. For, optimally, the mother's face is a reflection of what she has seen when gazing upon her child. Indeed, the mother's own visage is transformed by the vision of her child, and in turn, the child's unwitting capacity to thus transform the mother establishes the condition sine qua non of his or her own emergence as a *true* self. True, because the child sees reflected in the mother what was and is there in the child for the mother to see. It is a reflection of the child's own creation waiting to be (re)discovered by that child.

In this way does the baby create itself. For the image found on the mother's face is an image of what the child's own being has caused to be there; the mother's face, to the extent that it reflects the child, is thus the child's first creation. The baby's own being has fashioned the face upon which she or he, in turn, will discover the self. In this way the baby genuinely creates his or her own self by blindly casting being upon the "face of the deep," there to grasp, in the mother's transformed image, the rudimentary *knowledge* of that being. It is the "good-enough" face of the mother which shows the child the self which was there but which could not otherwise have been apprehended. If what is upon the mother's face is the child's being, then the self the child sees is his or her authentic or "true" self. Thus does Winnicott (1967) unambiguously respond to his own query, "what does the baby see when he or she looks at the mother's face? I am suggesting that, ordinarily, what the baby sees is himself or herself" (p. 112).

In this way it is possible to envision the mother's face serving as the canvas upon which the baby's own spontaneous gesture fashions his or her own particular image, there to be discovered by its creator. But the child cannot make this discovery of his own spontaneously created self without the reliable participation of the reflecting mother. For it is only the mother who is able to organize the baby's unwitting gestures, she renders them continuous by their regular appearance upon the face, thus affirming and reaffirming not only the child's existence, but his sense of omnipotent influence upon the realness of his being.

It is the mother's reliable availability as a sensitive reflection of the child's own gestures which nurtures genuine being and fosters its emergence. Thus, "it is an essential part of my theory that the True Self does not become a living reality except as a result of the mother's repeated success in meeting the infant's spontaneous gesture . . . " (Winnicott, 1960b, p. 145). Thus is the true and authentic self, the child's own spontaneous creation, held by the mother, there for the child to behold.

But what of the mother who does not, who perhaps cannot, reflect her child? Whose face displays her own mood, or need, or defense? What does the baby see in such instances? When there is a regular failure to find the self in the mother "they look," Winnicott (1967) asserts, "and they do not see themselves" (p. 112). Rather, the child sees the mother's actual face and becomes accustomed to the notion that it is what will be found at the end of his looking. In such cases "the mother's face is not then a mirror. So perception takes the place of apperception, perception takes the place of that which might have been the beginning of a significant exchange with the world, a two-way process in which self-enrichment alternates with the discovery of meaning in the world of seen things'' (Winnicott, 1967, p. 113). The child in such a situation cannot find himself in the world; at least not his spontaneously experienced self.

Instead, if an unrecognized, and effectively ''foreign,'' that is, nonreflective, image is persistently substituted for the child's own gestures, the child, Winnicott (1960b, 1967) says, will eventually begin to conform his gestures to accommodate what is presented. ''This compliance on the part of the infant is the earliest stage of the False Self'' (Winnicott, 1960b, p. 145). The extent to which the false or compliant self, marked by varying degrees of living by imitation, comes to predominate, depends upon a number of circumstances which will not be discussed in this context. We will note, however, that under all circumstances it is the overriding role of the false self system to protect and even to foster the true self system. Thus, ''the False Self, if successful in its function, hides the True Self, or else finds a way of enabling the True Self to start to live'' (Winnicott, 1960b, p. 148).

The source of the Winnicottian self, the font from whence one's sense of realness, or lack thereof, derives, is quite literally contained in the gaze of the mother. Indeed, if the spontaneous self is repeatedly given back to the child upon the face of the mother, or the ''good-enough analyst,'' then the baby or the client ''will find his or her own self, and will be able to exist and to feel real. [And] feeling real is more than existing; it is finding a way to exist as oneself, and to relate to objects as oneself, and to have a self into which to retreat for relaxation'' (Winnicott, 1967, p. 117).

A Mediate Vision

Thus, as we have seen, the self is, in this view, a derivative of the reflecting face; the outcome of indirection. It is known only through the mediation of the mirror that is the mother. Unlike Lacan (1949), whose influence if not his conclusions in this respect are readily acknowledged, Winnicott (1967) does not subscribe to the formative impact of the actual mirror. Whereas Lacan (1949), we recall, asserted that it is to the child's ''jubilant assumption of his specular image . . . before it is objectified in the dialectic of identification with the other''

(p. 2), that an early, indeed presocial, self may be attributed, Winnicott (1967) concludes that "the actual mirror has significance mainly in its figurative sense" (p. 118). Nonetheless, for both Lacan (1949) and Winnicott (1967), these significant differences notwithstanding, the self is the result not of direct, but of mediated, that is, reflected experience. Both seem to suggest that the reality of the self, not unlike Kantian reality generally, can only be mediate, not immediate, knowledge.

In addressing the significant distinctions between Lacan's (1949) and Winnicott's (1967) disparate visions, however, we reiterate that it is rather to the actual mother, and thereby to the actual relation to the object, that Winnicott credits the self. Herein rests the Winnicottian paradox, for the self, we see, cannot come to fruition without the stimulus of the mother, specifically, though not exclusively, in her reflection of that self. But it is also of the essence of this selfhood that "at the centre of each person is an incommunicado element" (Winnicott, 1963, p. 187). The self is an interpersonally established being which communicates, and often enjoys such communication, yet at the same time "each individual is an isolate, permanently non-communicating, permanently unknown, in fact unfound" (Winnicott, 1963, p. 187). The self is interpersonal; the self is an isolate; it must be discovered in the other yet is, at its core, inaccessible to the other. Let us see how this antinomy obtains.

The "Secret Self"

Winnicott (1960b, 1963) developed the concept of a true self in order to explain the pathological phenomenon of hollow, compliant, and imitative, that is, "false" being. The true self, Winnicott (1963) suggests, is the outcome of primitive defensive operations, called into play specifically to protect against felt threats to the "isolated core" of the personality. And "the defense consists in a further hiding of the secret self" (Winnicott, 1963, p. 187), such that it will avoid being violated by invasive communication.

Thus, the true self is a construct designed to render comprehensible "false," or imitative, behavior. The true self is the psychological "reason" that compliant and empty behavior manifests itself. It is a kind of decoy performance, distracting the would-be mother, foiling attempts to reach one's essential, or "true," being. Winnicott extrapolates from the symptomatic, but seeks to reach beyond it to fashion a statement in which "real health need not be described only in terms of the residues . . . of what might have been illness-patterns" (Winnicott, 1963, p. 184). Winnicott (1963) asserts that all individuals, not only those who must divide existence into true and false constellations for protective purposes, come to possess an aspect of being which is not available to communication with the external, or objective, world. This inaccessible, isolated center of being engages only in a kind of silent, internal communication. Thus does Winnicott (1963) postulate a kernel self whose initial and eternal character is unremediably isolated.

Importantly, this silent communication engaged in by the core self "concerns the subjective aspects of objects" (p. 185). Subjective objects, Winnicott (1963) suggests, are essentially autistic in character; possessing no capacity for generalization. Such "objects," or constellations of experience, are based largely upon bodily phenomena and are described by Winnicott (1963) as "cul-de-sac communication," for they lead "no where" so far as can be *objectively* determined. Nonetheless, such communication is intimately associated with one's knowledge of one's "realness," bound up as it is with that which is profoundly idiosyncratic.

In fact, what Winnicott (1963) is here suggesting is the idea that there is an early core of selfness which is entirely subjective and which is experienced, both at the outset, and henceforth, as that aspect of one's being which is most genuinely actual or real. We note that self is not an admixture; but rather a pure culture of subjectivity. In this we recall many of the theorists discussed herein, most notably Kernberg, Kohut, and Stern in the American tradition, whose work both singly and in the aggregate attests to the original impact of the subjective. In this Winnicott (1963) shares in what we are discovering is a consistent, if not regularly revealed, commitment to a self coincident with subjectivity.

Now, in suggesting a self whose initial, and forever central, aspect coheres in the course of silently communicating with its own being, Winnicott (1963) is, in effect, introducing a phase in psychic development which is prior to Klein's "internal world" and indeed serves as a forerunner of it. For, as Winnicott (1963) maintains, Klein's internal world asks a level of mastery over such mental mechanisms as introjection and projection, for example, which cannot have yet been achieved during the earliest period of infantile life of which they both speak. Thus, while not repudiating her claims about the nature and complexity of the internal psychic life, Winnicott's (1963) object is "to get to a very early version of that which Melanie Klein referred to as 'internal' " (p. 185). Most interestingly, Winnicott's (1963) early version comes to characterize the internal as coterminous with the nascent self. It is not, at first, an interpersonal self, but rather a wholly personal and subjective self, which emerges. Thus, "at this early stage 'inner' only means personal, and personal in so far as the individual is a person with a self in process of becoming evolved" (Winnicott, 1963, p. 185).

Thus we observe that Winnicott (1963) posits a self whose genesis is subjective; and an infant whose first experiences of being, and of being *real*, are founded in phenomena not subject to modification by the external. And one of his explicitly intended consequences in so positing was to retain, by chronological modification, the efficacy of Klein's internal world. But what of our initial contention that the Winnicottian self is an anomalous construct? We have seen that it is a self which is sparked into being as it is reflected on the mother's actual face, and also a self which is most authentic when it is essentially idiosyncratic and incommunicable. How is the interpersonal to be reconciled with the personal in seeking the origins of the self? Perhaps the beginning of understanding rests in the Winnicottian paradox that *"it is a joy to be hidden but disaster not to be found"* (Winnicott, 1963, p. 186).

On Being Alone

Authentic contact with the self, we have seen, is largely a secreted event; hidden from external impingement, the self is most real only when it is most solitary. The self establishes contact with itself, is able to *be*, as it is able to be alone. But the ability, the capacity, to be alone, Winnicott (1958) avows, is a developed, not an inherited, capacity. It, and with it the self, must be *achieved*. Thus, though there is a hidden, core self in silent communication with subjective phenomena, it is not yet an actual, but more truly a potential self. The actual self, the self which possesses the capability to achieve its essential reality in exclusive communication with its own subjectivity, can only evolve interpersonally. How does Winnicott (1958) construct and maintain this paradox?

The Language of Interiority

Despite his avowed intent to explore the individual's capacity to be
alone, Winnicott (1958) allows that "it will be appreciated that *actually*
to be alone is not what I am discussing" (p. 30; emphasis added). In
fact, Winnicott (1958) is discussing the developed capacity to function
in a solitary or exclusively subjective state, but he is not thereby implying that to do so means to be without the mother. Indeed, that is
the Winnicottian paradox upon which the capacity rests: for "although
many types of experience go to the establishment of the capacity to
be alone, there is one that is basic . . . [and] *this experience is that of
being alone, as an infant and small child, in the presence of mother*"
(Winnicott, 1958, p. 30).

The mother is an indispensable element in the equation which
yields the mature ability to seek out and enjoy a relationship solely
with one's self. Thus we see that the most authentic facet of the Winnicottian self is that which faces inward and converses with its own
subjectivity. Yet at the same time, this conversation can only occur if
it is the face of the mother with whom one subjectively speaks. Now,
in constructing this paradox in which aloneness requires the presence
of the other, Winnicott (1958) "attempt[s] to use another language"
(p. 31); a language which builds upon Melanie Klein's conceptual
contribution, the internal object.

In resting his paradox upon the internal world of objects it becomes possible to see that in a psychological sense the self is never
alone, for the inner life is "peopled" with internalized others; the
subjective self is composed of objective others, transformed as they
become part of the subjective world, into thoroughly personal, or subjective objects. (We recall here the transmuting effect of internalization
to which Kohut referred, and the metaphor of metabolic absorption via
internalization on which Kernberg drew, for example.) Thus,
"aloneness," and with it the singular subjective experience of one's
"real self," rests with the successful transformation of the objective
world into the subjective. "The capacity to be alone depends on the
existence of a good object in the psychic reality of the individual"
(Winnicott, 1958, pp. 31–32). The "true" and authentic experience of
self as a private subjectivity, inaccessible to others, insists upon the
internalized presence of the mother in the child's inner world. That
world must be experienced as the baby's own creation.

On Creating the World

The transformation of which Winnicott (1958, 1959) speaks does not involve, on the baby's part, any experience with the object, or knowledge of it other than as an aspect of interiority. This is important, for it underscores the subjective nature not only of the self, but of existence in its entirety. Winnicott (1958, 1959) appears to be asserting that, in effcct, the only reality is that which is internally generated; that which is able to be felt as part of the "inside." Indeed, he asks the reader to consider the fact that even in adulthood "an external object has no being for you or me except insofar as you or I hallucinate it, but being sane we take care not to hallucinate except where we know what to see" (Winnicott, 1959, p. 54). The world of objective reality is lately and developmentally achieved, and does not supplant, but rather takes a place alongside of, an antecedent and more authentic experience of subjective reality. And this transition occurs, Winnicott (1958, 1959, 1963) maintains, as the mother actively participates in the baby's hallucinatory creations.

Thus, in the beginning, Winnicott (1958, 1959) seems to suggest, there is no objective other; there is only the subjective, to which everything that is encountered belongs. To the extent that the good-enough mother participates in this infantile illusion, the baby is able to make use of external objects, experiencing them as "real" and "mine" and subject to personal use. It is in this sense that Winnicott (1959) refers to the infant self's omnipotent creation of the object, for if the mother is able to present the object to the child as the child is imagining it, then "by letting a real object be just where the infant is hallucinating an object . . . the infant gains the illusion that the world can be created and that what is created is the world" (Winnicott, 1959, p. 53). This early omnipotence is optimally modified such that it becomes an experience of personal efficacy; the sense that one is the author of his or her own ineffable privacy; the true creator of the (internal) world.

Summary

We have seen that in elaborating his notion of the self Winnicott (1958, 1959, 1960a,b, 1962, 1963, 1967) tempers, and then builds upon, the Kleinian internal world. First he suggests that Klein's internal world is too complex to be present from the outset, and posits an anterior phase in which there is only the purely personal experience associated with one's own body which is not subject to external influence. This, Winnicott suggests, is the self, but in an evolving, potential state. The actual self requires the environmental trigger that is the mother, specifically in her capacity to reflect the child's own being upon her face, there for the child to find.

Further, we have noted that the Winnicottian self is most genuinely felt to be real when experienced as a solitary exchange with one's own subjectivity. But at the same time, it is ultimately a paradoxical self, for in order to attain this condition of realness, there must have been, and must continue to be, a regularly available mother present, first actually and then psychically. It is a singular and subjective self whose emergence and sustenance calls for the continued availability of many objective (m)others.

The next chapter will engage a discussion of Winnicott's contemporary, Balint, who was exploring many related facets of the development of the self.

Chapter 11

THE BASIC SELF OF MICHAEL BALINT

Michael Balint (1937, 1958a,b, 1968), not unlike Winnicott, concentrated his theoretical efforts upon the earliest stages of infantile development, seeking there some more fundamental explanation of psychological being than instinctual gratification appeared to provide. Balint (1952), again in conceptual kinship with Winnicott (1960a,b), did not subscribe to the notion that the infant becomes psychologically related to the object only gradually. Indeed, in keeping with an evolving theoretical Weltanschauung, largely fashioned by the definitive work of Melanie Klein, Balint (1937, 1958a,b 1968) was also proposing that a state of interpersonal relatedness is present nearly from the outset, and is a necessary precondition in the evolution of the individual. Let us see how the self emerges under Balint's clinical scrutiny.

A Primary Connection

Writing in 1937, Balint was in the midst of the theoretical furor, or what he referred to as "the confusion of tongues" (p. 103), then extant among the "Londoners," or Kleinians and the "Viennese," or Anna Freudians over the nature of the earliest state of infantile being. Whereas the "Londoners," briefly, subscribed to the view that the infant comes into the world in an utterly self-absorbed condition, that is, of primary narcissism, and whose behavior is very quickly "driven" by intense sadistic and aggressive impulses, the "Viennese" were skeptical regarding the pervasive presence and intensity of such impulses, and were inclined to doubt as well whether the human mind was even capable of recalling, let alone lending verbal expression to, such early experiences.

Balint (1937) entered into the midst of this controversy in the characteristic garb of the "middle" or "independent" minded theoreticians then evolving among British psychoanalysts, to offer an alternative hypothesis which, he believed, would account for the observed data which pointed to a greedy, insatiable infant given to unmistakable bouts of hostility, without having to embrace primary narcissism or the Kleinian commitment to sadistic and aggressive depictions of the psyche. At the same time, Balint's (1937) proposal will, he asserts, offer some insight into the earliest state of mind, something not, in his view, adequately addressed by the "Viennese."

Extrapolating from clinical observation, Balint (1937) suggests that infantile frustration and expressions of aggression, not unlike the hostile and sadistically colored phantasies of his adult patients, may be more accurately explained by the mother's, or analyst's, failure to gratify what is perhaps best described as intimacy needs, or wishes for intimate association. This does not, Balint (1937) emphasizes, refer so much to the intimacy of libidinal satisfaction. On the contrary, and quite importantly for his development of a distinct object relations explanation, the nature of the earliest infantile wishes are, first, "*without exception . . . directed towards an object,* and second *never go beyond the level of fore-pleasure*" (Balint, 1937, p. 98).

That is to say, the frustrations and hostilities observed in the infant, not unlike the ofttimes vehement sadistic and aggressive expressions of the adult patient, are theoretically explained in terms of an unsuccessful experience of relatedness to the mother in the earliest developmental phase of infantile life. The infant does not begin life as a narcissistically self-involved being, driven by impulses alone, but is, instead, object-seeking, and specifically in need of the purely psychological experience of security and contented well-being that only another object imparts. Balint (1937) rather unequivocally asserts that "in my opinion a very early, most likely earliest, phase of the extra-uterine mental life is not narcissistic; *it is directed towards objects*" (p. 98; emphasis added).

Balint (1937) refers to this early phase as one of "primary or primitive object-love," and reiterates that "this form of object-relation is not linked to any of the erotogenic zones . . . *but is something on its own*" (p. 101; emphasis added). The object is sought in its own right, for its psychological value to the emerging infantile self. Thus, in positing a condition of primary object love to supplant primary narcissism, Balint (1937), like Winnicott, and other object relations theorists generally, removes the development of human being from a primary reliance upon the vicissitudes of the drive. They assert instead that the infantile self is a product of the quality of relatedness achieved in this early, even primary, phase of development.

In what follows we shall take a closer look at the different levels of self experience proposed by Balint (1958b, 1968), but first we shall undertake a brief review of an infrequently discussed paper in which Balint (1958a) draws some interesting semantic distinctions among subject and object and sets the psychoanalytic stage for his assertions regarding the nature of self.

Harmonious "Mix-Ups" and the Nature of Self

In "The Concepts of Subject and Object in Psychoanalysis" (1958a), Balint undertakes to discuss the psychoanalytic object as a secondary phenomenon, only gradually manifest along the infant's horizon of discovery; a relative "late-comer" psychologically, having been ontologically preceded by a primary state of subject–object blur. This argument buttresses his earlier assertion of a state of primary object-love but seems to suggest that while the object is *sought*, it is not yet *known*.

Briefly stated, Balint's (1958a) semantic introduction includes his observation that for a considerable time nature, or life, was conceived of as a collection of clearly delineated, separate, and durable entities, termed *objects*, derived from the Latin sense suggesting that which "lies against," or has resistance. Regarding the characteristics imparted by the sense of object, Balint makes the interesting observation that "we conceive the objects, the ultimate constituents of the world, as we wish to see ourselves, or perhaps even as we really see ourselves: firm, unchangeable, indestructible, in fact, eternal" (p. 84). Although he does not elaborate upon this thought-provoking statement, it is possible to read in it the suggestion that the self seeks to affirm its tangible, enduring *presence*, that is, its *objective* status.

The term *object* connotes that which is firm and resistant in the world. Those aspects of the same world which are not solid, however, do not tend to offer resistance, and possess no exact contours, and are known by words such as *substrate* and *substance*, both of which denote that which constitutes the essential matter of a phenomenon, rather than what is incidental. Substances or substrates lend support to that which is accidental or serve as a foundation for it. Balint (1958a) points out that such words clearly share a linguistic root with *subject*, frequently used when indicating ourselves (i.e., our *selves*), thereby suggesting that self shares in the qualities of foundation and "essentialness." Finally, Balint reminds the reader that *matter* and *matrix* also share a common root denoting *mother*.

All this is to say, with Balint (1958a), that "the inescapable inference is that at one time there must have been a harmonious mix-up in our minds between ourselves and the world around us and, that our 'mother' was involved in it" (p. 85). Thus the certain inference, if not the assertion, that the "subject-matter," the "self-mother/matrix," is the essential antecedent of the object; indeed, is the necessary foundation for its emergence. The subjective sustains the objective, and it is only from within the subjective and embracing matrix of self and mother that the object is distinguished. Now, although the "mix-up" of which Balint (1958a) spoke may "strike us as childish and primitive, we must admit," he asserts, "that it preceded our 'modern,' 'adult,' or 'scientific,' picture of the world which, so to speak, grew out of it" (p. 85). From this semantic prologue Balint (1958a) proceeds to elaborate a developmental schema which suggests that the ontological elaboration of the individual self follows a psychic path already foreshadowed in the very words by which we speak the subject of the self.

Thus, as suggested earlier, Balint (1958a) reaffirms his assertion that there is an early developmental phase of primitive or primary object-love which indeed does presuppose an experience of the external world, the world of objects, "but assumes that there exists a harmony between the individual and his world, that there cannot be any clash of interest between the two" (Balint, 1958a, p. 87). As such, if harmony prevails, there is no psychological knowledge of objects, there is only, in this early stage, experiential knowledge of the self.

The rudimentary self, not unlike the regressed patients from whom Balint (1958a, 1968) has drawn his more generalized explanations, is unaware of anything but self experience, and indeed, the self in Balint's (1958a) view antedates the yet to be discovered object. For in the period of primary object-love "there are as yet no objects, although there is already an individual who is surrounded by and floats in substances'' (Balint, 1958a, p. 87). The object awaits discovery. Now, it is precisely when Balint's (1958a, 1968) postulated harmony is disrupted that the object is encountered. The ruptured unity reveals the undeniably sharp-edged, immovable object and it is, paradoxically, in this discovery of the tangible, and present, object, that the self, essentially as an experience of emptiness or absence, is also first encountered in a psychologically reflective sense. This rupture is, in Balint's coinage, the area of the *basic fault*, and it represents one critical area, or level of being. We turn now to an investigation of the nature of these realms of the mind.

Levels of Being

At more or less the same time that Winnicott (1958a, 1960a, 1971) was suggesting that the self may be described as a Januslike entity, revealing one "false" face to the world, and obscuring, at an inaccessible level of the mind, the other "true" face, Balint (1958b, 1968) was also pursuing the idea that there are areas or levels of the mind which are characterized by different qualities of internal relationship, and which speak to different qualities, or aspects, of self. Like Winnicott (1958a, 1960a, 1971), Balint's (1958a,b, 1968) work extended the explanatory reach of psychoanalytic investigation by ranging into the psychological period prior to that of the oedipal, seeking, in effect, to speak with more authority about the emergence of a self not primarily characterized in terms of libidinal domination.

Thus, Balint (1958b, 1968) went on to theorize that there are three areas of the mind, two of which characterize states of the self not associated with instinctual conflict, and a third describing the ambivalent and conflicted experience of the self associated with oedipal strife. Balint (1958b, 1968) designated these three areas as the oedipal level, the level of the basic fault, and the level of creation. Each is characterized primarily by the number of people involved in relationship and the quality of their relatedness.

The oedipal level, which is not the primary focus of Balint's (1958b, 1968) extended investigation, is recognized by a triangular relational configuration; that is, the subject and at least two other objects are involved with each other. As well, the quality of relatedness is here marked by conflict as the child seeks to sort out the complexities of his libidinal attachments.

The area or level of the basic fault is perhaps most often associated with Balint's (1968) contribution to psychoanalytic theory development, and it is under this rubric that he seeks to explain not only the clinical phenomena of "emptiness," or "deadness," experienced by many patients, but even the discovery of the object and of the self. In the area of the basic fault relationships are characterized as "two-person" only, and the presence of a third is experienced as an unwelcome burden. Relatedness is not characterized by conflict, nor is it inspired by instinct. Rather, it is in the area of the basic fault that primary object-love predominates, and it is in this area as well that such unbounded, "mixed-up," love encounters the introduction of more or less severe irregularities (i.e., "fault lines") impacting upon this otherwise seamless psychological experience.

A basic fault, then, is a rent in the harmoniously patterned fabric of relationship between infant and caretaker which results in the simultaneous discovery by the infant of the object and of an experienced threat to security. Not unlike Winnicott's (1960a) infant, faced with the alternatives of being or annihilation, Balint's (1958b, 1968) infant knows either "fit" or "fault."

In this sense there is a differentiation which emerges within each infant–mother matrix as it inevitably endures the normative disruptions which prompt the emergence of a differentiated self. The distinction between "fault" and differentiation "may be traced back to a considerable discrepancy in the early formative phases of the individual between his . . . needs and the . . . care and affection available . . . " (Balint, 1958b, p. 337). Thus, we cannot fail to note that here, as in the Winnicottian elaboration, and indeed the evolving object relational view of the self generally, the quality of self experience relies almost entirely upon the vicissitudes of the object world. "I put the emphasis," Balint (1958b) advises, "on the lack of 'fit' between the child and *the people* who represent his environment" (p. 337).

We turn now to Balint's (1958b, 1968) area of creation, an infrequently discussed realm in which "the subject is on his own and his main concern is to produce something out of himself" (p. 337). This level of the mind is characterized by the complete absence of an external object; relatedness is exclusively to the self. The area of creation is not the center of Balint's (1958b, 1968) theoretical attention and he has said comparatively little in the way of elaborating upon this idea. Nonetheless, it remains interesting in that its primary character seems to be that it is virtually inaccessible to the other. In the analytic setting it is not amenable to transferential manifestations, and one may only infer this state of being by the subject's ambiguous silence. Thus, while in many cases, Balint (1958b) allows, a patient's silence indicates an effort to avoid, or run away from, a difficulty, "it is equally correct that he *is running towards* something, i.e., a state in which he feels relatively safe" (p. 338). Such a state is precisely the area of creation; an area neither visible nor tangibly available to the observing other. Rather, it would seem to be a dimension of self whose presence is inferred by absence.

This feature of self experience is, not unlike aspects of Winnicott's (1958, 1960a) self, paradoxical in nature. For as Balint (1968) asserts, "we know that there are no 'objects' in the area of creation, but we know also that . . . the subject is not entirely alone there" (p. 25). Thus we encounter again the phenomenon of the subject which absolutely requires the "good-enough" object, as in Balint's (1952) state of primary object love. It is most creative, or spontaneously authentic in Winnicott's (1960a) sense, when engaged in the solitary act of creation or what Winnicott (1958) might have referred to as "being alone." Parenthetically, creativity and aloneness are frequent, if not exclusive, psychic companions.

Balint (1968) suggests that the area of creation is marked not, as we have noted, by the presence of objects, but of preobjects, entities so primitive that they possess no organization or sense of wholeness. Indeed, exchanges between the articulating self and actual objects is predicated upon what amounts to the subjective creation of the objective world. For, "only after the work of creation has succeeded in making them [preobjects] 'organized,' or 'whole,' can a proper 'verbal,' or 'Oedipal,' interaction [with] external objects take place" (Balint, 1968, p. 25). The subject must, by a solitary act of creation, transform preobjects into objects, thus constituting the idiosyncratically known world.

Summary

Thus we see that Balint (1952, 1958a,b, 1968) proposes a tripartite schema of mind which descriptively and dynamically addresses the variety of self experience. We note that Balint (1952, 1958a,b, 1968), like Winnicott (1958, 1960a,b, 1962, 1967, 1971), proposes a self utterly reliant upon the object mother, yet asserts that an important and ongoing feature of that subject remains inaccessible to that object. It is the object, then, that creates the condition for the subject, which in turn creates from the preobject the object. This, we recall, bears a marked similarity to Winnicott's (1967) own assertion that the infant creates its own self in the mirrored gaze of the mother.

Perhaps the pivot upon which both Balint's (1958b, 1968) and Winnicott's (1958, 1960a, 1967) self turns is the common commitment to the notion of "self-in-waiting," that is, a potential self, which must be awakened, whether within Balint's (1952) matrix of primary object-love or Winnicott's (1960a,b) holding environment, by a proactive and responsive actual object. The core experience of self is reliant upon the presence of the other.

Yet it is equally so, for Balint as for Winnicott, that the essence of authenticity, the experience of creation or of the true self, occurs beyond the reach of that selfsame mother object. Thus it is that the self is made present by the mother and realized in her absence, for the object must be present for the subject to emerge, yet the subject most authentically emerges as it is most truly alone, and apart from the object.

Both Winnicott and Balint conceive of the self as the developing differentiation of a psychic entity from an encompassing matrix; and both draw upon extensive clinical observation in fashioning their respective statements. However, neither explicitly extends the implications of their assertions, both of which contain at least an implied questioning of the libidinal origins of the self, into a fully developed alternate theory of the structure of the mind and the nature of the self.

Chapter 12

THE PERSONAL SELF OF HARRY GUNTRIP

Guntrip (1971, 1975), not unlike Fairbairn, was committed to the view that impersonal instincts were not the fundamental structuring elements of the self. Rather, like his colleagues, Guntrip (1971, 1975), asserted that it is relationship which gives rise to an increasingly elaborated psychic structure, and sought to draw a clear distinction between biology and psychodynamics.

In comity with Winnicott (1965), for example, he held that the maturational processes, such as biological ones, were of central importance in accounting for the innate potential that could, in part, determine the quality and kind of object relationships the baby might have. However, such considerations were unquestionably, in his view, secondary to the "proper business" of psychoanalysis, which was "studying the unique individual person growing in the medium of interpersonal relations" (Guntrip, 1971, p. 103).

Guntrip (1971, 1975) was an unambiguous champion of the theoretical views of both Fairbairn and Winnicott, and undertook in his own work to fashion some interesting elaborations and modest extensions to those contributions. Thus, in the case of Fairbairn, Guntrip (1971) believed that the endopsychic situation did not adequately account for the regressed states he himself observed in his own work with schizoid individuals. Thus did Guntrip (1971) speculate that, by way of a split in Fairbairn's libidinal self, one internal aspect of the self in fact withdrew from all object relationships while another engaged in increasingly furious, even compulsive, internal object relations in an effort to avert the disastrous loss of self threatened by the withdrawal. In this we note that Guntrip's (1961) proposal implies, perhaps even more strongly than Fairbairn's (1952b), the role of the internal object relationship, not only in establishing states of the self, but in its very survival as well.

Interestingly, in postulating that a facet of the self breaks away entirely from the object, occasioning an experience of basic existential terror for the individual, Guntrip (1971) seems to suggest that there is a self experience totally devoid of the other. It is, we may say, an experience of self as "lost," or "empty," or even "absent." It is an experience made possible precisely because a second remnant of self remains attached to the object, and thus seems to be able to retain a slippery psychological foothold from which to observe, and experience, the terrible psychological demise of another part of the self.

Guntrip (1975) integrated his views concerning this primitive self experience by employing Winnicott's (1961) notions of being and doing, extending them into a more fully evolved draft addressing the development of the self. In so doing, Guntrip (1971, 1975) amplified the view that the self was found not in action, but in being. While the individual surely has bodily demands, and vast mental capacities, the overriding human imperative, Guntrip (1971) avows, is to discover one's own self and, in an ongoing fashion, bring that self into association with the world of others. Thus, "the latent self is [the individual's] *raison d'etre* to find and be in the process of relating to his complex material and human environment. This involves that being is more fundamental than doing, quality more fundamental than activity" (Guntrip, 1971, p. 111).

But perhaps, in general terms, the most sweeping assertion that can be made with respect to Guntrip (1971) is that he unmistakably personalized the psyche, claiming without the reservations of biological determinism or the inhibitions of objective confirmation, that the psychoanalytic problematic is a purely psychological one. In contrast to Hartmann's biological foundation for psychoanalysis, and surely combining the influences of both Fairbairn (1952b) and Winnicott (1965), Guntrip (1971) rather asserts that "the individual whose nature contains latent maturational processes requires a facilitating environment in which to grow and this is first and foremost the infant's own mother if a healthy . . . person is to emerge" (p. 104). Psychoanalytic theory, Guntrip (1971) will say, describes the development and cultivation not of functional, adaptive capacities of impersonal agency, but of a subjective, even spiritual, person, that is, a self, which is the guiding and explanatory force of psychological life. For "a human being is a psychosomatic whole in which the soma provides the basis of material existence and the machinery for carrying out the purposes of the psychic self" (Guntrip, 1971, p. 111).

In drawing the argument in such "personal" terms, Guntrip (1971) challenges the explanatory efficacy, and thus the theoretical primacy, of Hartmann's notion of adaptation as the central concept upon which the psychological life of the individual turns. Rather, if psychoanalysis purports to study *human* being, then " 'adaptation'," Guntrip (1971) insists, "is replaced by a higher concept, that of a *meaningful relationship* (Guntrip, 1971, p. 107). It seems apt, as we draw this study to a close, to come around again to our beginnings, and so we shall here briefly explore the manner in which Guntrip (1971) resolves the issue of the self by replacing Hartmann's (1950) functional ego with the personal self.

The "Secret Critical Issue"

We recall that Hartmann (1939, 1950) modified, and in fact significantly affected the subsequent direction of the psychoanalytic understanding of the psyche, and of human behavior, when he asserted that not all ego processes derive from conflict. Rather, some ego procedures evolve outside the orbit of instinctual turmoil, but very much within the compass of the external environment. Hartmann's (1939, 1950) contribution, of course, served as an important counterweight to an otherwise "id centered," and determinist view; asserting that the ego was in goodly portion shaped by that external environment to which it had to adapt. It was nonetheless, Guntrip (1971) insisted, a "theory [which] is rooted on the one hand in the biological id, and on the other hand in the equally biological concept of 'adaptation' " (p. 106).

It was Guntrip's (1971) view that a concept more closely tied to the uniquely human attributes of being was required to adequately account for human behavior. Thus, in kinship with other theoreticians of the self we have discussed, and again it is Stern (1985) who comes readily, but not solely, to mind, Guntrip (1971) shifts the focus of inquiry from what he has referred to as a "system-ego" to a "person-ego." In proposing this shift he suggests that the crucial target of psychoanalytic theory is not the economic vicissitudes of energy, neutralized or otherwise, as it is distributed and redistributed among psychic systems. Indeed, like Fairbairn (1952b), Guntrip (1971) sees no theoretical need to maintain the idea of neutralized energy because he also does not adhere to the view that original energy is instinctual and id-derived. On the contrary, all energy is initially located within the person, the dynamic totality of the psyche, and is in its nature aimed at, even desirous of, the other for ontologically specific reasons, not phylogenetically universal and impersonal ones. Thus, "the truth appears to me," Guntrip (1971) asserts, "to be that there is one basic psychophysiological life-drive toward the object-world" (p. 133).

Nor, in Guntrip's (1971) view, ought psychoanalytic inquiry to spotlight the efforts of an "organism" seeking to effect an ecologically adequate adaptation to its environment, but rather the evolution of an originally unified psychosomatic person as she or he seeks to organize experience in terms of meaningful relationships with others. Thus not only does Guntrip (1971) dispute the conceptual need for a separate theory of neutral energy, but, as well, takes direct issue with the adaptational view of human being, vigorously maintaining that "*personal relationship cannot be reduced to the level of adaptation*" (p. 107; emphasis added).

Thus, for Guntrip (1971) "the problem of having an unquestioned possession . . . of a sense of personal reality and selfhood . . . is the biggest single issue that can be raised about human existence. It has always been the secret critical issue" (p. 119). And the subject of the "secret" has all along been the subject. The "secret," as our investigation of theorists in all traditions reveals, has always been the subjective self. And indeed, Guntrip (1971) speaks the "secret," defining as the "critical issue" the determination whether the individual is to be conceived in terms of what he refers to as the "*system*-ego," or the "*person*-ego."

Thus, the heart of the matter for Guntrip (1971) is constructing an analytic explanation of the self, and he unambiguously employs the term *ego* to mean the self, that is, the person. "The ego," he contends, "is the whole psychic person . . . [and] this person-ego has its own energy or life-drive, and develops a structural identity and individual characteristics by organizing its experiences as it goes along" (Guntrip, 1971, pp. 133–134). And here we may recall that Guntrip (1961, 1971) argues that the healthy self has avoided the abyss of schizoid unrelatedness; that the achievement of "selfhood" is the concomitant achievement of relatedness. The self is called into being by the enabling environment of the other, and conversely, may remain forever an untapped potential when left to languish in unresponsive surroundings.

"Thus we arrive," Guntrip (1971) says, "at the radical theory of the object-relational origins of the person-ego" (p. 118), and it is precisely in these origins that the core psychoanalytic concern rests. For the idiosyncratic problematic of psychoanalytic theory is not described within the measurable and palpable parameters of objective soma alone, but within the experiential and immaterial arc of subjective psyche as well. The issue does not concern an essentially biological adaptation, though adaptational capacity is a necessary, if not sufficient, condition for self-realization. Nor is the issue simply a matter of social, or interpersonal, relatedness, though such mutuality is essential to the emergence and maintenance of the self. Instead, it is the unique task of psychoanalysis to comprehend the self as it journeys, within the medium of mutuality, toward the realization of "a spiritual independence . . . on the level of its *own special significance*, that of the person-ego" (Guntrip, 1971, p. 111).

Guntrip's (1971) essential and uniquely human self is not found in the successful fit of organism to environment; nor even in relationship to the other, though such relationship is the absolutely necessary condition for the uniquely human self. Rather, it appears that the distinctive feature of human "selfness" is a virtually ungeneralizable, for being an elusive and averbal "spiritual," experience, carrying exclusive (i.e., nonreplicable) significance for the single and singular individual. In what follows we shall see that Bollas (1987, 1989, 1992) makes fertile use of a notion which may fairly be called a kind of "spiritual," or what he refers to as "transformational," experience in accounting for the origin of the self. Indeed, we shall employ his notion as one possible way in which to span the apparent theoretical gulf among the views addressed in this work.

Chapter 13

THE CONTAINED SELF OF DIDIER ANZIEU

Anzieu (1985), as we have seen all other psychoanalytic theoreticians do, calls upon the authority of Freudian texts to legitimately launch his own innovative enterprise. Unlike his compatriot, however, Anzieu turns toward the theoretical birthplace of the very ego which we have seen Lacan (1949, 1953, 1960) so vigorously disavow. Thus, Anzieu begins his elaboration by suggesting that the ego as it begins to emerge in Freud's (1923) reformulated theory of the psyche corresponds to what he calls the *skin ego*.

The essence of Anzieu's argument is perhaps best revealed in his persistent reference to the tenets outlined in "The Ego and the Id" (1923) as the "second topographical theory," rather than the more frequently employed title of "structural theory." In doing so Anzieu provides a somewhat different slant to the reading of Freud's (1923) work. Rather than emphasizing the structured aspects of the psyche, Anzieu understands the ego and the id as psychical apparatuses superimposed upon the preexistent, or earlier topography of conscious, preconscious, and unconscious. Thus, while the id corresponds to the deeper aspects of the psyche, that is, the unconscious, the ego is more closely associated with the *surface*, with consciousness. In this way a *second* topography of id, ego corresponds to the first alignment.

But in this second topography the ego is not merely at the surface, but maintains as well its connection, via the preconscious, to the inner aspects of the psyche. In this way, the ego has the dual capacity to experience the inner and to perceive the outer. Thus the ego, Anzieu

The discussion in this chapter centers on Anzieu's 1985 book and all Anzieu references are to that work.

here asserts, functions as an interface between the external and internal worlds. This, he will go on to argue, is precisely the function of the skin, in that it also functions to allow one to feel the external and the internal. We are reminded here of Freud's (1923) assertion that although perception, that is, the visual, is a factor in the formation of the ego, there is yet "another factor." This factor, Freud (1923) avows, is "a person's own body, and above all its surface," for the body is "a place from which both external and internal perceptions may spring." And in addition to being seen, Freud (1923) goes on, the body "to the *touch* . . . yields two kinds of sensations" (p. 25).

Thus, while overall the 1923 topography is associated with the supersession of the visual, in the ego's capacity to see reality and thus initiate critical psychic modifications, Anzieu argues for the antecedent influence of tactile phenomena in the origin of the psyche. "In relation to all other sensory registers," he maintains, "the tactile possesses a distinctive characteristic which not only places it at the origin of the psyche, but allows it permanently to provide the latter with something which one might also call the mental background" (Anzieu, p. 84). That is, the "distinctive characteristic" of the tactile as a "doubling agent" capable of providing both internal and external "perception" serves, in this view, literally as the background upon which psychical events may stand out as figures, or, as Anzieu's metaphor has it, as "the containing envelope which makes it possible for the psychical apparatus to have contents" (p. 84).

Now we may describe Freud's (1923) interest, in "The Ego and the Id" as well as elsewhere, as being principally focused upon the "core" or the "kernel," the nucleus, of psychic experiences. It is thus that we may understand his theoretical devotion to the unconscious, for example, or to the Oedipus complex as a central experience in the definition of character. Anzieu, on the other hand, by underscoring the formative influence of the skin, shifts the focus of inquiry from the deep interior of the psyche to its surface. In doing so he, quite paradoxically, highlights the periphery as a central organizing principle.

Thus, Anzieu's ideas regarding the ego and the self derive from his elevation to determinative authority of the boundaries or outer margins of early experience. Those outer margins include the body and specifically the skin. And he places his theoretical claim upon the Freudian belief that every psychic function traces its origin to a bodily function which is "rearticulated" mentally. Anzieu reminds the reader that the id as a mental apparatus has biological roots in the instincts; that the superego derives from "acoustical roots." Here we recall Freud's (1923) assertion "that the ego wears a 'cap of hearing' " (p. 25). Finally, the ego, in the well-known Freudian dictum, is "first and foremost a body-ego" (p. 27), and though it is primarily reliant upon the perceptual, it is, at least in part, derivative of the experience of touch.

In this way does Anzieu make the argument for the anaclitic roots of the ego, generally in the body, but specifically, in his innovative contribution, in the tactile. It is his view that the ego is first and foremost a "skin ego," which provides the initial stimulus for psychic differentiation; an "epidermal sac," transposing the actual containing function of the physical skin to the psychical plane.

Now it is in light of these considerations, particularly the tactile origins of the ego, that Anzieu arrives at those specific propositions which are of direct interest to our inquiry into the formulations of the self concept manifest in the various psychoanalytic schools of thought. For having reaffirmed the topographical location of the ego upon the surface, and underscored its reliance upon the tactile, Anzieu goes on to suggest that the awareness of self experience is both different from the full differentiation of the ego and takes place prior to it.

Indeed, Anzieu suggests that the self, unlike the ego, does not develop initially from tactile contact, but is rather contained in an antecedent experience of olfactory and auditory sensuality. "It seems to me," Anzieu asserts, "that we need to add to this account [of the topographic evolution of the ego] the existence of a more archaic, perhaps even original, topology [sic] in which the subject is aware of the existence of the Self, a Self that corresponds to the auditory and olfactory envelope" (pp. 97–98). Thus, the origin of the self, he here proposes, is distinct from the topographical evolution of the ego and takes place prior to it. The self, it is suggested, derives from the more primitive, that is, earlier, immersion in smell, and in sound.

It should be emphasized here that when Anzieu asserts that the self develops prior to the ego he distinctly refers to the ego which "comes into being when the visual envelope . . . takes the place of the tactile envelope in providing the Ego with essential support" (p. 98). The earlier "tactile ego" actually develops, in Anzieu's view, alongside the self, thereby making it possible to characterize the latter as "a Self on to whose exterior all the stimuli, whether exogenous or endogenous, are projected'' (p. 98). The skin ego, then, is not the same as the self, but its functional presence allows the self to establish its outer limits, its boundaries. The self is anaclitically dependent upon the tactile in order to delimit and shape, literally, its first *sense* of itself. The self is psychologically held together by the skin ego in its analogous role as a psychic container, or ''sac.'' We reiterate, however, that Anzieu's self does develop prior to the more fully elaborated ''visual ego.''

Anzieu assigns nine functions to the skin ego. The scope and intent of this work precludes an investigation of these functions, except to note that among them is, for our purposes, the essential role of the skin ego as a ''unifying envelope for the Self'' (p. 98).

Thus, Anzieu argues, just as the skin contains and supports the skeleton and the muscles, the skin ego, in parallel fashion, serves to contain and support, that is, to maintain, the self as a coherent psychic entity. An entity capable, by virtue of the already noted doubling capacity of the skin, to delimit that which is actually self and nonself; inside or outside. The bodily functions of the tactile, as they are translated by Anzieu from the physical to the psychical, by analogy serve to erect the necessary and defining psychological borders that denote the self.

We note in this construction a valuable insight into the multideter-mined bodily mutilations so prevalent in the pathology of the borderline personality. For the containing function of the skin ego possesses an explanatory power in regarding the superficial but frequent scratching of the wrists and body with sharp objects as an effort to reestablish (temporarily) lost boundaries. While surely self-destructive, such ''au-totactile'' expressions may also be understood as desperate and primitive attempts at self-*construction*. The archaic experience of pain is, in the sense that Anzieu seems to imply, affirming the presence, in its capacity to feel, of the very self so at jeopardy in the borderline individual.

Thus, we see that Anzieu has, to this point, proposed a self concept which, in tandem with the functional support of the skin ego, serves as an bifocal interface between inner and outer, serving to demarcate the experience and knowledge of one from the other. Now, parallel to this tactile ego ''there forms, through the introjection of the universe of sound (and also of taste and smell), a Self as a pre-individual psychical cavity possessing a rudimentary unity and identity'' (p. 157). It is to this self that we now turn our attention.

"The Sound Mirror"

We have already alluded to the predominantly "visual centric" organization of many theoretical explanations of the formation of the self. Thus, we recall, for example, the attribution by Kohut (1971, 1977) of constituting impact to the experience of being "mirrored" by the other; of seeing its own actions reflected in the object, with whom the budding self will psychologically "fuse," establishing in his way the first Kohutian selfobject. We note, as well, our recently concluded discussion of Lacan's (1949) hypothesis that the self is constituted by taking as its model and fusing (i.e., identifying), with the image seen in the mirror. In this connection we also recall Winnicott's (1967) formulation, in which the self is organized not in the mirror but in the mother's *gaze*. For Winnicott (1967), as we know, the self is constituted in the "gleam in the mother's *eye*," after all. Ultimately, of course, the originally mythic notion of self as discovered by Narcissus, was the outcome of catching sight of one's own image.

Anzieu, unlike these theorists, chooses not to accentuate the visual. Rather, he proposes "to demonstrate the existence at an even earlier stage of a sound mirror or of an audio-phonic skin" (p. 158). This "skin" will, Anzieu goes on, play a significant role in the psyche's capacity to produce meaning, beginning as it does in the creation of the illusion of "oneness" or unity produced by the enveloping sound. Such illusion is an early harbinger of the later imaginary and psychologically necessary fusion. It is through the mediation of sound, Anzieu argues, that the self is prefigured as a unified entity. For the child is first enveloped, and is first aware of being enveloped in sounds of its own breathing, as well as of those sounds which accompany nursing, notably those of the mother.

It is in the sound, Anzieu argues, that the infant first encounters himself and the mother. In the cacophony of external noises, both loud and soft; in the assortment of internal gurgles and breathing; in the cries, from the moment of birth, and later in response to hunger and pain, arises what Anzieu asserts is the first psychic space, a "sound space." Out of this noisy disorder there arises the "melody" of the human voice, quickly taken as indicative of a particular individual in the idiosyncratic inflections of the voice. "This is the moment, the state," Anzieu avows, "in which the baby experiences a first harmony (prefiguring his unity as a Self across the diversity of his sensations and emotions)'' (p. 171). In addition to the initial experience of harmony out of chaos, the infant also encounters what Anzieu calls his ''first enchantment,'' that moment when the harmonics suggest the illusion of unity between the self and the environment. Sound establishes the first and illusory boundary which forms the earliest sense of self. It is a boundary which, perforce, will be pared back as the child successively enters the psychic spaces dominated by the tactile, the visual, the locomotor, and ultimately the verbal.

The ''sound mirror'' works, Anzieu suggests, by providing the infant with information both about what he is experiencing and what the mother may be experiencing in connection to him. The infant ''mirrors'' these sounds by his babbling, in this way finding himself in the sounds which emanate from him; and, as well, learns to ''find'' the mother by these sounds and smells.

In terms of chronological evolution, then, the earliest psychic formulation is of a self emerging from immersion in resonance which predates not only the ''visual ego,'' but the ''tactile ego'' as well. Prior to both of these psychic manifestations ''the Self forms as a sound envelope through the experience of a bath of sounds'' (Anzieu, p. 167).

This ''sound envelope'' creates a common psychic space, inhabited by the nascent self and the resonant mother. It provides the first ''image'' of the body, though it does not rely upon the visual, but rather the auditory, to fashion the self in this (very particular) sense. As we noted, it is within this envelope of sound that there is an actual fusion of the sounds of self and other which establishes the foundation for the imaginary fusion later on. The early ''articulation'' of meaning, of thinking, we see, is first sounded out here, as sensory events are transposed to the mental plane (i.e., to the level of mentation). Thus, the ''sound envelope'' shapes and contains the first sense of the self, and prepares the ground for the construction of first meanings in the imagination.

In conclusion, we see that Anzieu has taken the self concept back to the very moment of entry into the world beyond the womb, in the sounds of the infant's first cry, and the background of noises *cum* harmony that accompanies that first cry.

This ''preindividual'' self is shaped in the discrimination of increasingly familiar sounds, his own and mother's, lifted from the background, and contained by nondiscriminatory fusion of these two sources of familiarity. Here, the self in the "sound mirror" arrives prior to the visual ego, but alongside of the tactile ego which contains it. Thus, the self is originally formed by sound, while the ego, simultaneously, is originally formed by touch. It is the tactile, or skin ego, we reiterate, that contains this particular configuration of the self mirrored in sound.

Anzieu's work, we cannot fail to observe, represents a significant modification of the topographic trinity (of id, ego, superego) outlined by Freud (1923). It is Anzieu's view that to his original schema of conscious, preconscious, and unconscious, Freud (1923) superimposed a "second" topography of ego and id. Anzieu, in turn, has proposed the addition of an antecedent topography which consists of the auditory and olfactory self, coincident with the tactile ego which contains it, and which is subsequently superseded by the visual ego but not eradicated in the process. It is the visual ego, in its turn, which heralds the advent of the "second topography."

We observe in closing, that Anzieu, in this like his compatriot Lacan (1953, 1960), attributes a formative influence to speech. Thus, while he surely does not emphasize the structuring impact of the word, he surely does, on the other hand, underscore the seminal significance of the first utterance, the unformed sound which precedes and makes possible the formed word; sound, which accompanies and is the essence of all words. Anzieu seeks the more archaic form of the word, in the first infantile cry which is, after all, the first assertion of "I am."

Part IV:

THE THOUGHT OF THE UNKNOWN

And so each venture is a new beginning, a raid on the inarticulate . . .

[T. S. Eliot, *East Coker*, p. 128].

Having tracked the self concept through a series of differentially organized formulations reflecting the play of presence and absence, we arrive at that paradoxical juncture wherein it becomes possible to entertain some thoughts about what cannot be known and cannot be spoken. For what rests at the heart of this extended review of the literature, it seems to me, is an elucidation of the variety of ways in which theoreticians have engaged the essential conundrum of being a self: the simultaneous existential knowledge of being and of nonbeing. As we have observed, they have done so by employing some variation upon the notion that the self is essentially a presence to its own knowing, and a knowledge of its fundamental absence.

In what follows the British psychoanalyst Bollas will be seen to suggest that the self, in true paradoxical fashion, is a product of the impersonal and unknowable made known. That is to say, the reflective and conscious self that knows itself to be is in the first instance a thoroughly unknowing, but fully sensate and experiential being which encounters and comes to prearticulately know its own being through a series of profoundly transformative manipulations by the mother. These alterations in the infant's state of being, as she or he is turned from belly to back, or bathed, or fed, these essentially proprioceptively induced transformations are, despite their being administered by the particular infant's particular mother, effectively impersonal in nature.

They are impersonal, Bollas suggests, because they cannot yet be named. The actions, while providing the first knowledge of being, are attached to no one in particular. Without words, the actions belong to the vast and linguistically unknown regions of existence which come to be experienced, as language struggles to capture the prearticulate,

261

as "what once was," as "paradise lost," as, that is to say, the absent at the heart of the linguistically present being.

The self in its "true" sense is the outcome of these early transforming experiences by what Bollas calls the "transformational object," but that object has no particular or present identity. It is "found" in certain sounds, aromas, and sights, which evoke an acute feeling of wordless recognition that, Bollas asserts, is the momentary capture of what might be called "selfness."

So we note that Bollas' self is, in its most fundamental origins, the result, and eternal container, of the impersonal; of what is recognized and known, but not capable of being thought. Indeed, Bollas' concept of the *unthought known* addresses precisely this notion that there are things of which the self has knowledge, but not thoughtful knowledge. Rather, the knowledge is existential and precognitive in nature; and precisely because it is so, it is experienced by the cognitive and linguistic self as forever elusive and absent.

Because the transformational object cannot be actually recalled to imagined memory or captured by verbal wiles, it is most often sought in some (long) awaited future, with which, I suggest, it has much, conceptually, in common. For the transformational object, actually long past, like the future, cannot be seen; and like the future is only a thought of the unknown. As Nick Carroway says of Gatsby, so we may say of our knowledge of the "true" self and our (psychological) search for it, that "[we] did not know that it was already behind [us], somewhere back in that vast obscurity . . . " (Fitzgerald, 1925, p. 182). When, within or without the walls of the consulting room, we encounter the frequently heard plaint that, "I don't know what I'm looking for; something is missing from my life," we may do well to recall the seductive lure of the long heralded and long absent transformative other already behind us.

Allusions

By way of gathering the strands of this discussion together, and making the point that what is conceptually asserted is merely the manifest face of the many formulations of self we have here encountered, we shall revisit some central concepts within the literature of the developing self, such as object constancy and delayed gratification, to discover how they may speak of both manifest presence and latent absence.

Supplemental Thoughts

Finally, in concluding this survey of the self as it has manifested and eluded its variably conceived nature, I propose that we consider, in a certain variation upon Bollasian themes, the *thought of the unknown* as an effort to conceptually contain the absent, and to speak the inarticulate. I will present the notion that within all concepts of the self there is the allusion to what is not; that all concepts of self which bespeak presence contain and allude to absence, and conversely, all knowledge of absence must, perforce, be a manifestation of presence. In this connection I will introduce the idea of a *supplemental object* which may serve the dual purpose of adding to, and so supplementing, what is already present, and substituting for what is always absent, and so also supplementing it. In this way we seek to suggest a kind of reconciliation with what cannot be known by supplementing, and so acknowledging, our lack. We also, perforce, recognize that any effort to articulate the absent will inevitably fall short, for "naming achieves presences and controls absences" (Sokolowski, 1978, p. xvi) but cannot realize absence without relinquishing it.

Chapter 14

THE UNTHOUGHT SELF OF
CHRISTOPHER BOLLAS

Differences in emphasis notwithstanding, the British tradition of psychoanalytic inquiry, most particularly as it is manifest in the "independent school," is predominantly a theoretical effort to characterize the essential nature of psychological being, or what Winnicott (1960b) aptly characterized as the "true self." As we have seen, the "true" is largely synonymous with the elusive, the arcane, and even the objectless.

The British thematic is, in this sense, somewhat of a paradox. For while its major motif asserts the causative impact of the object in the formation and myriad incarnations of the thus interpersonal self, the less than fully articulated minor key declares that there is another, and *"truer,"* feature of the self which is, as Bollas (1989) characterizes it, an "essential aloneness." That is, despite its interpersonal origins in the object-other, the self which emerges in consequence of that object-other is, at heart, curiously and strikingly unknowable by the other; inaccessible and profoundly idiosyncratic.

For we have seen in Balint's (1958a, 1968) "area of creation," and Guntrip's (1971) regressed self state, as well as Winnicott's (1960b) true self configuration, a recognition that ultimately there is a facet of being a self which is unknowable. Like his predecessors, Bollas (1992) concurs that finally the other, in this case the analyst other, is "fundamentally excluded from the patient's inner experience" (p. 5).

However, and also in close kinship with his British forerunners, perhaps especially Winnicott, Bollas (1987, 1989, 1992) conceives of a self very much in the formative debt of the object. But as his work unfolds we are struck by the particular uses he makes of the object, and of the unique formulation of self which emerges in consequence of that use. For Bollas has combined the implications of his predecessors—notably those of an ultimately unknowable aspect of self, and the transformative capacities of the object—to suggest that "in our true self we are essentially alone" (Bollas, 1989, p. 21). Let us see what the nature of this self is, and how it bears upon our efforts to reconcile the epistemological polarities of presence and absence.

A Transformational Self

From the outset, Bollas' work has been characterized by a preoccupation with process rather than product; with the dynamic aspects of perpetual becoming, rather than the relatively static states of realization. And in thus concentrating upon a self which *will be*, and only momentarily *is*, he offers a referentially ambiguous concept. For, as we shall see, Bollas' self is rarely discoverable in the particulars of its rather transitorily recoverable mnemic *contents*, but may be briefly palpable in the elusive interstices of its idiosyncratic psychic *forms*, which are eternally subject to the transformative influence of objects.

Bollas (1992) pursues and elaborates the argument for the mutational impact of objects upon the formation and ongoing experiences of the self, asserting that particular psychic states of being are elicited or evoked by the selection of particular objects. It is an important argument whose fundamental assumption, that the self is formed and transformed by the object, has been at the center of some of his earliest conceptualizations.

Thus, Bollas (1979, 1987) has consistently maintained, in true Winnicottian fashion, that the self is essentially transmitted to the infant through the particular patterns of nurturance of the child's particular mother. These patterns, or styles, of mothering become fundamental aspects of the infant's being and are imparted in a silent and preverbal dialogue, a language of gaze and of gesture.

Now what is particularly interesting about Bollas' (1987) formulation is the assertion that this private, gestural discourse is the infant's first encounter with the object. Further, this encounter is transformational; the object's significance resting not so much in its being identifiable as mother as in its capacity to produce transformation. Here we observe the curious proposition that the object's initial and perhaps most lasting impact is not specifically personal; and in some sense is actually rather impersonal.

For it is not yet the fixed and irreplaceable mother who is making herself felt, and thus experientially "known," to the infant. Indeed, "the mother is less significant and identifiable as an object than as a process" (Bollas, 1987, p. 14). It is rather the mother's *procedures* which the child first experiences; sensate encounters which cannot be referred to a discoverable location. Thus, the initial self experiences are objectless and *im*personal, that is, without an identifiable personal source. Nonetheless, this "procedural mother" brings about a series of profoundly intimate and deeply felt experiences of the personal; experiences which are, Bollas (1987) says, transformational in character.

These experiences are transformational because the mother soothes the infant, and thus transforms distress to calmness; transformational in changing a diaper and thereby exchanging one (wet) self-state for another (dry) one. So from hunger to satiation, and the many proprioceptive transfers of the infant from belly to back, and crib to lap—all these functional and emotional ministrations represent radically disparate states of being for the infant. The qualities of these states (i.e., the particular techniques employed by the mother in effecting these necessary activities) become the affective bedrock of the emerging personality. These experiences are the basic background of mood upon which the subsequent characteristics of self are inscribed.

Bollas (1987) has termed this early meeting with the other the *transformational object*, for its capacity to alter states of self experience. These alterations are actually the infant's first knowledge of the world, and it is not a *representational* knowledge, for the infant cannot yet image, or imagine, but rather, an *existential* knowledge. And the first existence is a symbiotic one, in which being is bonded to the unspoken procedures of the mother. Thus, the nascent self begins with a kind of mnemically fused knowing which antedates articulation and so remains forever beyond the reach of verbal capture. But not beyond a kind of (temporary) capture.

For in adult life such "transformational" experiences of self are sought, and even achieved, in what Bollas (1987) has called the "aesthetic moment," a time in which one realizes a wordless rapport with an object, perhaps a painting or a piece of music, evoking a state of being which prevailed in one's psychic prehistory. This "sense of being reminded of something never cognitively apprehended but existentially known" (Bollas, 1987, p. 16) retains the force of personal veracity precisely because it escapes consensual capture. The very elusiveness which marks the transformational also nominates it as the sign of the "true" self, just beyond grasping, forever absent over the next horizon.

Interestingly, the notion of transformation, notably, but not exclusively, in a religious sense, is conceptually oriented to the future while experientially seeking the past. Thus, like the dissolution of difference and confusion that is slated to accompany the long-heralded, but never yet present, messianic age, the psychological alterations of self are sought in yet to be discovered, and so *still absent*, aesthetic, erotic, but always inarticulate experiences. While all along these wordless fusions are as *revenants*, ghostlike remnants of an *already absent* past. What marks this experience, we suggest, is that the self originates in a sensation of transformation which was never (representationally) present, and so whether sought in the perpetually absent future, or the irremediably absent past, the self seeks to reestablish the experience of its own completeness by striving to embrace the wind, touch the dark.

In this observation we return again to the important notion that the transformational experience of self, a characteristically subjective, personal, experience, is at heart an impersonal undertaking. For these most authentic of selfstates, in which one feels touched by some "otherness," is not the caress of another *person*, but a brush with the unutterable strangeness, the "not me-ness," of existence; with the trace of the literally unimaginable. What is transformative is elusive; and the experience imparted by the transformational "object" is a passing sign precisely of what is *not* an enduring feature of self, but rather an indication of the self's inconstancy. Thus, "there is something impersonal and ruthless about the search for . . . all objects nominated as transformational" (Bollas, 1987, p. 27) because Bollas' formulation of the self owes its origins to the truly objective procedures of imageless existence, and the particular object is incidental to its capacity to transform the self. We recall in this context that Anzieu's (1985) early self experiences are also distinctly prerepresentational, that is, previsual, as are Stern's (1985).

Thus, one seeks Mahler's Ninth Symphony not for Mahler's sake, but for the sake of the ultimately idiosyncratic transformative powers of the sound. The self seeks to *be*, to exist, in the absent place of the transforming other. Interestingly, "true subjectivity," Bollas (1987) observes, is "that understanding of oneself that permits us sentient knowledge of the originating activity behind our experiences of ourself" (p. 63). Bollas' work, we are suggesting, implies that the originating activity of subjectivity is ultimately attributable to an impersonal objectivity. This theme, of the self-transformative influence of the absent other object, plays a significant role in the balance of Bollas' (1989, 1992) work and we shall continue to highlight these aspects as we proceed.

But a Dream

In his effort to discover the self, Bollas has actively undertaken a quest for the other, opening a theoretical dialogue with the obscure and, from the standpoint of the familiar I, strange objective, the better to grasp the nature of the subject of psychoanalysis. In so doing, Bollas (1987, 1992) suggests, as we have already noted in his construction of the transformational object, that the essentially subjective and interpersonal self is a fabrication of the impersonal.

Now the particular nature of the object-other is further elucidated as Bollas (1987, 1992) investigates the origin and nature of the self through the vehicle of the dream. In following his idea that the self is a product of its own dreaming, we encounter some important formulations regarding the unique and characteristically human exchange between the other and the self. We begin, then, with Bollas' (1987) assertion that the cardinal contribution of the dream to an understanding of the particular nature of human being is "its offering a place for this interplay of self and Other" (p. 68).

For the dream is, Bollas (1987) argues, primarily an aesthetic space, a theater in which the story of the self is narrated by the Other. This narration is the depiction, and the experience, in the dream, of a particular kind of object relationship in which the self as subject is the object of the other's desire. The dream, like the joke or the parapraxis, is the voice of the other; and a stage upon which the subject is spoken, handled, directed, and ultimately possessed by that which is other than the subject. Indeed, "the ego sponsors a character who plays the self in the recurrent theatre of the dream" (Bollas, 1987, pp. 64–65). The dream, we thus underscore, is ultimately a mirror in which the self is made manifest to its own other self. But in order to more adequately grasp Bollas' (1987) meaning here, we must pause to clarify his use of the terms *subject* and *ego*.

In asserting that the "*ego* sponsors a character" which plays the role of the self, Bollas (1987) appears to argue for a rent in the fabric of being; a split in which one aspect of self is subject while another aspect of self is object. If this is so, than Bollas (1987) is suggesting that the other of whom he speaks is the "other self." How is this conceived? In fact, Bollas (1987) makes precisely this distinction, saying that "by subject I mean the arrival of *self-reflective consciousness*" while "by *ego* I mean the *unconscious organizing processes* determined by a mental structure that evolves from the inherited disposition of the infant . . . the ego long precedes the arrival of the subject" (p. 285, n. 2 and 3; emphases added), and is its progenitor.

Thus we see that the other to which Bollas (1987) has been referring is none other than that aspect of self which remains unconscious and thereby, of course, unavailable to conscious knowing and absent from it. The conscious self, on the other hand (i.e., the subject), is, in large and essential aspects, the character which has been sponsored by this (ego) other. The conscious and knowing subject-self is thus the creature of what Bollas (1987) has termed the "unthought known," the unconscious ego aspects of the self. At the same time, however, the unconscious, and thus "unthought," is effectively created by the knowing subject in its capacity to speak the meaning of the (unconscious) Other. The dream is that psychic space in which Bollas' (1987) "Other" invents the subject; while, on the other hand, it is only the articulating subject which is in a position to relate the Other's story, and so invest it with meaning. Thus, "the dream *text* . . . is nothing more than the awakened subject's transcription of the dream experience into language," whereas during the actual dream time "the subject was inside the Other's fiction—*without memory of any alternative existence*" (Bollas, 1987, p. 70; emphases added).

Indeed, the oneiric is a distinct realm of being in which the self is, albeit transitorily, solely other. Upon awakening to a realm of conscious being, the subjectself seeks to capture that other self by speaking its meaning. It is inevitably, not unlike the recounting of the dream itself, a displacement of otherness to the region of consciousness; and a condensation of oneirically dispersed subjectivities, gathered by consciousness into constructed coherence. This self is both subject and object; both the known and the unknown; the (consciously) present and the (unconsciously) absent.

In his introduction of the term *unthought known*, Bollas (1987) conveys this dual essence of the self; for it is a formulation which asserts that the self is not wholly accessible to its own knowing. This self consists of the subject which consciously speaks a thoughtful (i.e., cognitively constructed) meaning; and the ego, which unconsciously shapes that meaning according to the inherited forms, or dispositions, of the infant. These forms are bestowed by the particular, and as we have seen, transformational proclivities of the private infant–parent discourse. Importantly, the ego's procedures are also known, but not, as we have also observed in transformational experiences, representationally. Ego knowledge is existential knowledge. Thus, the "unthought known," Bollas (1987) says, stands for "that which is known but has not yet been thought" (p. 280). It is, no less than conscious, or "thought," knowing, an aspect of self; but an elusive, even largely absent, for being *un*conscious, aspect. What is unthought, yet existentially sensed, is another feature of the self; indeed, it is the "other" within.

We pause here to observe that Bollas (1987) has undertaken an interesting denotational reversal, in which he employs the term *subject* to indicate what Lacan (1949) meant by *ego*, that is, the conscious element of being. Lacan (1949), as we have seen, chose to employ the quintessentially analytic, and since Hartmann the functional and adaptational term, *ego* to convey precisely that which is, in his view, a *distortion* and a misapprehension of veridical, that is, unconscious being. Bollas (1987), however, determines to retain ego as the semantic carrier of the same psychoanalytic shibboleth contained by Lacan's (1949) subject, a curious instance, it would appear, of a conceptual consensus obscured by the loyalties implied in linguistic usage.

Thus, for Lacan (1949), using ego as the manifestation of distortion was likely also a way of speaking his rejection of Hartmannian functionalism in favor of what he believed to be the original, and radically self deconstructing, intent of the Freudian unconscious. No less so for Bollas (1987), who also speaks of the formative "otherness" of the unconscious; and in reserving ego to point the way, seems also to disavow a circumscribed functional and adaptational meaning for the self. Both effect a distance from the Hartmannian ego, but Lacan (1949) does so by "reinventing" the "language of psychoanalysis," while Bollas (1987, 1992), less extremely, reaffirms his view of "original intent." Bollas (1992) seems to confirm this when he asserts that in using the dream as a paradigm for the articulation of the self, he wishes to "suggest a different fate—or at least a more complex fate—for the human subject than is suggested by the ego-psychological ideal of a progressive adaptation to reality" (p. 50).

Varieties of Self-Experience

The dream stands as one significant manifestation of the manner in which Bollas (1987, 1992) conceives the emergence of the subjectself in consequence of the formative procedures of the objectother. But it is one manifestation only; Bollas (1992) has more recently enlarged his fundamental proposition, that the subjectself is formed by, is contained by, and itself contains, the objectother, to reflect the deconstructive principle that the self is not a phenomenological unity. Indeed, "it cannot be, because, in the first place, the true self is not an integrated phenomenon but only *dynamic sets of idiomatic dispositions* that come into being through problematic encounters with the object world" (Bollas, 1992, p. 30; emphasis added). The *sense* of unity, Bollas adds, results from a kind of "unconscious rapport" among the many and diverse states of experiential being, what he refers to as "simple self states," and the organizing properties of the subject, the I—what Bollas is here calling the "complex self position."

Now, Bollas (1992) makes the thought-provoking assertion, to which we shall return in our concluding remarks, that "although these [disparate] senses [of self] do not add up to a sum of the many parts, they may yield *a kind of 'spirit' of place* . . . leaving psychoanalysis in the challenging position, it seems to me, of honoring such a human spirit with a place in its theory" (p. 30; emphasis added). This somewhat mysterious sounding "spirit of place," we shall suggest, may prove a step in the direction of conceptually containing presence and absence within a dynamic dialectic of self. But first, let us see what Bollas (1992) intends by this variety of self-experiences.

Lexical Being

We have already noted, in the concept of the transformational object, Bollas' (1987) description of the subject's use of the structured object, such as a painting or a musical score, to invoke, or even resurrect, a particular experience of self. Here, we observe, the object is intentionally selected for its capacity to recapture a desired experience of self. We observe, as well, that particular memories, or what Bollas (1992) calls the "mnemic object," serve as containers in which aspects of self are stored, and may also be recalled.

In these instances the self selects its objects for the specific self-resonating properties they possess; they serve as the language by which the self is expressed. Thus do the selected objects compose the subject's vocabulary of being, serving as the voice by which the self may utter its other. Thus, "objects can be said to have a lexical function when we employ them to 'speak' our idiom" (Bollas, 1992, p. 21).

The object world is thus in part conceived as a vast thesaurus of evocations, from among which the self selects those of a particularly nuanced demeanor, best suited for the experience of self which is sought. In this way does the self become what it intends to contain of the other; employing the object as a self-selected vernacular of being. But the self's use of the object is only one way in which the object defines the self. For purpose is often displaced by promiscuity.

And Aleatorical Being

Chance, of course, plays a sizable role in the unfolding of self, "and certainly the aleatory object has its own integrity and capacity to play upon us" (Bollas, 1992, p. 30). Thus, even when the self anticipates the lexical, the unanticipated may conjure the arbitrary. It is precisely in such moments that the self *is* as it is fashioned by the random, and handled by the "unthought." Not unlike the hidden, or absent, handling of the subject by the dreamwork, the unbidden object also "speaks," and shapes, discrete and aleatorical moments of being.

Bollas' (1992) proposals led him to suggest a series of stages in the experience of self, all of which are object derived. Thus, in the intentional selection of the object, for example, as in choosing to attend a concert rather than read a book, the self *uses* a selected object.

However, the self is also used, or "played by," the object, as in those moments when the object's own particular integrity, whether intended or randomly appearing, transforms the self. Here, as it unfolds, the concert "plays," and may transform, the self. Here, the object speaks the self.

In a third stage, Bollas (1992) asserts that the self is "lost" in its own experiencing. In such instances, the self is inside what Bollas (1992) has referred to as "the third area," a psychological region akin to Winnicott's (1951) transitional space, in which the object has become experientially coterminous with antecedent states of being. This zone cannot be characterized by either the properties of the self in any other state, nor the integral features of the object. Rather, it is a combinative region, in which the shared impact of each upon the other establishes a different order of being, neither objective nor subjective, but bordering in a "third area" of transition. An area of illusion, Winnicott (1951) has declared, of which *"it can be said that it is a matter of agreement . . . that we will never ask the question: 'Did you conceive of this or was it presented to you . . . the important point is that no decision on this point is expected"* (p. 12).

Finally, we come to a stage of "observation," in which the self effects a detachment from its recent experiential encounters in order that it may contemplate, and construct the meaning of, what has transpired. "This," Bollas (1992) allows, "is the place of the complex self" (p. 31).

Here, in sum, is a formulation which declares the fundamental multiplicity of the self, attributing its experiential diversity to the manifold resonances derived in encounter with the other. The self is a momentary, but palpable and thus present, experience of the object as it disperses and blends its own objective effects with the unconscious forms of the subject. The experience of self is in the transitory meeting of the knowing subject(ive) and the "unthought" object(ive); the mixing of conscious presence and unconscious absence. How is such a paradox rendered meaningful? Bollas' (1992), we note, comes close to providing a response.

The Spirit of Self

Bollas has long argued the thesis that the self as a subjective, a conscious presence, is a series of fleeting instances which emerge briefly to knowing awareness from the dynamic interplay of objective, unconscious and absent, unknown forces. We have seen that this objective is the true vocabulary of the speaking subject; the knowing self's unknown and absent other, residing at the heart of subjective being.

For Bollas (1992), as we have noted, asserts that this "Otherness" of which he speaks is the self's own unconscious, absent, and unthought existence. Contained at the very core of subjectivity, in the place where the self knows that it knows, and so knows that it *is*, rests the unknowable and unlocatable objective other. Present in no place, this absent and missing objective psychic link (theoretically) speaks the explanation of the subjective. Just where the self is, in its own subjectivity, there too is all that is irremediably strange to that subjectivity, and yet, by its very objective otherness, sparks the ephemeral realization of self which Bollas (1992), like Lacan (1949), speaks of as "the *jouissance* of the true self" (p. 51). How is it that this objective otherness, this absence, is at the same time such a central presence at the heart of being? How can we reasonably speak of that which is absent as present, and that which is present as unutterably absent?

We perhaps begin to detect the germ of a response to this conundrum in Bollas' (1992) comment that "the self does not evolve unconsciously; rather, the self *is* unconsciousness, a particular inner presence" (p. 51). Now it turns out that this "inner presence" to which Bollas (1992) alludes is a quality of "itness," a pure extract of impersonality, expressed psychoanalytically in the theory of the unconscious id. This "itness" is the true riddle of the self, this otherness that psychoanalysis names the unconscious, sitting at the defining center of what has been, at least since Descartes, the reigning *cogito*. The unknown at the heart of knowing; the objective threaded through the fabric of the subjective; and unfamiliar "otherness" patterning the weave of the most familiar and selfsame I.

Is it any surprise, Bollas (1992) rhetorically ponders, that as we mature:

> [W]e come to believe more and more in life's mystery and the strangeness of being human, as we are in possession of—or is it possessed by?—these inner realities, which we know, but which we truly cannot think. . . . And yet they are there. Not only there, but the inner senses we have when we think of our inner objects seem more a part of us than anything else. How do we name them? [p. 61].

Bollas (1992) quite unapologetically names them "spirits." For these "inner realities," these unthinkable presences, which move within, and are spoken of in the aggregate as self, affirming the palpably animate and seemingly material existence of being, are neither available to the image, nor to the word; they are, after all, *immaterial*, that is, spiritual.

In this way we arrive at Bollas' (1992) assertion that to be a self is to contain, and to be, a spirit. That a self is insofar as it is apprehended in its effect upon others, and otherness; and as otherness plays transformatively upon the experientially "lost" subject. Momentarily sensed in the other's gaze, barely discernible in a lingering aroma or fading sound; cloaked in the object's shadow, the palpable experience of self is apprehended only in what is left behind as a sign of its passing. Evidenced in the altered spaces where it *was*, but never held in the *here*, the self is recognized as a presence only in the traces it leaves; remnants which imply its *past presence*, or suggest its *future presence*, but always affirm its *present absence*.

This absence, the darkness which punctuates the spoken self, and wherein being anticipates the spark of the other, is an integral feature of being. For "we are as often waiting in the interiors of silence and darkness as we are informed by the projections of psychic news" (Bollas, 1989, p. 22). As in the imaged presence of the act, so too in the penumbral intermissions between, is the self in attendance. For it is in the unfulfilled waiting, devoid of presence and substantially empty that the self may touch its own singular and transient other. "There, in the solitary space, we repeatedly contact that essential aloneness that launches our idiom into its ephemeral being" (Bollas, 1989, p. 22).

Chapter 15
THE ALLUSIONAL SELF

We suggested at the outset of this book that psychoanalysis engaged the question of the self, and its nature, in the coincident moment that Breuer and Freud (1893–1895) encountered Anna O. We further suggested that a survey of the principal theoretical statements regarding the self concept would reveal that theory building had diverged, taking two distinctly different epistemological paths toward an understanding of the self. And we asserted that the two major, and seemingly antithetical, organizing ideas were presence and absence.

Indeed, we have seen that the traditions examined have formulated the self, more or less, either from the viewpoint of a progressively imperial and knowing subjective, increasingly able to appropriate mother objects to its own selfsame substance, and thus master the external world; or from the hypothetical vantage of the vast and unknown objective which more closely expresses the true and unconscious self. In the former instance we have here spoken of the *self of presence*, composed of all that was initially experienced as foreign but has been "metabolized" into the psychic bloodstream of the subjective, thus becoming one and the same with the self, and "filling" the psychic interior. The latter instance describes a *self of absence*, a self which cannot be grasped in sameness, and is radically *un*identical to the knowing subject.

We propose that the thetic formulations of each of the traditions discussed herein contain its latent antithetic; and that the analytic self concept, broadly conceived, is an *allusive self*. That is to say, the "theorists of realization" and of "anticipation," no less than those of "paradox" nor of "postmodern multiplicity," contain allusions to

277

their conceptual opposites, and the full sense of the concept is most often implied, or hinted at.

Thus we recall, for instance, that the self of the American tradition came gradually but surely to claim a subjective explanatory cast, as highlighted in the work of Kernberg (1976, 1982a,b), Kohut (1959, 1971, 1977), and perhaps especially Stern (1985), whose "senses of self" are unambiguously rooted in a form of subjective knowing. We reiterate, the self *became*, as it became a metabolic byproduct of the "ingested" (i.e., introjected) other object. The self increasingly *was*, as it was known to itself, and filled by its "transmuted" internal objects. The self was a presence.

The theoretical emphasis, we know, was not solely upon the knowing and progressively ascending subjective, self. While this was the manifest thrust of the work in the American school, the unconscious other was being accorded its conceptual due by the French, particularly Lacan (1949, 1953). Here the argument was for the formative influence of this ultimately unknowable and impersonal otherness that resides within the very fabric of the psychological self. Indeed, the unconscious, that is, the self's other, is structured along the lines of a language, one that speaks the self. From this theoretical standpoint the (true) self is as it is "other," and the "true" subject of psychoanalysis is unconscious otherness.

The British occupy a curious position within the psychoanalytic tradition, for they invite us to consider, on the one hand, the highly personal and subjective origins of the self—origins largely attributable to the idiosyncratic procedures of the infant's particular mother; while on the other hand, all the major theorists of this tradition have included some variant of "otherness" within their formulations. The British, perhaps more so than either the French or the Americans, were able to conceptualize the self's ambiguity.

Nonetheless, all traditions contain both presence and absence, though where one epistemology is dominant, the other is inferred. Thus, absence, otherness, and the formative impact of the objective upon the emergence, maintenance, and uniquely human character of the subjective self is, we suggest, a more or less latent substrate in those theories which manifestly organize the self in terms of presence. That presence, on the other hand, becomes the allusive but necessary component in those theories in which absence is the dominant theme, as it is in Lacan's work.

Let us pause here to examine the absence which sits at the heart of some key ego psychological notions whose achievement is a manifest assertion of the self's growing presence; and, as well, to explore the necessary presence which sustains the veracity of Lacan's absent self.

A Functional Absence

Perhaps foremost among the hallmarks of a maturing, and adequately adapted, individual from the standpoint of Hartmannian (1939, 1950) ego psychology is the functional capacity to tolerate frustration by delaying gratification. From within the cognitive matrix of progressive mastery which conceptually organizes much that characterizes ego psychological principles, these attributes, and the associated aptitude for anticipation, bespeak the evolution of an increasingly present self. Present in that toleration, delay, and anticipation are all functional acquisitions, properties of being which are obtained, achieved, and possessed. They are attributes of self which, in being acquired, attest to their once having *not* been but now *are*. As such, they constitute demonstrable evidence that the self is an increasingly palpable presence, known by its progressively complex effects in and upon the material world. At the same time, however, we suggest that realization of these very skills which seem to vouchsafe the vital actuality of the self, equally attest to an increasingly ample absence.

A reconsideration of these functional attributes suggests an obverse, and other, reading. In reflecting upon the condition implied by the delay of gratification, for example, we cannot fail to note that it conjures what is not, namely, absence. For to delay is to put off, to pause prior to realization, and to *suspend the arrival of gratification.* During this interregnum, when gratification-fulfillment, after all, is held in abeyance, it has not yet been actualized, or made present; it *is* absent. May we not say that in mastering the skill to tolerate and endure this frustration of desire that the self is able to contain and abide absence? May we not say, within the ego psychological frame of reference itself, that the self increasingly *is* (i.e., becomes evermore capable of engaging in a variety of masterful and mature actions) as it is capable of sustaining the experience of absence, which is here conceptualized as a kind of temporary forswearing of fulfillment, or ''delay in gratification?''

The developed capacity to anticipate consequences serves to make the same assertion, to wit, that as the functional abilities of the ego grow in complexity there is an accompanying aptitude, which is indeed heralded as a welcome affirmation of the psychologically sound self, to sustain the experience of absence. For here again we note an arresting feature of anticipation: it describes a state of *awaiting*, or looking forward to. Anticipation is a *contingent* condition, describing events which stand unfinished and incomplete. Like delay, anticipation is a suspended state, characterized by, indeed is, the condition of "waiting for" that which is *not here*. Being able to anticipate is, quite simply, being able to be in a state of psychological absence. Anticipation is also something more.

In being able to anticipate, one indeed conjures a psychic absence, but does so in a curiously present manner. For what happens in anticipation is that the self imagines (i.e., quite literally *images*, or pictures) what is not, and in this way establishes a kind of intangible presence. This paradox of "immaterial presence" is a trademark human solution to the perpetual lure of desire; to wit, making the absent present by "calling it to mind." For in thinking it, we presence it; yet because it is, and can only be, made present by calling it to *mind*, which is the essence of the insubstantial, it is substantially and irremediably, not present, but is absent. The Freudian *fort-da* is itself "called to mind," as is the quintessentially ego psychological concept, object constancy.

For, generally conceived, object constancy is, we recall, that developed capacity to sustain an internal image of the absent object, and thus represents an acquired psychic mechanism for making present that which is not present. And so, in this way, does the increasingly mature self come to master a range of actual and felt losses—absences—by capturing them mnemically. In this way it is possible to see that object constancy is yet another mechanism for asserting (psychic) fulfillment, but this concept as well contains its antithesis.

Thus, object constancy also testifies to what is absent, for the mnemic image is but the *indicator*, the sign, of the actual and absent object. For when the other object is vitally and tangibly before one, accessible to sensate experience, it is never "called to mind." Such substitutive maneuvers are employed only in the absence of the object, and ultimately can only serve as evidence of that absence. In this way object constancy is also a psychological statement about the developed capacity to sustain and contain absence as a feature of the self.

Indeed, a phenomenological account of object constancy is less likely to yield descriptions of an actually *constant*, and pictorially available, mnemic image. Instead, such narrative depictions are more apt to produce renderings of internal objects as "flickering" and indeterminate impressions, oscillating in the uncertain intervals highlighting an otherwise tenebrous psychic theater. And "the darkened screen is as much a part of our life as is the play of images across its illumined surface" (Bollas, 1989, p. 22). Less reliably available to visual resurrection, the "constant" object is more closely conceived as a "sense"—akin to Stern's (1985) subjective, or Anzieu's (1985) sensate skin ego—in which the self experiences the presence of the other as the "ghostlike" breeze of the transformational object.

Thus we suggest that object constancy, along with the affiliated formulations of delayed gratification and the anticipation of consequences, attest to the conceptual presence of the idea of absence in the ego psychological tradition. All serve to indicate how the psyche manages absence, either in its endurance or temporary mnemic defeat, but in any event attesting to its formative and persistent influence.

It is significant to note that each of the capacities we have discussed here are *developed* capacities; acquired in the course of progressive movement toward the realization of selfhood. That these are developed skills which serve, in part, to master absence, and its psychological concomitant, desire, speaks to the notion that the self is most fully realized in the realization of its perpetual desire. That tolerance of frustration does sustain absence; and the ability to do so is one enduring feature of the self.

A Self Deferred

Federn's (1926, 1928a,b, 1934) formulations, we recall, make a significant and somewhat ambiguous contribution to the idea of the self both as a materially fulfilled presence and the manifestation of continuous lack. Thus, Federn's is a self which is not apprehended by an abstract and intangible conceptual knowledge, but rather, is "located" in the very palpable feeling of one's being.

Federn's tradition and intellectual commitment were very much to the classical Freudian paradigm, and the "reality" of his self is expressed and assessed in terms of the extent to which it is cathected with narcissistic libido. It is the tangible, felt presence of this energic investment which renders the conviction of one's existential "realness." His concept of ego feeling is a manifestation of his theoretical allegiance to a self which is recognized through its capacity to make itself *felt*; and to *fill* consciousness with the libidinal tension of being.

On the other hand, Federn's (1926, 1928b) work contains a number of conceptual indicators of the self of absence. Thus, for example, we recall his modification of narcissism to include an "objectless" variety. Such narcissism is literally self-sustaining, and is Federn's (1928a,b) economic counterpart to what he has conceived of as the "medial," or "intransitive," voice of the self. Here, the self simply is, but has no idea of the objective. This is a self absent the other, and absent even the idea of its own self. For to conceive of *self*, Federn (1928b) asserted, there must be an initial idea of an object. In this early ego state there is only I. But simply because the self cannot desire its own object self, nor yet satisfy that desire in an autoerotic fashion, does not preclude Federn (1928b) from claiming that this "medial" state is a kind of desire.

Indeed, it is not desire which is absent in this early self, but satisfaction. The I *does* desire, and this is an exemplary Freudian notion, because it is imbued with libidinal, which is to say in psychoanalytic terms erotic, energy. But this I lacks for satisfaction, for the object of desire, whether the self or the other, is absent. Indeed, this is not a pathological, but an existential lack, for we recall that Federn (1928b) asserts that this lack is not commensurate with displeasure. On the contrary, while it is an absence of satisfaction, it is also a kind of presence of anticipation, or what Federn (1928b) referred to as an "agreeable forepleasure." Even as this objectless, medial self comes to be overlaid by the psychological complexities associated with the advent of the object and the acquisition of its internal image, this feeling of forepleasure persists as a continuous psychic undercurrent. Thus we see that Federn's (1926, 1928a,b) healthy I feeling is characterized by absence (of the object) and lack (of satisfaction). The latent source of the I's material and experiential apprehension of its "realness," then, rests in the sustained tension of its own deferred satisfaction. If in many other important respects Federn's theoretical work bears little resemblance to Lacan's, in this instance of conceptual allegiance to the sustaining, and even presencing influence, of lack there is a curious kinship.

A Consuming Desire

We alluded above to the ingestive metaphors of ego psychological theory which suggest that the healthy self does metabolize, or otherwise blend, the objective other's nonself strangeness into the seamless weave of subjective experience. We have seen also that this is accomplished by a variety of psychological mechanisms, including introjection, internalization, identification, and transmuting internalization.

This assortment of descriptors notwithstanding, the inclusive and operative metaphor which obtains in all instances suggests that psychological being demands a mentational variation upon the long-standing actual ritual of physically ingesting the threatening other, thereby winning its strength for one's self. One "hungers" after the absent objective of desire; its possession the fulfillment of the subjective self. The object is the subject of a consuming desire.

We observed the theoretical consequences of a failure to thoroughly partake of the psychic substance of the other in Kernberg's (1976) and Kohut's (1971, 1977) work, both of which are metaphorically digestive in nature. Thus, we recall, for example, Kernberg's (1976) assertion that profoundly disturbed object relations signify "the persistence of 'nonmetabolized' early introjections" (p. 34).

We noted a similar principle operating in the clinical observations and theoretical conclusions of, for example, Guntrip (1971), who addressed the "regressed," and objectless core of the profoundly schizoid individual. We note here the same inclination in Fairbairn (1952a,b) who, though he begins with a fully present, "unitary," and whole self, demonstrates that significant portions of that self are lost to conscious and thus present knowing because they are consigned to the nether world of impersonal unconsciousness. Interestingly, some of the very features of self which are repressed are those which are engaged in a perpetual struggle with the frustrations of the tantalizing but ungratifying libidinal object.

These too are manifestations, here conceived as pathological instances, of the failure to blend the ephemeral essence of objective otherness with the material experience of subjective sameness. Of course we reiterate that Lacan (1949) stands as a definitive instance of the dominating impact of absence, drawn in Kojevian terms as an unceasing desire for what is forever lacking.

Lacking for Nothing

Lacan (1949) also employed the idea of absence in elaborating a notion of the pathological. But whereas the American and British traditions largely conceived of pathology in terms of the failure to effectively metamorphose strange otherness by an act of psychic metabolism which effectively enfolds, and thus obscures, strangeness within the embrace of subjective identity; Lacan (1949) took the reverse tack.

Indeed, Lacan (1949), as we have noted, argued that a "distorted" (i.e., pathological) self results precisely when the voice of desire is silenced; when what is lacking is sublated by the misapprehensions of the deceptive ego. For we recall that the Lacanian self is initially constituted in the false light of the mirror image, suggesting a tangible presence which is merely imaginary and serves only to alienate the self from its essential character. And this essential character, the "true self" in the Lacanian sense, is most completely realized as it most closely approaches the "full speech" of the unconscious other. Lacan's (1949) self is wholly encountered as it most knowingly pursues what is lacking and absent. Thus, a "healthy" self, from this theoretical standpoint, is one which joyfully courts "no*thing*," and thus always lacks for nothing.

But this true absent self of unconscious otherness could not be sustained without the intercession of language which, Lacan (1953, 1960) argues, is a distortion of the essence of the unconscious, but a necessary distortion. For without the presence of the symbolic, the unrepresentable, and otherwise unknowable, unconscious self could not be approached. Absence requires presence, and this is indeed alluded to in Lacan's (1953, 1960) formulations regarding the impact of speech upon the birth of the subject. For we recall that while Lacan (1953) argued that the defining characteristic of the human self is its desire for what is absent and *gone*—we recall his use of the *fort-da* paradigm—he nonetheless asserted that the actual I of the subjective is only realized when it can *speak* its desire. The true Lacanian subject, the self, is encountered in the assumption of language. For language, the word makes the self *known* and hence present to itself. Thus, although the essence of self is in its lack of, and desire for, what is not, this only has meaning as it is made present in the capacity to speak, to symbolically represent, the unconscious. The "full speech" of the unconscious is only known through the culturally transmitted word.

Like Freud (1915), Lacan (1953) appears to suggest that nothing can be certainly known unless and until it is "transformed" by conscious knowing, a form of speech, and thus recognized by the self as its own and not its other.

Janusian Views

Like the Roman guardian of gates, the British theorists of the self have managed to face at once in two directions, proposing formulations which contain the characteristics of both presence and absence; concepts which embrace the knowing and thoughtfully conscious self, whose "true," and paradoxical, nature is unthought, unconscious, and perhaps only known in the "spiritual" sense to which Bollas (1992) has alluded.

It is a self variously expressed in terms of its objectless, primitive, or solitary core—here we think of Balint's (1958a, 1968) "area of creation," Guntrip's (1971) "regressed core," and Bollas' (1992) "essential aloneness," for example. Or a self which is frankly divided, as the emblematic formulation of this tradition, the dichotomous "true" and "false" selves, attests. Finally, there is a self which candidly endows the unrepresentable, even as it is literally the unspeakable, with manifestly self-defining capabilities, as in the traces left by Bollas' (1987, 1992) transformational object, or more recently his object "spirits," which "can neither be seen nor described" (Bollas, 1992, p. 62). Perhaps the paradigmatic expression of the impact of the unrepresentable, however, is still Winnicott's (1951) transitional space, wherein the objective and the subjective conjoin to create an "intermediate" area whose substance is neither actual nor phantastic, but *is* illusory.

However, the British formulation is also a depiction of the self as it becomes increasingly constituted by internally imaged, that is, made present, variants of other objects. In fact, we have seen that the self is, in significant proportion, created in the mother's gaze, and in her handling. As the object is increasingly assimilated, the self develops a growing psychic substantiality. That is to say, the self becomes more of a felt and palpable actuality, and its objects become more of a felt and palpable familiarity. Thus does the self become experientially and cognitively known, or present, to itself as it is shaped by and comes to know as identical and "mine" the ministrations of the object. In this way it is possible to say that the self is created in its own other image. We think here of Winnicott's (1958) assertion that the capacity to be alone requires the presence of the other, a presence which, in time, becomes an ''inner'' presence.

Supplemental Thoughts

Thus, we conclude that the American formulations of the self are fashioned in the manifest light of a predominantly knowing, aware, and consciously present subject; but we have seen that the latent content of this formulation acknowledges the force of absence, alluding to its formative influence by, in effect, claiming that the developed self will have learned to tolerate that absence, giving it its due in, for example, the delay of gratification.

On the other hand, the conceptualization of the self elaborated by Lacan (1949) elevates the impact of ''otherness,'' (indeed, to ''Otherness'') and the perpetual lack of completion that desire imposes, to an explicit position. Nonetheless, the necessity for the symbolic ''presencing'' impact of language in establishing the self is recognized as a certain necessity if the defining role of absence is to be sustained.

Finally, the British have emphasized both the ''presencing'' elements in the emergence of the self as well as the ''absencing'' elements, asserting thereby the essential ambiguity of the self. Here we encountered a concept of the self which seeks to acknowledge, and contain within the parameters of one formulation, the fundamental split which has shadowed the object, and the subject of psychoanalysis since the advent of the unconscious.

Now all the theories discussed in this project, irrespective of originating tradition, have conceptually acknowledged the indispensable role of the objectother in the construction of the self. Whether as the functional activator of the self's existential, and later subjectively known, presence or as the unrepresentable experience of lack and absence at the self's ''core,'' the objectother plays the pivotal role in defining the character of the subjectself. As this discussion has implied, the object thus appears to play two incommensurate roles. Let us see how we may reconcile these seemingly incompatible conceptions of the object.

I propose that we reformulate the idea of the internal object, combining in a single concept its dual nature, first as an internal (re)*presentation* to the self of what is outside the self, a manner in which it has been traditionally employed in object relations theories of the self. Second, in its character as an objective, and thus unavailable to the metabolizing mechanisms of subjective assimilation. This latter is a use to which the object has been put largely as a descriptive manifestation of psychological pathology—as in swallowing the object whole in psychotic illness. Indeed, "madness" is often conceived as the experience of being inhabited by "others"—whether other voices or demonized other beings. The object as the unassimilable objective is, we have seen, also employed in the relatively unintegrated notions of Lacan (1949, 1953), who conceived of self in terms of an unrelenting desire for what is lacking.

Combining these two features of the internal object, that is, its roles as a presencing agent, bearing a sense of psychic fulfillment, and as an affirmation of the unidentifiable and even objectlessness within the psyche requires that we concede the incalculable. For the *supplemental object*, as I propose we refer to this notion for the originating debt owed to the formulations of Jacques Derrida (1967a,b), will, in one maneuver, serve as the instrument of addition *and* subtraction; that is, of presence and of absence.

For a supplement contains these two ideas: that which is added to, and as such contributes more to an already present plenitude; and that which compensates, and in this way serves to make up for, and take the place of, that which is not present, filling a space where there is no thing.

Considered in this supplementary fashion, the internal object image is that which is added to the sensate self as a contribution to that which is already present. We think here, for example, of Jacobson's (1964) "primal psychophysiological self," Stern's (1985) early "senses" of self, or Anzieu's (1985) previsual "skin ego." But precisely because it is here regarded as a supplement, the internal object image is also that which compensates for, and serves as a *substitute* for what is not present.

In this simultaneously enacted role it is called upon, indeed psychically relied upon, as an alternative for what is absent. But as an alternative, indeed, a "stand-in," for what is absent, and if it were present it would not require substitution, the supplement can never gratify desire. The object of desire is exactly not where a substitute *is*; nor can it actually, but only approximately, fill the void where absence is.

A third feature of the supplemental object is its fundamental exteriority. For whether as an addition or a compensation, the supplement originates in otherness; it necessarily comes from outside of that which it is either being added to or compensating for. Were it already of the subject, for example, it could not then be added to what it already was; nor, in like fashion, could that which is the same as serve to substitute for. Thus, the supplemental object, like the essence of the objective in itself, can never be identical to the subject-self and yet remain itself. There is thus always some supplementary core in which the self may experience its true *alien*ation.

Thus conceived, the supplemental object may explain Lacan's (1949) self, which can speak its lack, but because of the interposition of the (supplementary) word, can never achieve coincidence with the (unconscious) object of its desire; and accounts as well for Balint's (1968) "area of creativity," and Winnicott's (1960a) unreachable "true self." Bollas' (1992) similarly conceived "third area" is also addressed by the notion of the supplement which speaks, in all these instances, to the conceptualization of the self's *thought of the unknown*.

By the thought of the unknown I intend to suggest that we cognitively consider, that is, knowingly articulate, what can never be existentially apprehended, thereby seeking to conceptualize the thought unknown. Unlike the "unthought known," which is the unconscious within the self, the "thought unknown," I suggest, is the articulate capture of the unspeakably alien within the self; that is, the conscious apprehension of what is literally unidentifiable and thus unknowable within the self. It is an idea which seeks to express, and engage, the subject of "foreign (object) relations."

The supplement says that in order to sustain a psychologically present self we must supplement it with additional images. But inevitably, as that supplement is, in its inherent and immutable nature as a supplement, outside of, alien to, and other than self, it can never add to the substance of self, but only signify, by its *substitutive presence*, that it is nonself. In this way does the supplement, in its additive function, contribute to presence, but as a subtractive testify to what Derrida (1967a) has characterized as "the anterior default of a presence" (p. 145). That is to say, the very appearance of the image signifies the antecedent failure of presence, for immanence has no iconography.

REFERENCES

Alexander, F., & Szasz, T. (1952), The psychosomatic approach in medicine. In: *The Impact of Freudian Psychiatry*, ed. F. Alexander & H. Ross. Chicago: University of Chicago Press, 1961, pp. 260–286.

Allport, G. (1955), *Becoming*. New Haven, CT: Yale University Press.

Anzieu, D. (1985), *The Skin Ego. A Psychoanalytic Approach to the Self*, tr. C. Turner. New Haven, CT: Yale University Press, 1989.

Arendt, H. (1966), *The Origins of Totalitarianism*, 3rd ed. New York: Harcourt, Brace & World.

Balint, M. (1937), Early developmental states of the ego. Primary object-love. In: *Primary Love and Psycho-Analytic Technique*. New York: Liveright, 1965.

———— (1952), *Primary Love and Psycho-Analytic Technique*. New York: Liveright, 1965.

———— (1958a), The concepts of subject and object in psychoanalysis. *Brit. J. Med. Psychol.*, 31:83–91.

———— (1958b), The three areas of the mind: Theoretical considerations. *Internat. J. Psycho-Anal.*, 39:328–340.

———— (1968), *The Basic Fault*. London: Tavistock.

Barrett, W. (1986), *Death of the Soul*. Garden City, NY: Anchor Press/Doubleday.

Barthes, R. (1972), *Critical Essays*. Evanston, IL: Northwestern University Press.

Bettelheim, B. (1982), *Freud and Man's Soul*. New York: Alfred A. Knopf.

Bion, W. (1962), *Learning from Experience*. New York: Jason Aronson.

Bollas, C. (1987), *The Shadow of the Object*. New York: Columbia University Press.

———— (1989), *Forces of Destiny*. London: Free Association Books.

———— (1992), *Being a Character*. New York: Hill & Wang.

Breuer, J., & Freud, S. (1893–1895), Studies on Hysteria. *Standard Edition*, 2. London: Hogarth Press, 1955.

Brown, N. (1966), *Love's Body*. New York: Random House.

Cooley, C. (1902), *Human Nature and the Social Order*. New York: Scribner's.

Derrida, J. (1967a), *Of Grammatology*, tr. G. Spivak. Baltimore: Johns Hopkins University Press, 1976.

———— (1967b), *Writing and Difference*, tr. A. Bass. Baltimore: Johns Hopkins University Press, 1976.

Descartes, R. (1641), Meditations of first philosophy. In: *Descartes Philosophical Writings*, tr. N. K. Smith. New York: Modern Library, 1958, pp. 91–144.

Eagle, M. (1984), *Recent Developments in Psychoanalysis. A Critical Evaluation*. New York: McGraw-Hill.

Eliot, T. S. (1943), East coker. In: *Four Quartets*. New York: Harcourt, Brace, pp. 11–17.

Epstein, S. (1973), The self-concept revisited: Or a theory of a theory. *Amer. Psychologist*, 28:404–416.

Erikson, E. (1950), *Childhood and Society*, 2nd ed. New York: W. W. Norton, 1963.

———— (1968), *Identity Youth and Crisis*. New York: W. W. Norton.

Fairbairn, R. (1952a), *Psychoanalytic Studies of the Personality*. London: Routledge & Kegan Paul, 1957.

———— (1952b), *An Object-Relations Theory of Personality*. New York: Basic Books.

Federn, P. (1926), Some variations in ego feeling. In: *Ego Psychology and the Psychoses*, ed. E. Weiss. New York: Basic Books, 1952, pp. 25–37.

———— (1928a), Narcissism in the structure of the ego. In: *Ego Psychology and the Psychoses*, ed. E. Weiss. New York: Basic Books, 1952, pp. 38–59.

———— (1928b), The ego as subject and object in narcissism. In: *Ego Psychology and the Psychoses*, ed. E. Weiss. New York: Basic Books, 1952, pp. 283–322.

———— (1932), Ego feeling in dreams. In: *Ego Psychology and the Psychoses*, ed. E. Weiss. New York: Basic Books, 1952, pp. 60–89.

———— (1934), The awakening of the ego in dreams. In: *Ego Psychology and the Psychoses*, ed. E. Weiss. New York: Basic Books, 1952, pp. 90–96.

Fitzgerald, F. S. (1925), *The Great Gatsby*. New York: Scribner's.

Foucault, M. (1965), *Madness and Civilization: A History of Insanity in the Age of Reason*, tr. R. Howard. New York: Random House.

———— (1977), *Discipline and Punish: The Birth of the Prison*, tr. A. Sheridan. New York: Random House.

Freud, A. (1926), Introduction to the technique of analysis of children. In: *The Psychoanalytical Treatment of Children*. New York: Schoken Books, 1964, pp. 3–62.

———— (1936), *The Ego and the Mechanisms of Defense*, rev. ed. New York: International Universities Press, 1966.

———— (1959), Clinical studies in psychoanalysis. Research project of the Hampstead Clinic. *The Psychoanalytic Study of the Child*, 14:122–131. New York: International Universities Press.

Freud, S. (1900), The Interpretation of Dreams. *Standard Edition*, 4 & 5. London: Hogarth Press, 1953.

———— (1911), Formulations on the two principles of mental functioning. *Standard Edition*, 12:213–226. London: Hogarth Press, 1958.

———— (1914), On narcissism: An introduction. *Standard Edition*, 14:67–102. London: Hogarth Press, 1957.

———— (1915), The unconscious. *Standard Edition*, 14:161–204. London: Hogarth Press, 1957.

———— (1917), Mourning and melancholia. *Standard Edition*, 14:237–258. London: Hogarth Press, 1957.

———— (1920), Beyond the pleasure principle. *Standard Edition*, 18:1–64. London: Hogarth Press, 1955.

———— (1923), The ego and the id. *Standard Edition*, 19:1–59. London: Hogarth Press, 1961.

———— (1924), The economic problem of masochism. *Standard Edition*, 19:157–172. London: Hogarth Press, 1961.

———— (1930), Civilization and its discontents. *Standard Edition*, 21:57–145. London: Hogarth Press, 1961.

———— (1937), Analysis terminable and interminable. *Standard Edition*, 23:209–253. London: Hogarth Press, 1964.

———— (1940), An outline of psychoanalysis. *Standard Edition*, 23:139–207. London: Hogarth Press, 1964.

Fromm, E. (1941), *Escape from Freedom*. New York: Avon.

———— (1947), *Man for Himself*. Greenwich, CT: Fawcett.

———— (1955), *The Sane Society*. Greenwich, CT: Fawcett.

Gergen, K. (1985), The social constructionist movement in modern psychology. *Amer. Psychologist*, 40:266–275.

———— (1990), Toward a postmodern psychology. *Human. Psychologist*, 18:23–34.

———— (1991), *The Saturated Self: Dilemmas of Identity in Contemporary Life*. New York: HarperCollins.

Green, A. (1972), *A Private Madness*. New York: International Universities Press.

Greenacre, P. (1957), The childhood of the artist: Libidinal phase development and giftedness. *The Psychoanalytic Study of the Child*, 12:27–72. New York: International Universities Press.

Greenberg, J., & Mitchell, S. (1983), *Object Relations in Psychonalytic Theory*. Cambridge, MA: Harvard University Press.

Greenwald, A. (1980). The totalitarian ego: Fabrication and revision of personal history. *Amer. Psychologist*, 35:603–618.

Guntrip, H. (1961), *Personality Structure and Human Interaction: The Developing Synthesis of Psychodynamic Theory.* New York: International Universities Press.

———— (1971), *Psychoanalytic Theory, Therapy, and the Self.* New York: Basic Books.

———— (1975), My experience of analysis with Fairbairn and Winnicott. *Internat. Rev. Psychoanal.,* 2:145–156.

Hartmann, H. (1939), *Ego Psychology and the Problem of Adaptation,* tr. D. Rapaport. New York: International Universities Press, 1958.

———— (1950), Comments on the psychoanalytic theory of the ego. In: *Essays on Ego Psychology.* New York: International Universities Press, 1964, pp. 113–141.

———— (1952), The mutual influences in the development of ego and id. In: *Essays on Ego Psychology.* New York: International Universities Press, 1964, pp. 155–181.

———— (1953), Contributions to the metapsychology of schizophrenia. In: *Essays on Ego Psychology.* New York: International Universities Press, 1964, pp. 182–206.

———— (1956), The development of the ego concept in Freud's work. In: *Essays on Ego Psychology.* New York: International Universities Press, 1964, pp. 268–296.

———— Kris, E., & Loewenstein, R. (1946), Comments on the formation of psychic structure. *The Psychoanalytic Study of the Child,* 2:11–38. New York: International Universities Press.

Hegel, G. W. F. (1807), *The Phenomenology of Mind,* 2nd ed., tr. J. B. Baillie. New York: Humanities Press, 1931.

Hoffer, W. (1950), Development of the body ego. *The Psychoanalytic Study of the Child,* 5:18–23. New York: International Universities Press.

Horney, K. (1937), *The Neurotic Personality of Our Time.* New York: W. W. Norton.

———— (1939), *New Ways in Psychoanalysis.* New York: W. W. Norton.

Jacobson, E. (1954), The self and the object world. *The Psychoanalytic Study of the Child,* 9:75–127. New York: International Universities Press.

———— (1964), *The Self and the Object World.* New York: International Universities Press.

James, W. (1890), *The Principles of Psychology,* Vol. 1. New York: Henry Holt, 1950.

Kelley, G. (1955), *The Psychology of Personal Constructs,* 2 vols. New York: W. W. Norton.

Kernberg, O. (1975), *Borderline Conditions and Pathological Narcissism.* New York: Jason Aronson.

———— (1976), *Object Relations Theory and Clinical Psychoanalysis.* New York: Jason Aronson.

————— (1980), Developmental theory, structural organization and psychoanalytic technique. In: *Rapprochement: The Critical Subphase of Separation-Individuation*, ed. R. Lax, S. Bach, & J. A. Burland. New York: Jason Aronson, pp. 23–38.

————— (1982a), Self, ego, affects, and drives. *J. Amer. Psychoanal. Assn.*, 30:893–917.

————— (1982b), The dynamic unconscious and the self. In: *Theories of the Unconscious and Theories of the Self*, ed. R. Stern. Hillsdale, NJ: Analytic Press, 1987, pp. 3–25.

Kohon, G. (1986), *The British School of Psychoanalysis: The Independent Tradition*. New Haven, CT: Yale University Press.

Kohut, H. (1959), Introspection, empathy, and psychoanalysis. *J. Amer. Psychoanal. Assn.*, 7:459–483.

————— (1971), *The Analysis of the Self*. New York: International Universities Press.

————— (1977), *The Restoration of the Self*. New York: International Universities Press.

————— (1980), Summarizing reflections. In: *Advances in Self Psychology*, ed. A. Goldberg. New York: International Universities Press, pp. 473–552.

————— (1984), *How Does Analysis Cure?*, ed. A. Goldberg. Chicago: University of Chicago Press.

Kojeve, A. (1947), *Introduction to the Reading of Hegel*, tr. J. H. Nicols, Jr., ed. A. Bloom. Ithaca, NY: Cornell University Press, 1969.

Kristeva, J. (1982a), Freud and love: Treatment and its discontents. In: *The Kristeva Reader*, tr. L. S. Roudiez, ed. T. Moi. New York: Columbia University Press, 1986, pp. 238–271.

————— (1982b), *Powers of Horror: An Essay on Abjection*, tr. L. S. Roudiez. New York: Columbia University Press.

————— (1982c), Psychoanalysis and the polis. In: *The Kristeva Reader*, tr. M. Waller, ed. T. Moi. New York: Columbia University Press, 1986, pp. 301–320.

Kuhn, T. (1962), *The Structure of Scientific Revolutions*, 2nd ed. Chicago: University of Chicago Press, 1970.

Lacan, J. (1949), The mirror stage as formative of the function of the I as revealed in psychoanalytic experience. In: *Ecrits. A Selection*, tr. A. Sheridan. New York: W. W. Norton, 1977, pp. 1–7.

————— (1953), The function and field of speech and language in psychoanalysis. In: *Ecrits. A Selection*, tr. A. Sheridan. New York: W. W. Norton, 1977, pp. 30–113.

————— (1960), The subversion of the subject and the dialectic of desire in the Freudian unconscious. In: *Ecrits. A Selection*, tr. A. Sheridan. New York: W. W. Norton, 1977, pp. 292–325.

Mahler, M. S. (1952), On childhood psychosis and schizophrenia: Autistic and symbiotic infantile psychoses. In: *The Selected Papers of Margaret S. Mahler*, Vol. 1. New York: Jason Aronson, 1979, pp. 131–154.

────── (1958), Autism and symbiosis: Two extreme disturbances of identity. In: *The Selected Papers of Margaret S. Mahler*, Vol. 1. New York: Jason Aronson, 1979, pp. 169–182.

────── (1963), Thoughts about development and individuation. In: *The Selected Papers of Margaret S. Mahler*, Vol. 2. New York: Jason Aronson, 1979, pp. 3–20.

────── (1966), Notes on the development of basic moods: The depressive affect. In: *The Selected Papers of Margaret S. Mahler*, Vol. 2. New York: Jason Aronson, 1979, pp. 59–75.

────── (1967), On human symbiosis and the vicissitudes of individuation. In: *The Selected Papers of Margaret S. Mahler*, Vol. 2. New York: Jason Aronson, 1979, pp. 77–98.

────── (1972), On the first three subphases of the separation-individuation process. In: *The Selected Papers of Margaret S. Mahler*, Vol. 2. New York: Jason Aronson, 1979, pp. 119–130.

────── Elkish, P. (1953), Some observations on disturbances of the ego in a case of infantile psychosis. In: *The Selected Papers of Margaret S. Mahler*, Vol. 1. New York: Jason Aronson, 1979, pp. 193–203.

────── Gosliner, B. J. (1955), On symbiotic childhood psychosis: Genetic, dynamic, and restitutive aspects. In: *The Selected Papers of Margaret S. Mahler*, Vol.1. New York: Jason Aronson, 1979, pp. 109–130.

────── LaPerriere, K. (1965), Mother-child interaction during separation-individuation. In: *The Selected Papers of Margaret S. Mahler*, Vol. 2. New York: Jason Aronson, 1979, pp. 35–48.

────── McDevitt, J. (1982), Thoughts on the emergence of the sense of self, with particular emphasis on the body self. *J. Amer. Psychoanal. Assn.*, 30:827–848.

────── Pine, F., & Bergman, A. (1975), *The Psychological Birth of the Human Infant*. New York: Basic Books.

Mead, G. H. (1934), *Mind, Self, and Society*, tr. C. W. Morris. Chicago: University of Chicago Press.

Oliner, M. (1988), *Cultivating Freud's Garden in France*. Northvale, NJ: Jason Aronson.

Orwell, G. (1949), *Nineteen Eighty-Four*. New York: Harcourt, Brace and Company.

Piaget, J. (1952), *The Origins of Intelligence in Children*, tr. M. Cook. New York: W. W. Norton.

Rayner, E. (1991), *The Independent Mind in British Psychoanalysis*. Northvale, NJ: Jason Aronson.

Rosenwald, G. (1988a), Toward a formative psychology. *J. Theory of Soc. Behav.*, 18:1–32.

——— (1988b), A theory of multiple-case research. *J. Personality*, 56:239–264.

Roudinesco, E. (1986), *Jacques Lacan & Co. A History of Psychoanalysis in France, 1925–1985*, tr. J. Mehlman. Chicago: University of Chicago Press.

Sampson, E. (1985), The decentralization of identity. *Amer. Psychologist*, 40:1203–1211.

——— (1988), The debate on individualism. *Amer. Psychologist*, 43:15–22.

——— (1989), The challenge of social change for psychology. *Amer. Psychologist*, 44:914–921.

Sandler, J. (1960), On the concept of superego. *The Psychoanalytic Study of the Child*, 15:128–162. New York: International Universities Press.

——— Holder, A., & Meers, D. (1963), The ego ideal and the ideal self. *The Psychoanalytic Study of the Child*, 18:139–158. New York: International Universities Press.

——— Rosenblatt, B. (1962), The concept of the representational world. *The Psychoanalytic Study of the Child*, 17:128–145. New York: International Universities Press.

Saussure, F. de (1915), *Course in General Linguistics*, tr. W. Baskin, ed. C. Bally & A. Secchehaye with A. Reidlinger. New York: Philosophical Library, 1959.

Schilder, P. (1935), *The Image and Appearance of the Human Body*. New York: International Universities Press, 1950.

Sokolowski, R. (1978), *Presence and Absence: A Philosophical Investigation of Language and Being*. Bloomington: Indiana University Press.

Spence, D. (1982), *Narrative Truth and Historical Truth*. New York: W. W. Norton.

Spiegel, L. (1959), The self, the sense of self, and perception. *The Psychoanalytic Study of the Child*, 14:81–109. New York: International Universities Press.

Spitz, R. (1965), *The First Year of Life*. New York: International Universities Press.

Stern, D. (1985), *The Interpersonal World of the Infant*. New York: Basic Books.

Stevens, W. (1957), *Opus Posthumous*. New York: Alfred A. Knopf.

Stolorow, R., & Atwood, G. (1979), *Faces in a Cloud: Subjectivity in Personality Theory*. New York: Jason Aronson.

——— Brandchaft, B., & Atwood, G. (1987), *Psychoanalytic Treatment: An Intersubjective Approach*. Hillsdale, NJ: Analytic Press.

——— Lachmann, F. (1980), *Psychoanalysis of Developmental Arrests*. New York: International Universities Press.

Sullivan, H. S. (1940), *Conceptions of Modern Psychiatry*. New York: W. W. Norton.

———— (1950), The illusion of personal individuality. In: *The Fusion of Psychiatry and Social Science*. New York: W. W. Norton, 1964.

———— (1953), *The Interpersonal Theory of Psychiatry*. New York: W. W. Norton.

Tolpin, M. (1971), On the beginnings of a cohesive self: An application of the concept of transmuting internalization to the study of the transitional object and signal anxiety. *The Psychoanalytic Study of the Child*, 26:316–354. Chicago: Quadrangle.

Turkle, S. (1992), *Psychoanalytic Politics. Jacques Lacan and Freud's French Revolution*, 2nd ed. New York: Guilford Press.

Wilden, A. (1968), Lacan and the discourse of the Other. In: *The Language of the Self*, tr. A. Wilden. Baltimore: Johns Hopkins University Press, pp. 159–311.

Winnicott, D. W. (1951), Transitional objects and transitional phenomena. In: *Playing and Reality*. New York: Basic Books, 1971, pp. 1–25.

———— (1958), The capacity to be alone. In: *The Maturational Processes and the Facilitating Environment*. New York: International Universities Press, 1965, pp. 29–36.

———— (1959), The fate of the transitional object. In: *Psychoanalytic Explorations*, ed. C. Winnicott, R. Shepard, & M. Davis. Cambridge, MA: Harvard University Press, 1989, pp. 53–58.

———— (1960a), The theory of the parent-infant relationship. In: *The Maturational Processes and the Facilitating Environment*. New York: International Universities Press, 1965, pp. 37–55.

———— (1960b), Ego distortion in terms of true and false self. In: *The Maturational Processes and the Facilitating Environment*. New York: International Universities Press, 1965, pp. 140–152.

———— (1962), Ego integration in child development. In: *The Maturational Processes and the Facilitating Environment*. New York: International Universities Press, 1965, pp. 56–63.

———— (1963), Communicating and not communicating leading to a study of certain opposites. In: *The Maturational Processes and the Facilitating Environment*. New York: International Universities Press, 1965, pp. 179–192.

———— (1965), *The Maturational Process and the Facilitating Environment*. New York: International Universities Press.

———— (1967), Mirror-role of mother and family in child development. In: *Playing and Reality*. New York: Basic Books, 1971, pp. 111–118.

———— (1971), Playing: Creative activity and the search for the self. In: *Playing and Reality*. New York: Basic Books, 1971, pp. 53–64.

Wolf, E. (1980), On the developmental line of selfobject relations. In: *Advances in Self Psychology*, ed. A. Goldberg. New York: International Universities Press, pp. 117–130.

NAME INDEX

SUBJECT INDEX

Absence, 276, 287–288
　articulation of, 263
　desire and, 3
　functional, 279–281
　impact of, 283
　of mind, 3
　object constancy and, 280–281
　pathology and, 284–285
　principle of, 6
　self of, 277–278
Absencing, 286
Absent other, 6–8
Adaptation, 21–22, 84
　impersonal, 248–249
　personal, 248–251
Aesthetic moment, 267–268
Affective experience, shared, 155–156
Affective subjectivity, 98, 99
　peak, 98, 101
Affectivity, diminished, 218
Aleatorical being, 273–274
Alienation, 288
Allusional self, 277–288
Alone, capacity to be, 227, 236, 245, 286
Aloneness, 235–236, 245, 276
Alterity, 3
Ambiguity, 133–134
American psychoanalytic tradition, 204,
　　208, 212, 278
The Analysis of the Self (Kohut), 113–114
Anarchic self, 172–173
Anna O case, 8, 16–17
Annihilation, 229–230, 244
Anomalous self, 201–209
Anticipation, 21, 277–278
　as agreeable forepleasure, 282
　capacity for, 280
　self of, 179–181, 201
Apperception, 231–232

Archaic object, 109
Ascendancy-dependency relationship,
　　185–186
Ascendant self, 91–140
Auditory sensation, 255, 257–258
Auditory/olfactory envelope, 202–203
Authenticity, 245, 246
Autism, 86
　normal, 80
Autoerotic instinct, 17–18
Autonomous function, 156–157
Average expectable environment, 84
Awareness
　definition of, 142–143
　experience of, 219
　invariant pattern of, 177
　language and, 162
　sentimental, 183

Basic fault level, 244
Being. See also Human being; Self
　aleatorical, 273–274
　dynamic experience of, xiii
　existential, 261
　levels of, 243–245
　lexical, 273
Beneffectance, 169, 170, 171
Biases, 167–170
　explanation of, 173–174
　versus organization, 170–175
Bipolar self, 117–118
Bodily functions, 254–255
Body ego, 85, 254–255
　representations of, 81–83
Body image, 79
Body representation, 60, 78
Body self, 71, 73–74
　origin of sense of, 78–79
　primacy of, 78–80

limits of, 223–225
linguistic deconstruction of, 5
mature, 131–132
medial or intransitive voice of, 282
mediated, 86–89
mental, 71–72
modification of, 11
mother's reflection and, 230–233
multiplicity of, 274
narcissism in, 32–34, 36
narrow sense of, 106–111
nature of man and, 127–132
objectless, 220–221
as organizing principle, 112–113
origin of, 78–79, 208, 278
otherness and, 8–9
in own other image, 285–286
paradigmatic, 176–177
paradoxical, 261–263
personal, 247–251
personality and, 14, 35
phenomenal, 85, 211–225
plurality of, 6
postmodern formulation of, 3–7
preindividual, 258–259
presocial, 198
preverbal, 162–163
primal psychophysiological, 69–70, 75
primary connection of, 239–241
primitive experience of, 248
primordial experience of, 98
as product of impersonal, 36–37
as psychic structure, 96
psychological essentials of, 120–127
realized, 9–10, 13–19, 201, 208
representational, 51–66, 70, 139–140
riddle of, 175–177, 275
rudimentary, 242–243
search for, 227
secret, 233–235
sense of, 141–165, 278
sensory origin of, 255–256
sexual overestimation of, 45
skin ego and, 255–256
spirit of, 274–276, 285–286
split, 247–248

spoken, 187–188
as stage, 60–62
as subject, 96–103
subjective, 102–103, 119–120, 154–155, 212–225
supraordinate, 91–96, 100, 134–135
symbolic function of, 101–102
theories of, xiii–xiv
totalitarian, 167–178
transformational, 266–269, 274
transforming, 161–162
transmuting, 109–111, 135
true, 230–232, 233–234, 265, 268, 288
unthought, 265–276
verbal, 158–160
virtual, 116–117
world and, 8
Self concept
  ambiguously certain paradox of, 133–134
  American tradition of, 132–135
  bounded, 6
Self feeling, 220
Self knowledge, 72–73
Self psychology, 103–140
Self representation, 38, 41, 60, 81–86
  averaged, 65, 88
  construction of, 72–73
  earliest, 78–79
  ego functions in, 60–62
  ego structure and, 71–72, 75
  good and bad, 99–100
  ideal self as, 63–64
  internalized, 94–95
  nature of, 64–65
  visual, 87
Self system, 95
Self-affectivity, 148
Self-agency, 148
Self-altering experience, 150
Self-assertiveness, 118
Self-awareness, 80–81
Self-cathexis, 33–34
Self-coherence, 148
Self-consciousness, 181
Self-ego relationship, 52–53
  ambiguity of, 81–86